Microsoft®

Windows Vista™
Step by Step

Joan Preppernau and Joyce Cox

PUBLISHED BY
Microsoft Press
A Division of Microsoft Corporation
One Microsoft Way
Redmond, Washington 98052-6399

Copyright © 2007 by Joan Preppernau, Joyce Cox, and Online Training Solutions, Inc.

Library of Congress Control Number: 2006937013

Printed and bound in the United States of America.

6 7 8 9 QWT 2 1 0 9 8

Distributed in Canada by H.B. Fenn and Company Ltd.

A CIP catalogue record for this book is available from the British Library.

Microsoft Press books are available through booksellers and distributors worldwide. For further information about international editions, contact your local Microsoft Corporation office or contact Microsoft Press International directly at fax (425) 936-7329. Visit our Web site at www.microsoft.com/mspress. Send comments to mspinput@microsoft.com.

Microsoft, Microsoft Press, Aero, ClearType, Dexterity, DirectX, Excel, Internet Explorer, MSN, OneNote, Outlook, PowerPoint, SharePoint, Windows, Windows Live, Windows Media, Windows Server, and Windows Vista are either registered trademarks or trademarks of Microsoft Corporation in the United States and/or other countries. Other product and company names mentioned herein may be the trademarks of their respective owners.

The example companies, organizations, products, domain names, e-mail addresses, logos, people, places, and events depicted herein are fictitious. No association with any real company, organization, product, domain name, e-mail address, logo, person, place, or event is intended or should be inferred.

This book expresses the author's views and opinions. The information contained in this book is provided without any express, statutory, or implied warranties. Neither the authors, Microsoft Corporation, nor its resellers, or distributors will be held liable for any damages caused or alleged to be caused either directly or indirectly by this book.

Acquisitions Editor: Juliana Aldous Atkinson
Project Editor: Sandra Haynes
Editorial Production: Online Training Solutions, Inc.

Body Part No. X12-48750

Contents

What do you think of this book? We want to hear from you!

Microsoft is interested in hearing your feedback so we can continually improve our books and learning resources for you. To participate in a brief online survey, please visit:

www.microsoft.com/learning/booksurvey/

What do you think of this book? We want to hear from you!

Microsoft is interested in hearing your feedback so we can continually improve our books and learning resources for you. To participate in a brief online survey, please visit:

www.microsoft.com/learning/booksurvey/

About the Authors

Joan Preppernau

Joan is the author of more than a dozen books about Windows and Office, including the popular *Microsoft Windows XP Step by Step,* and a contributor to the development of the Microsoft certification exams for the 2007 Office system and Windows Vista. Having learned about computers literally at her father's knee, Joan's wide-ranging experiences in various facets of the computer industry contribute to her enthusiasm for producing interesting, useful, and reader-friendly training materials. Joan is the President of Online Training Solutions, Inc. (OTSI) and an avid telecommuter. The power of the Internet and an obsession with technology have made it possible for Joan to live and work in New Zealand, Sweden, Denmark, and various locations in the U.S. during the past 15 years. Having finally discovered the delights of a daily dose of sunshine, Joan has recently settled in San Diego, California, with her husband Barry and their daughter Trinity.

Joyce Cox

Joyce has 25 years' experience in the development of training materials about technical subjects for non-technical audiences, and is the author of dozens of books about Office and Windows technologies. She is the Vice President of Online Training Solutions, Inc. (OTSI). She was President of and principal author for Online Press, where she developed the *Quick Course* series of computer training books for beginning and intermediate adult learners. She was also the first managing editor of Microsoft Press, an editor for Sybex, and an editor for the University of California. Joyce and her husband Ted live in downtown Bellevue, Washington, and escape as often as they can to their tiny, offline cabin in the Cascade foothills.

The Team

Without the support of the hard-working members of the OTSI publishing team, this book would not exist. Susie Bayers and Marlene Lambert guided the editorial process, and Robert (RJ) Cadranell guided the production process. Jan Bednarczuk copyedited the book and created its index, and Jaime Odell proofread the final content. Lisa Van Every laid out the book for print, using Adobe InDesign, and Jeanne Craver processed the graphics. Another important member of our team, Microsoft Press Series Editor Sandra Haynes, provided invaluable support throughout the writing and production processes.

Online Training Solutions, Inc. (OTSI)

OTSI specializes in the design, creation, and production of Office and Windows training products for information workers and home computer users. For more information about OTSI, visit

www.otsi.com

Introducing Windows Vista

Windows Vista is the latest and greatest in the illustrious line of Windows operating systems from Microsoft. The successor to Microsoft Windows XP, this operating system is specifically designed to fill the needs of both business and personal users. As soon as you turn on a computer running Windows Vista, you'll notice the slick look of the new user interface. If your computer has the hardware necessary to display the Windows Aero color scheme, the high-quality visual effects will contribute significantly to your overall computing experience.

But this new version of Windows isn't just pretty to look at. It takes secure computing to a new level. In addition to providing accessory programs that help you monitor and protect your computer, it works behind the scenes to help keep malicious programs and malicious people at bay, and alerts you if a program or a person tries to make any changes that might affect the stability of the system.

After you get used to its sophisticated design and you come to rely on its new security features, you will probably start noticing the many Windows Vista features that increase your efficiency and productivity. Finding files has never been simpler or faster; simply type a word you know exists in the file you are looking for, and Windows Vista instantly shows you all the files stored on your system that contain the word. Getting the information you need to complete the task at hand is a snap; simply click the help links in windows and dialog boxes to learn about the available choices. Need to see whether a particular date falls on a weekend, keep track of the time in another country, or remove the red-eye from the photograph you want to use on your new business card? Take advantage of the many programs that come with Windows Vista to take care of these and other tasks, all from your computer desktop.

See Also For more complete coverage of media-related features and accessories such as Windows Contacts, Windows Mail, Windows Live Messenger, and Windows Meeting Space, consult *Microsoft Windows Vista Step by Step, Deluxe Edition* by Joan Preppernau and Joyce Cox (Microsoft Press, 2007).

Because Windows Vista has so many new features, we don't identify them with a special margin icon as we did in previous versions of this book. We do, however, list the features here, categorized by Windows Vista edition.

Many of the features introduced in Windows Vista run behind the scenes and don't require you to do anything. We don't cover these features in this book because it is unlikely that you will have to work with them.

Windows Vista Editions

Windows Vista comes in five editions—three designed for varying levels of personal computing, two specifically tailored for business computing needs.

Windows Vista Home Basic

This edition is designed for home users with the most basic computing needs, such as Internet and e-mail access. It delivers security and reliability without the extra features that many home users might not need. Windows Vista Home Basic includes the following features:

- Integrated desktop search makes it easy to find files, folders, messages, programs, and Windows Vista tools and controls from the Start Search box at the bottom of the Start menu or from the Search box in the upper-right corner of every Windows Explorer window.

- Windows Internet Explorer 7, with multi-page browsing and enhanced security, offers many convenient new features to simplify the process of locating, displaying, and returning to information on the Internet, including a built-in RSS reader for subscribing to Web feeds.

- Windows Explorer displays information about the properties and contents of folders and files.

- Sleep mode, a fast-acting hibernation function that shuts down or starts up your computer in seconds, and Windows ReadyBoost, which borrows from USB flash drive memory to expand the available system memory (RAM), help increase your efficiency.

- Windows Sidebar displays "gadgets" that make information such as news, photos, notes, weather, and more available full time from your desktop.

- Windows Mail, the new version of Microsoft Outlook Express, provides e-mail functionality without the need for other software.

- Windows Calendar provides personal and shared schedules and task tracking.

- Windows Photo Gallery and personal and public Pictures folders make it easy to view, label, organize, and share digital images.

- Microsoft Speech Recognition provides the means to control your computer by using your voice rather than the keyboard and mouse.

- Parental Controls enable you to limit the time children spend on the computer and the programs and sites they can access.

- Windows Backup And Restore Center safeguards against lost information by automatically backing up information on your computer at regular intervals and before any major system change. If you experience system trouble after installing a program, you can restore your system to the previous version without losing changes you have since made to documents or other content on your computer.

- The Network File And Sharing Center provides real-time monitoring of network connections from your computer and options for controlling what areas of your computer can be accessed from other computers.

- The Ease Of Access Center provides accessibility features and a questionnaire for determining which features can help you to better interact with your computer.

- Sync Center provides a central location for synchronizing content between your computer and portable devices such as Microsoft Windows Mobile devices and personal music systems, and for monitoring synchronization activities.

- Enhanced protection features help you ensure the security of your computer and the information on it. Windows Security Center provides real-time monitoring of the security controls in place on your computer and whether your operating system files are up to date. Windows Firewall protects against unauthorized connections to and from your computer. Windows Defender protects against malicious software (malware) attacks. User Account Control (UAC) prevents unauthorized changes to your computer by requiring administrator permission to carry out restricted tasks.

Windows Vista Home Premium

This edition is designed for home users who use their computers for more than the basics. It includes all the features of Windows Vista Home Basic, plus the following:

- The Windows Aero (authentic, energetic, reflective, and open) user interface provides an enhanced visual experience with features such as transparent window frames, additional color schemes, and live previews of open windows from the taskbar and when switching between windows.

- Windows Media Center provides the means to enjoy all forms of digital entertainment—photos, videos, television, and music—from one central location. If your system includes a television tuner and Windows Media Center–compatible remote control, you can use your computer as an all-in-one entertainment center. With the addition of Windows Media Extender hardware units, you can broadcast content from your computer to multiple locations in your home or office.

- Windows Tablet and Touch Technology enables you to interact with a Tablet PC–compatible computer by using a digital pen or your fingertip. Continuous feedback helps your computer do an increasingly accurate job of recognizing your handwriting.

- Windows SideShow provides auxiliary display support for next-generation hardware with external displays, making it possible, for example, to check your schedule without opening the lid of your laptop.

Windows Vista Ultimate

This edition is designed for home users who want to do it all. Ideal for home-based businesses, Windows Vista Ultimate includes business, mobility, and entertainment functions, with all the features of Windows Vista Home Premium, plus the following:

- Windows Movie Maker enables you to create, edit, enhance, narrate, and package video clips.

- Windows BitLocker Drive Encryption protects your system by encrypting the entire hard disk on which Windows Vista is installed. BitLocker automatically encrypts the files you move to or save on the system drive, and it decrypts them when you move them from the system drive to another drive. BitLocker also protects against intrusion by monitoring the startup and logon processes; if it detects anomalies, it requires the entry of a special BitLocker password to gain access to the computer.

- Advanced networking capabilities allow you to join a domain as well as provide Group Policy support and features such as Remote Desktop.

Windows Vista Business

Designed for small, mid-sized, and large businesses, this edition includes all the features of Windows Vista Home Premium, plus the following:

● Windows Mobility Center provides access to all the settings you might want to adjust when using a mobile PC, so you don't need to search for them individually.

● Windows Meeting Space provides a convenient online meeting interface for sharing information with and among a group of people. Participants can collaborate on documents, share control of a computer, distribute handouts, and chat with each other.

● Business and technology resources designed for small businesses are available, along with enhanced networking, backup, and fax and scan capabilities.

Windows Vista Enterprise

This edition is designed for mid-sized and large enterprises with complex IT infrastructures. It is available only to Microsoft Volume License customers, through the Microsoft Software Assurance and Microsoft Enterprise Agreement programs. It includes all the features of Windows Vista Business, plus the following:

● Windows BitLocker Drive Encryption (see the earlier description under Windows Vista Ultimate).

● Virtual PC Express allows users to run two operating systems on one computer by using Microsoft Virtual PC technology.

● Subsystem for Unix-based Applications (SUA) makes it possible to run UNIX-based programs and scripts on Windows Vista.

● Support for all 35 available interface languages makes global deployment easier.

> **Tip** Some features of Windows Vista work only if you have the hardware to support them. For information, see "Using the Book's CD" later in this book.

See Also For detailed descriptions of the Windows Vista editions and features, visit *www.microsoft.com/windowsvista/getready/editions/*.

The exercises in this book cover the features of Windows Vista that you are most likely to use at home and at work, and assume that you have *administrative privileges* on your computer. Screenshots depict the Windows Vista Ultimate user interface.

Let's Get Started!

It might seem a bit strange to sing the praises of an operating system. In the past, a computer's operating system was supposed to do its job so unobtrusively that we only noticed it when something went wrong. Not so with Windows Vista. Its sophisticated design values and superior collection of tools and programs mean that after we've shown you around, you will be looking at this operating system in a whole new light.

The Microsoft Business Certification Program

Desktop computing proficiency is becoming increasingly important in today's business world. As a result, when screening, hiring, and training employees, more employers are relying on the objectivity and consistency of technology certification to ensure the competence of their workforce. As an employee or job seeker, you can use technology certification to prove that you already have the skills you need to succeed, saving current and future employers the trouble and expense of training you.

The Microsoft Business Certification program is designed to assist employees in validating their Windows Vista skills and 2007 Microsoft Office program skills. There are two paths to certification:

- A Microsoft Certified Application Specialist (MCAS) is an individual who has demonstrated worldwide skill standards for Windows Vista or the 2007 Microsoft Office suite through a certification exam in Windows Vista or in one or more of the 2007 Microsoft Office programs, including Microsoft Office Word 2007, Microsoft Office Excel 2007, Microsoft Office PowerPoint 2007, Microsoft Office Outlook 2007, and Microsoft Office Access 2007.

- A Microsoft Certified Application Professional (MCAP) is an individual who has taken his or her knowledge of the 2007 Microsoft Office suite and of Microsoft SharePoint products and technologies to the next level and has demonstrated through a certification exam that he or she can use the collaborative power of the Office suite to accomplish job functions such as Budget Analysis and Forecasting, or Content Management and Collaboration.

After attaining certification, you can include the MCAS or MCAP logo with the appropriate certification designator on your business cards and other personal promotional materials. This logo attests to the fact that you are proficient in the applications or cross-application skills necessary to achieve the certification.

Selecting a Certification Path

When selecting the Microsoft Business Certification path that you would like to pursue, you should assess the following:

- The program and program version(s) with which you are familiar
- The length of time you have used the program
- Whether you have had formal or informal training in the use of that program

Candidates for MCAS-level certification are expected to successfully complete a wide range of standard business tasks, such as formatting a document or spreadsheet. Successful candidates generally have six or more months of experience with Windows Vista or the specific Office the program, including either formal, instructor-led training or self-study using MCAS-approved books, guides, or interactive computer-based materials.

Candidates for MCAP-level certification are expected to successfully complete more complex, business-oriented tasks utilizing advanced functionality with the combined 2007 Microsoft Office suite of products. Successful candidates generally have between six months and one or more years of experience with the programs, including formal, instructor-led training or self-study using MCAP-approved materials.

Becoming a Microsoft Certified Application Specialist—Windows Vista

Every MCAS and MCAP certification exam is developed from a set of exam skill standards that are derived from studies of how Windows Vista and the 2007 Office programs are used in the workplace. Because these skill standards dictate the scope of each exam, they provide you with critical information on how to prepare for certification.

To become certified as a Windows Vista Product Specialist, you must demonstrate proficiency in these seven areas:

- **Protecting your computer.** You must demonstrate the ability to manage Windows Firewall, manage malicious software protection, configure Windows Update settings, lock a computer, manage Windows Internet Explorer security, and configure local user accounts.

- **Managing mobile and remote computing.** You must demonstrate the ability to manage the computer power state, network connections, and remote access to your computer; connect to another computer; and access files stored in shared network folders when your computer is offline.

- **Managing software, disks, and devices.** You must demonstrate the ability to manage software, storage disks, devices, and drivers; manage display settings; configure multiple monitors; and install and configure a printer.

- **Managing files and folders.** You must demonstrate the ability to manage Windows Explorer settings; manage, organize, and search for files and folders; secure and share folders; and back up and restore files and folders.

- **Collaborating with other people.** You must demonstrate the ability to collaborate in real time and present information to an audience through Windows Meeting Space, and to communicate in real time by using Windows Live Messenger.

- **Customizing your Windows Vista experience.** You must demonstrate the ability to modify the Start menu and the taskbar, personalize the desktop and system sounds, and manage Windows Sidebar.

- **Optimizing and troubleshooting your computer.** You must demonstrate the ability to increase processing speed, locate the information about your system needed to troubleshoot a problem, repair a network connection, recover from software errors, troubleshoot printing errors, recover the operating system from a problem, and request and manage Remote Assistance.

Taking a Microsoft Business Certification Exam

The MCAS and MCAP certification exams for Windows Vista and the 2007 Office programs are performance-based and require you to complete business-related tasks using an interactive simulation (a digital model) of the Windows Vista operating system or one or more programs in the Office suite.

Test-Taking Tips

- Follow all instructions provided in each question completely and accurately.

- Enter requested information as it appears in the instructions, but without duplicating the formatting unless you are specifically instructed to do otherwise. For example, the text and values you are asked to enter might appear in the instructions in bold and underlined (for example, **text**), but you should enter the information without applying these formats.

- Close all dialog boxes before proceeding to the next exam question unless you are specifically instructed otherwise.

- Don't close task panes before proceeding to the next exam question unless you are specifically instructed to do otherwise.

- If you are asked to print a document, spreadsheet, chart, report, or slide, perform the task, but be aware that nothing will actually be printed.

- Don't worry about extra keystrokes or mouse clicks. Your work is scored based on its result, not on the method you use to achieve that result (unless a specific method is indicated in the instructions), and not on the time you take to complete the question.

- If your computer becomes unstable during the exam (for example, if the exam does not respond or the mouse no longer functions) or if a power outage occurs, contact a testing center administrator immediately. The administrator will restart the computer and return the exam to the point where the interruption occurred with your score intact.

Certification

At the conclusion of the exam, you will receive a score report, which you can print with the assistance of the testing center administrator. If your score meets or exceeds the passing standard (the minimum required score), you will be mailed a printed certificate within approximately 14 days.

For More Information

To learn more about the Microsoft Certified Application Specialist exams and courseware, visit

http://www.microsoft.com/learning/mcp/mcas/

To learn more about the Microsoft Certified Application Professional exams and courseware, visit

http://www.microsoft.com/learning/mcp/mcap/

Information for New Computer Users

Windows Vista is the latest edition of the Microsoft Windows *operating system*. Your computer's operating system basically tells your computer what to do and how to do it. For your computer to work, Windows Vista must do the following:

- Coordinate interactions among its components, such as receiving input from your keyboard and mouse, displaying output on your monitor, and locating programs and files on your hard disk.

- Act as the interface between you and your computer, so that you can work in a visual way by clicking items on the screen instead of having to type precise sequences of commands.

- Enable your computer to communicate with other computers and peripheral devices such as printers, scanners, and modems.

- Interact with programs installed on your computer.

The programs you purchase and install on your computer run on Windows Vista, meaning that they call on the operating system whenever they need to work with your computer's components or peripherals (such as printers). They also build on the interface provided by the operating system to communicate with you. This relationship allows the programs to concentrate on their specialized tasks, such as word processing or performing calculations in a spreadsheet, while the operating system handles the basic behind-the-scenes tasks.

The Windows operating system has been around long enough that it has spawned its own jargon. If you are a new computer user, some of the terms associated with Windows Vista and the programs that run on it might be new to you, so we will briefly cover them here to bring you up to speed.

Using Your Mouse

For new computer users who are not familiar with the standard Windows mouse actions, here's a quick summary:

- *Pointing to* an object involves moving the mouse so that the cursor (the visible representation of the mouse location on the screen) is over the object.

- *Clicking* an object involves pointing to the object and quickly pressing and releasing the primary mouse button once. (By default, the primary mouse button is the left one, but you can change this.)

- *Double-clicking* an object involves pointing to the object and pressing and releasing the primary mouse button twice in rapid succession. You can adjust the speed at which Windows recognizes two clicks as a double-click.

- *Right-clicking* an object involves pointing to the object and clicking the secondary mouse button once. This action displays a *context menu* listing actions that can be performed with the object you right-clicked. You select the action you want by clicking it on the context menu.

- *Dragging* an object involves pointing to the object, holding down the primary mouse button, moving the mouse until the pointer is in the location where you want the object to appear, and releasing the mouse button. You can also drag through multiple objects in a list to select them.

If you prefer to click, double-click, and drag with the right mouse button, you can switch the buttons by adjusting the Mouse settings in Control Panel.

See Also For information about switching the action of the left and right buttons and adjusting the speed of a double-click, see "Changing the Way Your Mouse Works" in Chapter 5, "Installing and Configuring Devices."

Working with Windows

Windows Vista displays information in *windows*. A window can either fill the entire screen or occupy just part of the screen. Each window is encased in a *frame* displaying information about the window contents and containing controls for managing the window content. When a window is not maximized to fill the screen, you can drag the edges of the frame to change the size of the window.

At the top of the window is space allocated to a *title bar*, which might tell you the window's purpose or the name of the program running in the window. You can maximize or reduce the size of a window by double-clicking its title bar. When a window is not maximized, you can move it on the screen by dragging it by its title bar.

At the right end of the title bar are the Minimize, Maximize/Restore Down, and Close buttons. You click the Minimize button to collapse the window into a button on the Windows Vista taskbar (called *minimizing the window*); you click the Maximize/Restore Down button to switch the window from filling the screen (often *maximizing the window*) to occupying just part of it (*reducing* the window), and to switch it back again; and you click the Close button to close the window. If the window is displaying a program or file, closing the window might also quit the program or close the file.

Below the title bar, the window might have a *menu bar*, *toolbar*, or other visual representation of the instructions (commands) you can give Windows Vista regarding the contents of the window.

When a window is not big enough to show all its contents, vertical and/or horizontal scroll bars appear so that you can move the contents within the window. You use the vertical scroll bar to move the contents up and down and the horizontal scroll bar to move the contents from side to side, as follows:

- Clicking the arrow at either end of a scroll bar moves the contents one line or column at a time.
- Clicking directly on the scroll bar on either side of the scroll box moves the contents one "windowful" at a time.
- Dragging the scroll box on the scroll bar moves the contents in larger increments.

The position of the scroll box in relation to the scroll bar tells you where you are in the contents. For example, when the scroll box is in the middle of the scroll bar, the window is displaying the portion of its contents located about halfway through.

Giving Instructions

To get any useful work done, you have to be able to give your computer instructions about what to do. These instructions are called *commands*. Some commands are simple, and you can give them by clicking an item on a menu, clicking a button on a toolbar, or pressing a key combination on the keyboard. If Windows Vista needs information from you in order to know how to carry out a command, it might display a different window, a *task pane*, or a *dialog box*. These might present only one set of options, but they can also be quite complex, involving several layers of options you can use to refine your instructions. However, they all request information in consistent ways and use these common components:

- **Tabs.** If a dialog box contains too many options to fit in the dialog box window, the options are arranged in logical groups on separate tabs. You click a tab's label to display that set of options.

- **Command buttons.** Most dialog boxes have at least two command buttons: an OK button that carries out the command, and a Cancel button that cancels the command. Clicking either button also closes the dialog box. Other buttons might be available, such as the Apply button that applies changes without closing the dialog box. If a button label includes an ellipsis (...), clicking the button opens another dialog box. A dark border around a button indicates that you can press Enter rather than clicking the button to implement that command.

- **Option buttons.** In a group of mutually exclusive options where only one option can be selected at a time, each option is preceded by an option button (a small circle). When you click an option button, a dot appears in the circle to indicate that the option is *selected*. Because only one option in the group can be selected at a time, selecting an option removes the dot from the previously selected option.

- **Check boxes.** Options that can be either selected or not selected, but are not mutually exclusive, are preceded by a check box (a small square). Clicking an empty check box selects the associated option; a check mark appears inside the box to indicate that the option is *selected* or *turned on*. Clicking the box again removes the check mark to indicate that the option is *deselected*, *cleared*, or *turned off*. Check boxes operate independently, so if a dialog box presents a group of check boxes, you can select none, one, some, or all of the options, as required for the task at hand.

- **Text boxes.** You enter information, such as a file name, by typing it in a text box. To replace an existing entry, select the entry and delete it, or overtype the old text with the new.

- **List boxes.** When you need to select from several options, the options are sometimes displayed in a list box. When you have more choices available than can fit in the list box, the list box has a scroll bar. Regardless of the format of a list box, you select an option by clicking it. The option is then highlighted in the list.

- **Drop-down list boxes.** To conserve space, options are sometimes displayed in a drop-down list. A drop-down list appears initially as a text box containing an option. At the right end of the box is a down arrow that you can click to display a list of the other available options. To select an option, you simply click it in the list. That option then appears in the box.

- **Combo boxes.** Sometimes a text box and a drop-down list box are combined to form a combo box. You can either type the information or select it from a drop-down list.

- **Spin boxes.** If a text box must contain only one of a specific set of options (usually numbers), it sometimes has a pair of up and down arrows at its right end. You change the entry either by selecting the existing number and typing a new one or by clicking one of the arrows to increase or decrease the number.

- **Sliders.** Settings can also be represented by the position of a slider on a horizontal or vertical bar. To change the setting, you drag the slider.

- **Links.** Clicking a link in a window might open another window or it might take you to information stored on your computer or on the Web. When you point to a link, it becomes underlined and the pointer changes to a hand.

You can move between options in a dialog box by pointing to them with the mouse, or by pressing the Tab key.

Message Boxes

Windows Vista displays message and warning boxes when a command you have chosen can't be carried out, or to request confirmation of a potentially risky action that you might later regret (for example, when you delete files). You can click OK or Yes to acknowledge the message and continue the command. Click Cancel or No to close the message box and cancel the command.

Features and Conventions of This Book

This book has been designed to lead you step by step through all the tasks you are most likely to want to perform in Windows Vista. If you start at the beginning and work your way through all the exercises, you will gain enough proficiency to be able to work with all the common Microsoft Windows elements and manage and maintain your own computer. However, each topic is self contained. If you have worked with a previous version of Windows, or if, after completing all the exercises, you later need help remembering how to perform a procedure, the following features of this book will help you locate specific information:

- **Detailed table of contents.** A listing of the topics and sidebars within each chapter.

- **Chapter thumb tabs.** Easily locate the beginning of the chapter you want.

- **Topic-specific running heads.** Within a chapter, quickly locate the topic you want by looking at the running head of odd-numbered pages.

- **Quick Reference.** General instructions for each procedure covered in specific detail elsewhere in the book. Refresh your memory about a task while working with your own documents.

- **Detailed index.** Look up specific tasks and features and general concepts in the index, which has been carefully crafted with the reader in mind.

- **Companion CD.** Contains practice files you can use while working through the step-by-step exercises, as well as a fully searchable electronic version of this book and other useful resources.

In addition, we provide a glossary of terms for those times when you need to look up the meaning of a word or the definition of a concept.

You can save time when you use this book by understanding how the *Step by Step* series shows special instructions, keys to press, buttons to click, and so on.

Convention	Meaning
(CD icon)	This icon at the end of a chapter introduction indicates information about the practice files provided on the companion CD for use in the chapter.
USE	This paragraph preceding a step-by-step exercise indicates the practice files that you will use when working through the exercise.
BE SURE TO	This paragraph preceding or following an exercise indicates any requirements you should attend to before beginning the exercise or actions you should take to restore your system after completing the exercise.
OPEN	This paragraph preceding a step-by-step exercise indicates files that you should open before beginning the exercise.
CLOSE	This paragraph following a step-by-step exercise provides instructions for closing open files or programs before moving on to another topic.
1 2	Blue numbered steps guide you through step-by-step exercises and Quick Reference versions of procedures.
1 2	Black numbered steps guide you through procedures in sidebars and expository text.
→	An arrow indicates a procedure that has only one step.
See Also	These paragraphs direct you to more information about a given topic in this book or elsewhere.
Troubleshooting	These paragraphs explain how to fix a common problem that might prevent you from continuing with an exercise.
Tip	These paragraphs provide a helpful hint or shortcut that makes working through a task easier, or information about other available options.
Important	These paragraphs point out information that you need to know to complete a procedure.
(Save button icon) Save	The first time you are told to click a button in an exercise, a picture of the button appears in the left margin. If the name of the button does not appear on the button itself, the name appears under the picture.
Enter	In step-by-step exercises, keys you must press appear as they would on a keyboard.
Ctrl + Home	A plus sign (+) between two key names means that you must hold down the first key while you press the second key. For example, "press Ctrl + Home" means "hold down the Ctrl key while you press the Home key."
Program interface elements	In steps, the names of program elements, such as buttons, commands, and dialog boxes, are shown in black bold characters.
User input	Anything you are supposed to type appears in blue bold characters.
Glossary terms	Terms that are explained in the glossary at the end of the book are shown in blue italic characters.

Using the Book's CD

The companion CD included with this book contains practice files you can use as you work through the book's exercises, as well as other electronic resources that will help you learn how to use Windows Vista.

What's on the CD?

The following table lists the practice files supplied on the book's CD.

Chapter	Files
Chapter 1: Getting Started with Windows Vista	None
Chapter 2: Working Efficiently in Windows Vista	None
Chapter 3: Working with Folders and Files	01_AlbumSlides.pptx
	01_ColorSlides.pptx
	01_FabricSpecial.docx
	01_FengShuiSlides.pptx
	01_JournalSlides.pptx
	01_LoanPayment.xlsx
	01_OrgSlides.pptx
	01_Procedures.docx
	01_RoomMakeover.docx
	03_Costs.xlsx
	05_Cat.jpg
	05_Crow.jpg
	05_Figurine.jpg
	05_Frog.jpg
	05_Introduction.wav
	05_MusicBox.jpg
	05_TeaPot.jpg
	06_Bamboo.docx
	06_Bamboo1.jpg through 06_Bamboo3.jpg
	06_BookBeat.docx

Chapter	Files
Chapter 3: Working with Folders and Files *(continued)*	*06_BookSales.xlsx* *06_Lady.jpg* *06_PlanningSlides.pptx* *06_SalesMtgSlides.pptx* *06_TagAnnounce.docx* *06_TagIntroduce.docx* *06_TagSlides.pptx* *06_Welcome.docx* *07_ComparisonShop.docx* *02_Presentations* folder, containing: *02_TagTemplate.pptx* *02_Background.jpg* *03_Videos* folder, containing: *03_HouseHome.wmv* *03_YinYang.png* *05_Narrations* folder (empty) *05_Photographs* folder (empty)
Chapter 4: Personalizing Windows Vista	*00_Arizona01.jpg* through *00_Arizona10.jpg*
Chapter 5: Installing and Configuring Devices	None
Chapter 6: Safely and Efficiently Accessing the Internet	None
Chapter 7: Working with Programs	*03_MusicBox.bmp*
Chapter 8: Making Connections	*05_Changes.docx* *05_FindingWord.docx* *05_SavedText.docx*

Chapter	Files
Chapter 9: Working with Digital Media	*01_Arizona01.jpg* through *01_Arizona10.jpg* *01_Background.jpg* *01_Bamboo01.jpg* through *01_Bamboo03.jpg* *01_CakePlate.jpg* *01_Cat.jpg* *01_Crow.jpg* *01_Figurine.jpg* *01_Frog.jpg* *01_Home01.wmv* through *01_Home03.wmv* *01_MusicBox.jpg* *01_TeaPot.jpg* *01_YinYang.jpg*
Chapter 10: Managing Computer Security	*02_Angelic.jpg*
Chapter 11: Optimizing Your Computer System	None
Chapter 12: Identifying and Solving Problems	*04_BookBeat.docx*

In addition to the practice files, the CD contains some exciting resources that will really enhance your ability to get the most out of using this book and Windows Vista, including the following:

- *Windows Vista Step by Step* in eBook format
- *Microsoft Computer Dictionary*, 5th ed. eBook
- *First Look 2007 Microsoft Office System* (Katherine Murray, 2006)
- Sample chapter and poster from *Look Both Ways: Help Protect Your Family on the Internet* (Linda Criddle, 2007)

> **Important** The companion CD for this book does not contain the Windows Vista operating system. You should purchase and install that operating system before using this book.

Minimum System Requirements

Windows Vista

To run Windows Vista, your computer needs to meet the following minimum hardware requirements:

- 800 megahertz (MHz) processor
- 512 megabytes (MB) RAM
- DirectX 9–capable graphics processor
- 20 gigabytes (GB) hard disk drive capacity with 15 GB available space

Computers that meet these requirements may be labeled by their manufacturers as *Windows Vista Capable.*

To get an even better Windows Vista experience, including the Windows Aero visual effects, your computer needs to meet these minimum requirements:

- 1 GHz processor
- 1 GB of system memory
- DirectX 9–capable graphics processor with a Windows Vista Display Driver Model (WDDM) driver, 128 GB of graphics memory (if the GPU uses dedicated memory; otherwise, no additional graphics memory is required), Pixel Shader 2.0 and 32 bits per pixel
- 40 GB hard disk drive capacity with 15 GB available space
- Internal or external DVD-ROM drive
- Audio output capability
- Internet access capability

Computers that meet these requirements may be labeled by their manufacturers as *Windows Vista Premium Ready.*

See Also For information about the Windows Aero visual effects, see "Optimizing Visual Effects" in Chapter 4, "Personalizing Windows Vista."

The TV Tuning, Microsoft BitLocker Drive Encryption, and Tablet PC features available with certain editions of Windows Vista require additional hardware, as indicated in the following table:

Feature	Available in	Additional hardware requirement
Windows Media Center television functionality	Windows Vista Ultimate, Windows Vista Home Premium	A TV tuner card and a remote control that complies with the Windows Vista Remote Control specification
BitLocker Drive Encryption	Windows Vista Enterprise, Windows Vista Ultimate	Integrated Trusted Platform Module (TPM) 1.2 chip or USB 2.0 key
Tablet PC features	Windows Vista Enterprise, Windows Vista Business, Windows Vista Ultimate, Windows Vista Home Premium	A PC that meets the Tablet PC specification and includes an electromagnetic digitizer pen

Step-by-Step Exercises

In addition to the hardware required to run Windows Vista, you will need the following to successfully complete the exercises in this book:

- Windows Vista Home Basic, Windows Vista Home Premium, Windows Vista Ultimate, Windows Vista Business, or Windows Vista Enterprise

  See Also For information about the features available in different editions of Windows Vista, see "Introducing Windows Vista" earlier in this book.

- Monitor with minimum 800×600 screen resolution; 1024×768 or higher recommended

- Keyboard and mouse or compatible pointing device

- Internet connection, 128 kilobits (Kbps) or greater, for download and activation of products, accessing online Help topics, and any other Internet-dependent processes

- Access to the following peripheral devices:

  - Scanner
  - Printer
  - Speakers
  - Camera
  - External storage device
  - Microphone

- 40 MB of available hard disk space for the practice files

Installing the Practice Files

You need to install the practice files in the correct location on your hard disk before you can use them in the exercises. Follow these steps:

1. Remove the companion CD from the envelope at the back of the book, and insert it into the CD drive of your computer.

    The Step By Step Companion CD License Terms appear. Follow the on-screen directions. To use the practice files, you must accept the terms of the license agreement. After you accept the license agreement, a menu screen appears.

    > **Important** If the menu screen does not appear, click the Start button and then click Computer. Display the Folders list in the Navigation pane, click the icon for your CD drive, and then in the right pane, double-click the StartCD executable file.

2. Click **Install Practice Files**.

3. Click **Next** on the first screen, and then click **Next** to accept the terms of the license agreement on the next screen.

4. If you want to install the practice files to a location other than the default folder (*Documents\MSP\SBS_WindowsVista*), click the **Change** button, select the new drive and path, and then click **OK**.

    > **Important** If you install the practice files to a location other than the default, you will need to substitute that path within the exercises.

5. Click **Next** on the **Choose Destination Location** screen, and then click **Install** on the **Ready to Install the Program** screen to install the selected practice files.

6. After the practice files have been installed, click **Finish**.

7. Close the **Step by Step Companion CD** window, remove the companion CD from the CD drive, and return it to the envelope at the back of the book.

Using the Practice Files

When you install the practice files from the companion CD that accompanies this book, the files are stored on your hard disk in chapter-specific subfolders under *Documents\ MSP\SBS_WindowsVista*. Each exercise is preceded by a paragraph that lists the files needed for that exercise and explains any preparations needed before you start working through the exercise. Here are examples:

USE the *02_Angelic* image. This practice file is located in the *Chapter10* folder under *SBS_ WindowsVista*.

BE SURE TO log on to Windows and have an active Internet connection available before beginning this exercise.

OPEN Control Panel, and then display the User Accounts window.

You can browse to the practice files in Windows Explorer by following these steps:

Start

1. On the Windows taskbar, click the **Start** button, and then click **Documents**.

2. In your **Documents** folder, double-click *MSP*, double-click *SBS_WindowsVista*, and then double-click a specific chapter folder.

You can browse to the practice files from a dialog box by following these steps:

1. In the **Favorite Links** pane in the dialog box, click **Documents**.

2. In your **Documents** folder, double-click *MSP*, double-click *SBS_WindowsVista*, and then double-click the specified chapter folder.

Removing and Uninstalling the Practice Files

You can free up hard disk space by uninstalling the practice files that were installed from the companion CD. The uninstall process deletes any files that you created in the *Documents\MSP\SBS_WindowsVista* chapter-specific folders while working through the exercises. Follow these steps:

Start

1. On the Windows taskbar, click the **Start** button, and then click **Control Panel**.

2. In **Control Panel**, under **Programs**, click the **Uninstall a program** task.

3. In the **Programs and Features** window, click **Windows Vista**, and then on the toolbar at the top of the window, click the **Uninstall** button.

4. If the **Programs and Features** message box asking you to confirm the deletion appears, click **Yes**.

See Also If you need additional help installing or uninstalling the practice files, see "Getting Help" later in this book.

Important Microsoft Product Support Services does not provide support for this book or its companion CD.

Getting Help

Every effort has been made to ensure the accuracy of this book and the contents of its companion CD. If you do run into problems, please contact the sources listed below for assistance.

Getting Help with This Book and Its Companion CD

If your question or issue concerns the content of this book or its companion CD, please first search the online Microsoft Press Knowledge Base, which provides support information for known errors in or corrections to this book, at the following Web site:

www.microsoft.com/mspress/support/search.asp

If you do not find your answer at the online Knowledge Base, send your comments or questions to Microsoft Press Technical Support at:

mspinput@microsoft.com

Getting Help with Windows Vista

If your question is about Windows Vista, and not about the content of this Microsoft Press book, first consult the resources listed in Chapter 12, "Identifying and Solving Problems." If you do not find your answer in Windows Help And Support, or through the other resources listed, please search the Windows Vista Solution Center or the Microsoft Knowledge Base at:

support.microsoft.com

In the United States, Microsoft software product support issues not covered by the Microsoft Knowledge Base are addressed by Microsoft Product Support Services. Location-specific software support options are available from:

support.microsoft.com/gp/selfoverview/

Quick Reference

1 Getting Started with Windows Vista

To activate Windows manually, page 8

1. In **Control Panel**, click **System and Maintenance**, and then click **System**.
2. In the **System** window, in the **Windows activation** area, click **Activate Windows now**. In the **User Account Control** dialog box, if you are logged on as an administrator, click **Continue**. Otherwise, enter an administrator password, and click **OK**.
3. In the **Windows Activation** dialog box, click **Activate Windows online now**. Then after Windows verifies that your copy of Windows is genuine, click **Close**.

To automatically download and install critical updates, page 14

1. In **Control Panel**, click **Security**, and then click **Windows Update**.
2. In the left pane, click the **Change settings** task. Then select the **Install updates automatically** option, if it is not already selected.
3. In the second **Install new updates** list, select a time at which your computer will usually be on and online. If you want more control over the update process but still want automatic updates, select the **Download updates but let me choose whether to install them** option.
4. With the **Include recommended updates** and **Use Microsoft Update** check boxes selected, click **OK**. In the **User Account Control** dialog box, if you are logged on as an administrator, click **Continue**. Otherwise, enter an administrator password, and click **OK**.

To install available Windows updates, page 14

1. In **Control Panel**, click **Security**, and then click **Windows Update**.
2. If updates are available, click the **View available updates** task in the update status box. Then in the list of available updates, select the check box for any update you want to install.
3. Click **Install**. In the **User Account Control** box, if you are logged on as an administrator, click **Continue**. Otherwise, enter an administrator password, and click **OK**.

To log on to a user account while another is active, page 17

1. On the **Start** menu, click the **Shut Down Options** button, and then click **Switch User**.
2. On the **Welcome** screen, click the user account you want to log on to, and enter the password if one is required.

To lock your computer, page 19

→ On the **Start** menu, click the **Lock** button.

To unlock your computer, page 19

→ If your account is password protected, on the **Welcome** screen, enter your password in the **Password** box, and then press Enter. Otherwise, click your user account picture.

To put your computer into Sleep mode, page 19

→ On the **Start** menu, click the **Sleep** button.

To wake your computer from Sleep mode, page 19

→ Depending on your specific hardware, press Enter or press your computer's power button to wake your computer.

To log off from Windows, page 20

1. On the **Start** menu, click the **Shut Down Options** button, and then click **Log Off**.

2. If you don't have any unsaved work, click **Log off now** to complete the process and display the Welcome screen. Otherwise, click **Cancel** to return to your computing session; then save and close open files, shut down running programs, and click **Log Off** in the **Shut Down Options** list to complete the process.

To shut down your computer, page 20

→ If you've already logged off from your computer, in the lower-right corner of the **Welcome** screen, click the **Shut Down** button.

→ If you haven't yet logged off, on the **Start** menu, click the **Shut Down Options** button, and then in the **Shut Down Options** list, click **Shut Down**.

To open the Ease Of Access Center, page 23

→ In **Control Panel**, click **Ease of Access**, and then click **Ease of Access Center**.

2   Working Efficiently in Windows Vista

To change the number of recently opened programs displayed on the Start menu, page 33

1. Right-click the **Start** button, and then click **Properties**.

2. On the **Start Menu** tab of the **Taskbar and Start Menu Properties** dialog box, with the **Start menu** option selected, click **Customize**.

3. In the **Start menu size** area of the **Customize Start Menu** dialog box, type or select the number of programs you want displayed, and then click **OK**.

4. In the **Taskbar and Start Menu Properties** dialog box, click **OK**.

To start a program from the Start menu, page 35

1. On the **Start** menu, click **All Programs**.
2. In the **All Programs** list, click a program name, or click a folder containing a program you want to open, and then click the program name.

To add a shortcut to the pinned programs area of the Start menu, page 38

→ Right-click a program icon in the **All Programs** list of the **Start** menu, or in Windows Explorer, and then click **Pin to Start Menu**.

→ Drag a program icon from the recently opened programs area or **All Programs** list of the **Start** menu to the pinned programs area.

→ Drag a program icon from Windows Explorer to the **Start** button, and then when the **Start** menu opens, to the pinned programs area.

To remove a shortcut from the pinned programs area of the Start menu, page 39

→ In the pinned programs area, right-click the program icon, and then click **Unpin from Start Menu**.

To browse the folder structure of your computer, page 43

1. In the **Navigation** pane, display the **Folders** list.
2. Click the arrow beside a folder name or double-click the folder name to show its list of subfolders; or in the Address bar, click the arrow to the right of the folder name to display its list of subfolders, and then click the folder name you want in the list.

To resize a window, page 44

→ In an open window, click the **Maximize** or **Restore Down** button in the upper-right corner of the window.

→ In a non-maximized window, point to the window's frame. When the pointer changes to a double-headed arrow, drag the frame to the size you want.

To hide a window, page 44

→ In an open window, click the **Minimize** button in the upper-right corner of the window.

To close a window, page 45

→ Click the **Close** button in an open window, or if the window is hidden, click the window's taskbar button, and then click **Close**.

To switch between multiple windows, page 49

→ On the **Quick Launch** toolbar, click the **Switch between windows** button, and then click the window you want to display.

To minimize all open windows, page 50

→ On the **Quick Launch** toolbar, click the **Show desktop** button.

To view a group of windows at the same time, page 50

→ Right-click the taskbar button for a group of programs, and then click **Show Windows Stacked**.

To lock or unlock the taskbar, page 51

→ Right-click an empty area of the taskbar, and then click **Lock the Taskbar**.

To resize the taskbar, page 51

→ Point to the top of the taskbar. When the pointer changes to a double-headed arrow, drag the border up or down until it's the size you want.

To modify what appears on the taskbar, page 51

1. Right-click an empty area of the taskbar, and then click **Properties**.
2. In the **Taskbar and Start Menu Properties** dialog box, select the options you want on each tab, and then click **OK**.

To create a desktop shortcut, page 54

1. Right-click an open area of the desktop, point to **New**, and then click **Shortcut**.
2. In the **Create Shortcut** wizard, type in the location of the item; or click **Browse**, navigate to and click the program you want, and then click **OK**.
3. In the **Create Shortcut** wizard, click **Next**.
4. In the **Type a name for this shortcut** box, type a name, and then click **Finish**.

To rearrange items on the desktop, page 57

→ Drag a shortcut on your desktop to the location you want it to appear.

→ Right-click an empty area of the desktop, point to **View**, and then click **Auto Arrange**.

To delete an item from the desktop, page 58

→ Right-click the shortcut, click **Delete**, and then in the confirmation message box, click **Yes**.

3   Working with Folders and Files

To display the contents of folders, drives, and storage devices accessible to your computer, page 64

→ Point to **All Programs** on the **Start** menu, click **Accessories**, and then click **Windows Explorer** to display the contents of your Documents folder.

→ Right-click a folder and then click **Explore**.

→ Click a folder link on the **Start** menu to open that folder. For example, click **Computer** or **Network** to display an overview of all the hard disk drives and storage devices accessible to your computer.

To navigate recent files in Windows Explorer, page 68

→ Click the **Back** button or **Forward** button to display the contents of folders you have already viewed in the Content pane.

→ Click the **Recent Pages** button to see a list of folders you have viewed so that you can select the one you want to display.

To add a folder to the Favorite Links list, page 66

→ In the **Contents** pane of Windows Explorer, drag the folder you want to add to the list.

To map a drive, page 69

1. On the **Start** menu, click **Computer**.
2. On the toolbar above the Content pane, click **Map network drive**. Then in the **Map Network Drive** window, specify the letter by which you want to identify this drive.
3. Click **Browse**, navigate to the drive or folder you want to map, and then click **OK** to return to the Map Network Drive window with the path entered in the Folder box.
4. If you want to connect to this location only until the end of the current Windows session, clear the **Reconnect at logon** check box. Then click **Finish**.

To disconnect from a mapped drive or folder, page 69

→ In Windows Explorer, right-click the drive or folder, and then click **Disconnect**.

To display or hide panes in Windows Explorer, page 71

→ On the **Organize** menu, point to **Layout**, and then in the list, click the pane you want to change.

To change the view of folders or files, page 72

→ On the Windows Explorer toolbar, click the **Views** button to cycle through the four most common views; or, click the **Views** arrow, and then select the view you want by dragging the slider.

To change the sort order in a Windows Explorer list view, page 74

→ Click the heading that you want to sort by. Click it again to reverse the sort order.

To delete a column in a Windows Explorer list view, page 74

→ Right-click a column heading, and then in the attributes list, click the attribute you want to add.

To change the properties of a file, page 78

→ Display the folder containing the file in Windows Explorer. Click the file, and then modify its properties in the **Details** pane.

To remove properties from a file, page 79

1. Select a file in Windows Explorer, and then on the **Organize** menu, click **Remove Properties**.

2. In the **Remove Properties** dialog box, select the properties you want to remove.

To create a folder from Windows Explorer, page 82

1. On the **Organize** menu, click **New Folder**.

2. With the *New Folder* file name highlighted, type the name you want for the folder, and then press Enter.

To compress a file, page 85

→ In Windows Explorer, right-click the file you want to compress, point to **Send To**, and then click **Compressed (zipped) Folder**.

To delete multiple files, page 86

1. In Windows Explorer, click the first file you want to delete, hold down the Ctrl key, and then click the other file(s) you want to delete; or to select a range of files, click the first file, hold down the Shift key, and then click the last file.

2. Press the Del key. Then in the Delete Multiple Items message box, click **Yes**.

To permanently delete items from the Recycle Bin, page 86

→ Open the Recycle Bin, verify that you do not want to retain any items, and then on the toolbar, click **Empty the Recycle Bin**. In the **Delete Multiple Items** message box, click **Yes** to permanently delete all items.

→ On the desktop or in the **Folders** list, right-click the **Recycle Bin**, and then click **Empty Recycle Bin** to delete all items without first reviewing them.

→ Open the Recycle Bin, select specific items you want to permanently delete, press Enter, and then in the **Delete File** message box, click **Yes**.

To restore files from the Recycle Bin, page 86

→ Open the Recycle Bin, do not select any items, and then on the toolbar, click **Restore all items** to return all deleted items to their previous locations.

→ Open the Recycle Bin, select specific items you want to restore, and then on the toolbar, click **Restore this item** to return selected items to their previous locations.

To copy files to other folders, page 88

→ In Windows Explorer, click the file you want to copy, and on the **Organize** menu, click **Copy**. Then display the folder you want to copy the file to, and on the **Organize** menu, click **Paste**.

→ Using the secondary mouse button, drag the file to its new location. Then when you release the mouse button, click **Copy Here**.

→ Hold down the Ctrl key, and then drag the copy to its new location, releasing first the mouse button and then the Ctrl key.

To search for items on your computer and on the Internet, page 91

→ Click the **Start** button, and then in the **Start Search** box, type what you want to search for. To use the Internet for your search, at the bottom of the **Start** menu, click the **Search the Internet** link.

→ On the **Start** menu, click **Search**. Then in the **Search** box, type what you want to search for. To use advanced criteria to help focus your search, click the **Advanced Search** arrow, and fill in any extra information you want.

4 Personalizing Windows Vista

To switch between themes, page 98

1. In **Control Panel**, click **Appearance and Personalization**.
2. Under **Personalization**, click the **Change the theme** task.
3. Click the **Theme** arrow, and then in the list, click the theme you want to use. Then click **OK**.

To adjust the refresh rate and the color depth of your monitor, page 103

1. In **Control Panel**, under **Appearance and Personalization**, click the **Adjust screen resolution** task.
2. In the **Display Settings** dialog box, click **Advanced Settings**.
3. In the **Advanced Settings** dialog box, click the **Monitor** tab. In the **Monitor Settings** area, click the **Screen refresh rate** arrow to display a list of valid refresh rates for the selected monitor.
4. Select a screen refresh rate of at least 10 Hertz, preferably 70 or over. Then click **OK**. If your computer system includes multiple monitors on the same graphics adapter or multiple enabled graphics adapters, select the other monitors in turn, click **Advanced Settings**, confirm the available graphics memory, select an appropriate refresh rate, and click **OK**.
5. In the **Display Settings** dialog box, click the **Colors** arrow to display the available color qualities. Set the color quality to at least **32 bit**. Then click **OK**.

To change the color scheme, page 105

1. In **Control Panel**, under **Appearance and Personalization**, click the **Change the color scheme** task.

2. In the **Appearance Settings** dialog box, in the **Color scheme** list, click the color scheme you want. Then click **OK**.

To enable window transparency, page 107

1. Apply the Windows Aero color scheme.

2. In **Control Panel**, under **Appearance and Personalization**, click the **Change the color scheme** task.

3. On the **Window Color and Appearance** page, select the **Enable transparency** check box. Then click **OK**.

To change the desktop background to a Windows Vista picture, page 109

1. In **Control Panel**, under **Appearance and Personalization**, click the **Change desktop background** task.

2. In the **Picture Location** list, click **Windows Wallpapers**.

3. In the **Windows Wallpapers** gallery, click the thumbnail of the picture you want. Then click **OK**.

To change the desktop background to your own picture, page 110

1. Save the picture you want to use to your Pictures folder.

2. In **Control Panel**, under **Appearance and Personalization**, click the **Change desktop background** task.

3. In the **Picture Location** list, click **Pictures**.

4. Click the thumbnail of the picture you want. Then click **OK**.

To change the desktop background color, page 111

1. In **Control Panel**, under **Appearance and Personalization**, click the **Change desktop background** task.

2. In the **Picture Location** list, click **Solid Colors**.

3. In the **Solid Colors** gallery, click the color you want. Then click **OK**.

To use your photos as a screen saver, page 113

1. In **Control Panel**, click **Appearance and Personalization**. Then under **Personalization**, click the **Change screen saver** task.

2. In the **Screen Saver Settings** dialog box, click the **Screen saver** arrow, and then in the list, click **Photos**. Then click **Settings**.

3. In the **Photos Screen Saver Settings** dialog box, to the right of **Use pictures and videos from**, click **Browse**.

4. In the **Browse For Folder** dialog box, browse to the folder that has the photos you want to use, and then click **OK**. Adjust the slide show speed if you want, and then click **Save**.

To change the system time, page 116

1. Right-click in the notification area at the right end of the status bar, and then click **Adjust Date/Time**.

2. In the **Date and Time** dialog box, click **Change date and time**. In the **User Account Control** dialog box, if you are logged on as an administrator, click **Continue**. Otherwise, enter an administrator password, and click **OK**.

3. Drag the mouse pointer over the hour, minutes, or AM/PM setting displayed in the digital clock to select it, and then type or select (by clicking the arrows) the time you want.

4. Click **OK** in each of the open dialog boxes.

To connect to an Internet time server for an automatic update, page 114

1. Right-click in the notification area at the right end of the status bar, and then click **Adjust Date/Time**.

2. In the **Date and Time** dialog box, click the **Internet Time** tab, and then click **Change settings**. In the **User Account Control** dialog box, if you are logged on as an administrator, click **Continue**. Otherwise, enter an administrator password, and click **OK**.

3. In the **Internet Time Settings** dialog box, with the **Synchronize with an Internet time server** check box selected, click the **Server** arrow. In the list, click the server you want to use, and then click **Update now**.

To view the computer name, page 119

→ On the **Start** menu, click **Computer**. The computer name appears in the lower-left corner of the **Computer** window.

To change the computer name, page 119

1. On the **Start** menu, right-click **Computer**, and then click **Properties**.

2. In the **Computer name, domain, and workgroup settings** area of the **System** window, click **Change settings**. In the **User Account Control** dialog box, if you are logged on as an administrator, click **Continue**. Otherwise, enter an administrator password, and click **OK**.

3. On the **Computer Name** tab of the **System Properties** dialog box, click **Change**, and replace the existing computer name with the name you want. Then click **OK**.

To change the name of the link to your Computer folder, page 120

→ On the **Start** menu, right-click **Computer**, click **Rename**, type the name you want to appear, and then press `Enter`.

5   Installing and Configuring Devices

To change your screen resolution, page 127

1. In **Control Panel**, under **Appearance and Personalization**, click the **Adjust screen resolution** task.
2. In the **Display Settings** dialog box, drag the **Resolution** slider to the setting you want, and then click **Apply**.
3. In the **Display Settings** message box that appears, click **Yes**.

To configure your computer to display your Windows desktop across two monitors, page 130

1. In **Control Panel**, under **Appearance and Personalization**, click the **Adjust screen resolution** task.
2. In the preview area, click Monitor 2, select the **Extend my Windows desktop onto this monitor** check box, and then click **Apply**.
3. In the **Display Settings** message box that appears, click **Yes**.

To change the primary monitor, page 131

1. In **Control Panel**, under **Appearance and Personalization**, click the **Adjust screen resolution** task.
2. In the preview area, click the monitor you want as the primary.
3. Select the **This is my main monitor** check box, and then click **Apply**.
4. In the **Display Settings** message box that appears, click **Yes**.

To adjust the relationship of the displays to each other, page 131

1. In **Control Panel**, under **Appearance and Personalization**, click the **Adjust screen resolution** task.
2. In the preview area of the **Display Settings** dialog box, drag Monitor 2 to the location you want it to be in relationship to Monitor 1.

To change the way the mouse buttons work, page 133

1. In **Control Panel**, under **Hardware and Sound**, click **Mouse**.
2. On the **Buttons** tab of the **Mouse Properties** dialog box, in the **Button configuration** section, select the **Switch primary and secondary buttons** check box to change the default primary button from left to right.
3. In the **Double-click speed** area, drag the slider to the speed you want. Then click **OK**.

To change how the mouse pointer looks and works, page 134

1. In **Control Panel**, under **Hardware and Sound**, click **Mouse**.
2. On the **Pointers** tab of the **Mouse Properties** dialog box, in the **Scheme** list, click one of the 21 available system schemes to change the pointer set.

3. In the **Customize** list, click any pointer, and then click **Browse**. Then in the **Browse** dialog box displaying the contents of your Cursors folder, double-click any cursor to replace the selected pointer.

4. Click the **Pointer Options** tab, and set the pointer speed, movement, and visibility options. Then click **OK**.

To change how the mouse wheel works, page 135

1. In **Control Panel**, under **Hardware and Sound**, click **Mouse**.

2. On the **Wheel** tab of the **Mouse Properties** dialog box, in the **Vertical Scrolling** area, select either the **The following number of lines at a time** option (and then type or click the arrow keys to set the number of lines you want to scroll) or the **One screen at a time** option to control how much of the screen scrolls as you turn the mouse wheel.

3. If your mouse supports horizontal scrolling, in the **Tilt the wheel to scroll the following number of characters at a time** box, enter the number of characters you want to scroll horizontally when you tilt the mouse wheel left or right. Then click **OK**.

To configure your computer to enter keystrokes as though you are typing on a different-language keyboard, page 137

1. In **Control Panel**, click **Clock, Language, and Region**, and then under **Regional and Language Options**, click the **Change keyboards or other input methods** task.

2. In the **Regional and Language Options** dialog box, on the **Keyboards and Languages** tab, click **Change keyboards**.

3. In the **Text Services and Input Languages** dialog box, in the **Default input language** list, click the language you want. Or, to accept input from a language-specific keyboard not in the list, click **Add** in the **Installed services** area.

4. In the **Add Input Language** dialog box, in the list of languages, click the **Expand** button to the left of the language keyboard you want, and then click the **Expand** button to the left of **Keyboard**.

5. In the **Keyboard** list, select the language's check box, and then click **OK** in the **Add Input Language** dialog box.

6. In the **Text Services and Input Languages** dialog box, click **OK**.

7. On the **Language Bar**, click the input language button. Then in the input language list, click your chosen language.

To remove a different-language keyboard, page 141

1. In **Control Panel**, click **Clock, Language, and Region**, and then under **Regional and Language Options**, click the **Change keyboards or other input methods** task.

2. In the **Regional and Language Options** dialog box, on the **Keyboards and Languages** tab, click **Change keyboards**.

3. In the **Installed services** area, click the keyboard you want to remove, and then click **Remove**.

To change the screen orientation of your Tablet PC, page 142

1. In **Control Panel**, tap **Mobile PC**, and then tap **Tablet PC Settings**.

2. On the **Display** tab of the **Tablet PC Settings** dialog box, in the **Orientation** list, tap the orientation you want. Then click **Apply**.

To set the pen equivalents of various mouse actions, page 143

1. In **Control Panel**, tap **Mobile PC**, and then tap **Tablet PC Settings**.

2. Tap the **Other** tab, and then tap the **Go to Pen and Input Devices** link.

3. On the **Pen Options** tab of the **Pen and Input Devices** dialog box, select the options you want.

To change the position of the Input Panel, page 147

1. Tap the **Input Panel** tab.

2. On the **Input Panel**, tap **Tools**, and then in the list, tap the option you want.

To install a local printer and test the installation by printing a test page, page 148

1. Connect the printer to the appropriate port on your computer.

2. Connect the printer to a power outlet, and then if necessary, turn it on.

3. If Windows Vista does not recognize the printer, skip to Step 5. Otherwise, click the alert to display the progress of the printer installation.

4. After Windows Vista declares the printer ready to use, close the **Driver Software Installation** window. If the installation does not complete successfully, continue with Step 5.

5. Open **Control Panel**, and under **Hardware and Sound**, click **Printer**.

6. On the toolbar of the **Printers** window, click **Add a printer**.

7. On the **Add Printer** wizard's first page, click **Add a local printer**.

8. On the **Choose a printer port** page, select the port to which your printer is connected from the **Use an existing port** list, and then click **Next**.

9. If you have an installation CD for your printer, insert it in the appropriate drive, click **Have Disk**, and then follow the instructions on the screen to install your printer. Otherwise, in the **Manufacturer** list, click the brand name of your printer.

10. In the **Printers** list, click the model of your printer (which you can usually find printed on the top or front of the printer). Then click **Next**. (If the Printers list doesn't include your specific model, select a model with a similar name, or download the necessary drivers from the printer manufacturer's Web site, return to the **Install the Printer Driver** page, and click **Have Disk** to install the printer manually.)

11. On the **Type a printer name** page, change the printer name if you want, or accept the default name. If you want Windows and any programs you install, such as Microsoft Office Word, to print to this printer when you click the Print button, select the **Set as the default printer** check box. Then click **Next**.

12. On the wizard's confirmation page, click **Print a test page**.

13. In the confirmation message box, click **Close**. Then in the **Add Printer** wizard, click **Finish**.

To change your default printer, page 151

1. In **Control Panel**, click **Hardware and Sound**, and then click **Printers**.

2. In the **Printers** window, double-click the printer you want to set as the default. Then on the **Printer** menu of the printer's management window, click **Set as Default Printer**.

To share a printer, page 152

1. In **Control Panel**, click **Hardware and Sound**, and then click **Printers**.

2. In the **Printers** window, right-click the printer you want to share, and then click **Sharing**.

3. In the **Properties** dialog box, click **Change sharing options**. In the **User Account Control** dialog box, if you are logged on as an administrator, click **Continue**. Otherwise, enter an administrator password, and click **OK**.

4. On the **Sharing** tab, select the **Share this printer** check box. Then in the **Share name** box, type a simple name for the printer (or leave the default).

5. In the **Properties** dialog box, click **OK**.

To connect to a network printer, page 154

1. In **Control Panel**, under **Hardware and Sound**, click **Printer**.

2. On the toolbar of the **Printers** window, click **Add a printer**.

3. On the **Add Printer** wizard's first page, click **Add a network, wireless, or Bluetooth printer**.

4. On the **Select a printer** page, click the printer you want to connect to, and then click **Next**.

5. In the **Printers** message box, click **Install driver**. In the **User Account Control** dialog box, if you are logged on as an administrator, click **Continue**. Otherwise, enter an administrator password, and click **OK**.

6. On the **Type a printer name** page, change the printer name if you want, or accept the default name. If you want Windows and any programs you install, such as Word, to print to this printer when you click the **Print** button, select the **Set as the default printer** check box. Then click **Next**.

7. In the **Add Printer** wizard, click **Finish**.

To connect speakers to your Windows Vista computer, and adjust the audio output levels, page 157

1. Remove the speakers from their packaging, if you have not already done so. If you are using an alternate audio configuration, such as a headset microphone, connect the input and output cables appropriately, and then skip to Step 6.

2. Link the two speakers by using the connector cable.

3. Position the speakers to the left and right of your monitor to provide stereo sound quality.

4. Connect the speakers to a power outlet by using the AC adapter cord.

5. Plug the speakers into the speaker jack on the computer by using the connector cable.

6. Open **Control Panel**, click **Hardware and Sound**, and then click **Sound.**

7. In the **Sound** dialog box, click each of the tabs, and explore the options available. Then on the **Playback** tab, click your speakers, and click **Configure**.

8. On the **Choose your configuration** page of the **Speaker Setup** wizard, select the appropriate audio channel, and then click **Test**. Try testing each of the configurations to hear the different options. Finally, select the channel you want, and then click **Next**.

9. If the **Select full-range speakers** page appears, click **Next** to complete the configuration, and then on the **Configuration complete** page, click **Finish**.

To connect a microphone to your Windows Vista computer, and adjust the audio input levels, page 160

1. Remove the microphone from its packaging, if you have not already done so. If you are using a USB microphone, ensure that you are logged in as an administrator before connecting the microphone to the USB port.

2. Plug the microphone connector cable into the audio input jack on your computer, or into a USB port, depending on the connection type.

3. Open **Control Panel**, and then click **Ease of Access**.

4. In the **Ease of Access** window, under **Speech Recognition Options**, click **Set up a microphone**.

5. In the **Microphone Setup** wizard, select the option for the type of microphone you are using, and then click **Next**.

6. On the **Set up your microphone page**, read the instructions, and then click **Next**.

7. On the **Adjust the microphone volume** page, read the microphone test paragraph aloud in your normal speaking voice.

8. When you finish reading the paragraph, click **Next**. Then click **Finish** to complete the wizard.

6   Safely and Efficiently Accessing the Internet

To connect to the Internet through a broadband or dial-up connection, page 168

1. In **Control Panel**, click **Network and Internet**.
2. Under **Network and Sharing Center**, click the **Connect to a network** task.
3. At the bottom of the page in the **Connect to a network** wizard, click the **Set up a connection or network** link.
4. On the **Choose a connection option** page, click **Connect to the Internet**, and then click **Next**.
5. On the **How do you want to connect** page, click either **Broadband** or **Dial-up**, and then click **Next**.
6. Enter the requested connection information, and then click **Connect** to close the window and create the connection.

To start Internet Explorer, page 171

→ On the **Start** menu, click **Internet**.

→ If Internet Explorer is not your default browser, point to **All Programs** on the **Start** menu, and then click **Internet Explorer**.

To open Web sites, page 171

→ In Internet Explorer, click once in the **Address** box, type the address of the Web site you want to visit, and then click the **Go** button or press [Enter].

To open a recently visited Web site, page 171

1. Click the **Start** button, and in the **Start Search** box, type http://.
2. In the results shown on the Start menu, click the site you want to open.

To return to a previous Web page, page 173

→ In Internet Explorer, to the left of the **Address** box, click the **Back** or **Forward** button; or, to the right of the Back and Forward buttons, click the **Recent Pages** button, and then in the list, click the page you want to go to.

To change tabbed browsing settings, page 174

1. On the Internet Explorer **Tools** menu, click **Internet Options**.
2. In the **General** tab of the **Internet Options** dialog box, in the **Tabs** area, click **Settings**.
3. In the **Tabbed Browsing Settings** dialog box, review the types of changes you can make, and change any settings that you want. Then click **OK** in each open dialog box.

To modify Pop-up Blocker settings, page 177

→ On the Internet Explorer **Tools** menu, point to **Pop-up Blocker**, and then click **Pop-up Blocker Settings**.

To turn off Pop-up Blocker, page 177

→ On the Internet Explorer **Tools** menu, point to **Pop-up Blocker**, and then click **Turn off Pop-up Blocker**. Then in the **Pop-up Blocker** message box requesting confirmation, click **Yes**.

To change your home page, page 178

1. In Internet Explorer, display the Web page you want to set as your home page.

2. On the **Command** bar, click the **Home** arrow, and then in the list, click **Add or Change Home Page**.

3. In the **Add or Change Home Page** dialog box, select the **Use this webpage as your only home page** option, and then click **Yes**.

To add a second home page, page 179

1. In Internet Explorer, display the Web page you want to set as your second home page.

2. In the **Home** list, click **Add or Change Home Page**. Then in the dialog box, select the **Add this webpage to your home page tabs** option, and click **Yes**.

To display your home page, page 179

→ On the Internet Explorer **Command** bar, click the **Home** button.

To set a blank home page, page 179

→ In Internet Explorer, in the **Home** list, point to **Remove**, and click **Remove All**. Then in the **Delete Home Page** dialog box, click **Yes**.

To change the size of the text on Web pages that don't specify text size, page 180

→ On the Internet Explorer **Page** menu, point to **Text Size**, and then click the size you want: **Smallest**, **Smaller**, **Medium** (the default), **Larger**, or **Largest**.

To change the text and background colors used on Web pages without color specifications, page 180

1. On the Internet Explorer **Tools** menu, click **Internet Options**.

2. On the **General** tab of the **Internet Options** dialog box, in the **Appearance** area, click **Colors**.

3. In the **Colors** dialog box, clear the **Use Windows colors** check box.

4. Click the **Text, Background, Visited**, or **Unvisited** color button, select the color you want to use for that feature, and then click **OK** in each open dialog box.

To override the default color and font options on Web sites, page 180

1. On the Internet Explorer **Tools** menu, click **Internet Options**.

2. On the **General** tab of the **Internet Options** dialog box, in the **Appearance** area, click **Accessibility**.

3. In the **Formatting** area of the **Accessibility** dialog box, select the **Ignore colors specified on webpages** check box and the **Ignore font sizes specified on webpages** check box. Then click **OK**.

To search the Web, page 183

→ In the Internet Explorer **Live Search** box at the right end of the Navigation bar, type a plain-text query, and then click the **Search** button.

To add search providers to the Search Options list, page 183

→ At the right end of the Internet Explorer **Live Search** box, click the **Search Options** arrow. Then in the **Search Options** list, click **Find More Providers**.

To add a page to your Favorites list, page 183

1. In Internet Explorer, display the page you want to add. On the toolbar, click the **Add to Favorites** button, and then in the list, click **Add to Favorites**.

2. In the **Add a Favorite** dialog box, click **Add** to make the current page available from your Favorites list.

To view your Web browsing history, page 184

1. To the left of the page tabs, click the **Favorites Center** button.

2. In the **Favorites Center**, click the **History** arrow, and then click the sort order you want.

To display the Favorites Center as a pane, page 184

1. On the Internet Explorer toolbar, click the **Favorites Center** button.

2. In the upper-right corner of the **Favorites Center**, click the **Pin the Favorites Center** button.

To preview a Web page before printing, page 185

→ In Internet Explorer, display a Web page you want to print. Then on the **Command** bar, click the **Print** arrow, and click **Print Preview**.

To print a Web page, page 187

1. On the Internet Explorer **Command** bar, click the **Print** button.

2. Select the printer you want to use, and then click **Print**.

To send a Web page in an e-mail message, page 188

1. On the Internet Explorer **Page** menu, click **Send Page by E-mail**. Then in the **Internet Explorer Security** message box that appears, click **Allow**.

2. Address the e-mail message, and then send it.

To send a link to a Web page in an e-mail message, page 189

→ On the Internet Explorer **Page** menu, click **Send Link by E-mail**. Then address the e-mail and send it.

To configure the Content Advisor settings, page 194

1. On the Internet Explorer **Tools** menu, click **Internet Options**, and then in the **Internet Options** dialog box, click the **Content** tab.

2. In the **Content Advisor** area, click **Enable**. In the **User Account Control** dialog box, if you are logged on as an administrator, click **Continue**. Otherwise, enter an administrator password, and click **OK**.

3. In the **Select a category** list of the **Content Advisor** dialog box, click each category and then adjust the slider to the restriction level you want.

4. Then click the **Approved Sites** tab, and add any sites you want to this list.

5. Click the **General** tab, and set the options you want.

6. In the **Supervisor password** area, click **Create password**.

7. In the **Create Supervisor Password** dialog box, type a password in the **Password** and **Confirm password** boxes, and click **OK**. Then click **OK** in the message box confirming that the password was successfully created.

8. In the **Content Advisor** dialog box, click **OK**. Then click **OK** in the message box confirming that Content Advisor has been enabled, and close the open dialog box.

To display a Web page that Content Advisor has blocked, page 195

→ In the Content Advisor window that opens when you attempt to view a blocked Web page, select the **Always allow this website to be viewed** option, type the password in the **Password** box if necessary, and then click **OK**.

To disable Content Advisor, page 198

1. On the Internet Explorer **Tools** menu, click **Internet Options**, display the **Content** tab, and then click **Disable**.

2. If necessary, in the **Supervisor Password Required** message box, type the password in the **Password** box, and then click **OK**. If a message box appears, notifying you that Content Advisor has been turned off, click **OK**. Then close the **Internet Options** dialog box.

7 Working with Programs

To uninstall a program, page 205

1. In **Control Panel**, under **Programs**, click the **Uninstall a program** task.

2. On the Programs and Features page, select the program you want to remove.

3. On the toolbar, click **Uninstall**. Then in the message box asking you to confirm that you want to proceed, click **Yes**. In the **User Account Control** dialog box, if you are logged on as an administrator, click **Continue**. Otherwise, enter an administrator password and click **OK**.

4. If a message box informs you that you need to restart your computer to finish the uninstall process, click **Yes** to restart your computer now, or click **No** to complete the uninstall process when you next start or restart your computer.

To start a program automatically, page 207

1. On the **Start** menu, point to **All Programs**, right-click **Startup**, and then click **Explore All Users**.

2. In the **Folders** list, display the contents of the folder containing the program you want.

3. If necessary, scroll the **Navigation** pane until the *Startup* folder is visible.

4. In the **Content** pane, hold down the right mouse button, and drag the program to the **Startup** folder in the **Navigation** pane, releasing the mouse button when you see the *Move to Startup* ScreenTip.

5. On the context menu, click **Copy Here**. In the **User Account Control** dialog box, if you are logged on as an administrator, click **Continue**. Otherwise, enter an administrator password, and click **OK**.

To change the default program for a file type, page 211

1. In Windows Explorer, right-click the file for which you want to change the associated program, point to **Open With**, and then click **Choose Default Program**.

2. In the **Open With** dialog box, under **Recommended Programs**, click the program you want to use, or click **Browse** and then navigate to the program you want to use.

3. Select the **Always use the selected program to open this kind of file** check box, and then click **OK**.

To change the default middleware settings, page 212

1. On the **Start** menu, click **Default Programs**.

2. Click the **Set program access and computer defaults** task. In the **User Account Control** dialog box, if you are logged on as an administrator, click **Continue**. Otherwise, enter an administrator password, and click **OK**.

3. In the **Set Program Access and Computer Defaults** dialog box, select the **Microsoft Windows**, **Non-Microsoft**, or **Custom** option, make any necessary changes, and then click **OK**.

To add a Games link to the Start menu, page 220

1. Right-click the **Start** button, and then click **Properties**.

2. On the **Start Menu** tab of the **Properties** dialog box, click **Customize**.

3. Scroll the list in the **Customize Start Menu** dialog box, and under **Games**, select the **Display as a link** option. Then click **OK** in each of the open dialog boxes.

To display Windows Sidebar, page 223

→ On the **Start** menu, point to **All Programs**, click **Accessories**, and then click **Windows Sidebar**.

To change the appearance of the Sidebar clock, page 224

1. On **Sidebar**, point to the **Clock** gadget, and then click the **Options** button.

2. In the preview area, click the **Next** button until the clock face you want is displayed.

3. In the **Clock name** box, type a name for the clock. Then select the **Show the second hand** check box if you want to, and click **OK**.

To view current news headlines, page 225

1. On **Sidebar**, in the **Feed Headlines** gadget, click the **View Headlines** link.

2. Click any headline that interests you. To view an entire article, click the headline at the top of the synopsis window.

To add a gadget to Windows Sidebar, page 225

1. On the **Sidebar control** at the top of Sidebar, click the **Add** button (labeled with a plus sign).

2. Drag the gadget you want to add from the **Gadgets** window to Sidebar. Then close the **Gadgets** window.

To detach or reattach a gadget on Windows Sidebar, page 227

→ On **Sidebar**, right-click the gadget you want to detach or reattach, and then click **Detach from Sidebar** or **Attach to Sidebar**.

To change the Windows Sidebar properties, page 228

1. Right-click an empty area of **Sidebar**, and then click **Properties**.

2. Change any properties you want, click **Apply**, and then click **OK**.

8   Making Connections

To join your computer to a new workgroup, page 233

1. In **Control Panel**, click **System and Maintenance**, and then click **System**.

2. In the **System** window, under **Computer name, domain, and workgroup settings**, click **Change settings**. In the **User Account Control** dialog box, if you are logged on as an administrator, click **Continue**. Otherwise, enter an administrator password, and click **OK**.

3. On the **Computer Name** tab of the **System Properties** dialog box, to the right of **To use a wizard to join a domain or workgroup**, click **Network ID**.

4. On the first page of the **Join a Domain or Workgroup** wizard, with the **This computer is part of a business network** option selected, click **Next**.

5. Select the **My company uses a network without a domain** option, and then click **Next**.

6. In the **Workgroup** box, type a name to describe your workgroup. Then click **Next**.

7. On the wizard's final page, click **Finish**. Then in the **System Properties** dialog box, click **OK**.

8. Close any open files and quit any running programs. Then in the message box, click **Restart Now**.

To create a VPN connection over the Internet, page 236

1. Display **Control Panel**, and then click **Network and Internet**.

2. In the **Network and Internet** window, under **Network and Sharing Center**, click the **Connect to a network** task, and then at the bottom of the **Connect to a network** window, click the **Set up a connection or network** task.

3. In the **Connect to a network** wizard, scroll to the end of the **Choose a connection option** list, click **Connect to a workplace**, and then click **Next**.

4. On the **How do you want to connect** page, click **Use my Internet connection (VPN)**.

5. On the **Type the Internet Address to connect to** page, in the **Internet address** box, type the remote access server's host name or IP address, and in the **Destination name** box, type a name for the connection.

6. Specify whether you want to make the connection available to other users of your computer or keep it to yourself, and then click **Next**.

7. On the **Type your user name and password** page, enter your network credentials, click **Connect**, and then in the **Connect to a workplace** wizard, click **Close**.

8. If the **Set Network Location** window appears, click **Work**. In the **User Account Control** dialog box, if you are logged on as an administrator, click **Continue**. Otherwise, enter an administrator password, and click **OK**.

To set up an ad hoc network, page 240

1. On the **Start** menu, click **Connect To**.

2. In the **Connect to a network** window, click the **Set up a connection or network** task.

3. On the **Choose a connection option** page, click **Set up a wireless ad hoc (computer-to-computer) network**, click **Next**, and then, after reading the information on the page, click **Next** again.

4. Provide a network name, select whether the network is open or requires authentication, provide a security phrase if necessary, and then click **Next**.

To disconnect from an ad hoc network, page 240

1. On the **Start** menu, click **Connect To**.

2. In the **Connect to a Network** window, click the ad hoc network, and then click **Disconnect**.

To connect a computer to a domain, page 241

1. Connect your computer to your corporate network, either physically or through a VPN connection.

2. Display **Control Panel**, click **System and Maintenance**, and then click **System**.

3. In the **System** window, under **Computer name, domain, and workgroup settings**, click **Change settings**. In the **User Account Control** dialog box, if you are logged on as an administrator, click **Continue**. Otherwise, enter an administrator password, and click **OK**.

4. In the **System Properties** dialog box, click **Network ID**.

5. In the **Join a Domain or Workgroup** wizard, with the **This computer is part of a business network** option selected, click **Next**.

6. With the **My company uses a network with a domain** option selected, click **Next**.

7. Make sure you have all the necessary information, click **Next**, and then enter your user name, password, and domain name.

8. Click **Next**, and then in the message box, click **Yes**.

9. If you want to enable your user account, click **Next**. Otherwise, select the **Do not add a domain user account** option, and then click **Next**.

10. Unless you are the domain's network administrator, accept the default **Standard Account** option, click **Next**, and then click **Finish**.

11. In the **System Properties** dialog box, click **OK**. Then close any open files, quit any running programs, and in the message box, click **Restart Now**.

12. When your computer restarts, press `Ctrl`+`Alt`+`Del` to display the Welcome screen. Then type your password, and press `Enter` to log on to the domain.

To set up your computer so that it can be accessed via Remote Desktop, and then connect to it from another computer, page 245

1. In **Control Panel**, click **System and Maintenance**, and then under **System**, click the **Allow remote access** task. In the **User Account Control** dialog box, if you are logged on as an administrator, click **Continue**. Otherwise, enter an administrator password, and click **OK**.

2. In the **System Properties** dialog box, under **Remote Desktop**, to allow Remote Desktop connections from any other Windows computer, select the **Allow connections from computers running any version of Remote Desktop** check box. To restrict connections to computers running Windows Vista, select the **Allow connections only from computers running Remote Desktop with Network Level Authentication** check box.

3. If your computer is set up to go to sleep after a specific period of non-use, a **Remote Desktop** message box advises you that you won't be able to connect through Remote Desktop while the computer is in sleep mode. Click **OK** to close the message box.

4. In the **System Properties** dialog box, click **OK**.

5. From another computer on the network, on the **Start** menu, point to **All Programs**, click **Accessories**, and then click **Remote Desktop Connection**.

6. If the multi-tabbed dialog box area is not displayed, click **Options**.

7. On the **General** tab of the **Computer** box, type the name of the remote computer you want to access, and then click **Connect**.

8. In the **Windows Security** dialog box, enter your computer or domain credentials and, if you will be connecting to the remote computer from this computer on a regular basis, select the **Remember my credentials** check box. Then click **OK**.

To store a network password, page 249

1. In **Control Panel**, click **User Accounts and Family Safety**, and then click **User Accounts**.

2. In the **Tasks** list, click **Manage your network passwords**.

3. In the **Stored User Names and Passwords** dialog box, click **Add**.

4. In the **Stored Credential Properties** dialog box, enter the server, Web site, or program for which you want to store credentials in the **Log on to** box.

5. In the **User name** box and **Password** box, enter your credentials for the server or Web site.

6. Under **Credential type**, select the type of entity for which you are storing credentials. Then click **OK**.

To share a folder on your computer with everyone else on your network, page 251

1. In Windows Explorer, display the folder you want to share. Then on the toolbar, click **Share**.

2. On the first page of the **File Sharing** wizard, click the arrow to the right of the empty box, click the option you want, and then click **Add**.

3. Click **Share**. In the **User Account Control** dialog box, if you are logged on as an administrator, click **Continue**. Otherwise, enter an administrator password, and click **OK**.

4. After the folder is shared, click **Done**.

To customize permissions for a shared folder, page 253

1. Right-click the shared folder, and then click **Properties**.

2. On the **Sharing** tab of the **Properties** dialog box, click **Advanced Sharing**. In the **User Account Control** dialog box, if you are logged on as an administrator, click **Continue**. Otherwise, enter an administrator password, and click **OK**.

3. In the **Advanced Sharing** dialog box, select the **Share this folder** check box, and then click **Permissions**.

4. In the **Permissions** dialog box, with **Everyone** selected, click **Remove**. Then click **Add**.

5. In the **Select Users or Groups** dialog box, enter the Windows user account names or domain user account names of the people you want to have access to the shared folder, and then close the four open dialog boxes.

9   Working with Digital Media

To display a photo in Photo Gallery and then add the folder in which the photo is stored to the gallery, page 257

1. In Windows Explorer, browse to the folder in which the photo is stored. Then in the **Content** pane, double-click the image.

2. In Windows Photo Gallery, apply any changes you want, and then click **Add Folder to Gallery**.

To sort and filter files in the Photo Gallery window, page 259

1. In **Windows Photo Gallery**, navigate to the folder in which the files are stored.

2. In the **Navigation** pane, click **Tag**, **Date Taken**, or **Rating**.

To add a tag to a file, page 260

1. In **Windows Photo Gallery**, navigate to the file you want to add a tag to.

2. In the **Info** pane, click **Add Tags**. Then in the box that appears, type the tag you want to apply.

To change the Windows Media Player skin, page 267

1. In **Windows Media Player**, right-click a blank area of the bar at the top of the window or the **Player controls** area, and then click **Show Classic Menus**.

2. On the **View** menu, click **Skin Chooser**. For a broader selection, click **More Skins**. Scroll the list of skins, and follow the directions to download those you like; when you've finished downloading them, close the browser window.

3. In the **Skin Chooser** window, click the skin you want. Then click **Apply Skin**.

To burn a folder of picture files from Windows Explorer, page 272

1. In Windows Explorer, navigate to the folder containing the files you want to burn to CD or DVD. Select either the entire folder or individual files, and then on the toolbar, click **Burn**.

2. Insert a blank CD or DVD in the drive. Then in the **Burn a Disc** dialog box, enter a name in the **Disc title** box.

3. If you don't intend to burn more data to the disc or want to ensure that the disc is compatible with older operating systems and with CD or DVD players, click the **Show formatting options** button, and in the expanded **Burn a Disc** dialog box, select the **Mastered** option.

4. Click **Next**.

To burn music tracks to disc from Windows Media Player, page 274

1. Display Windows Media Player in full mode.

2. Click the **Burn** tab. Then drag the album, play list, or tracks you want to burn into the **Burn List** area of the **List** pane.

3. At the bottom of the **List** pane, click **Start Burn**. When prompted, insert a writeable CD or DVD into your computer's disc burner.

To use Windows Photo Gallery to share your media files with other people on your network, page 275

1. On the Windows Photo Gallery toolbar, click the **File** button, and then click **Share With Devices**.

2. Under **Sharing settings** in the **Media Sharing** dialog box, select the **Share my media** check box, and then click **OK**. In the **User Account Control** dialog box, if you are logged on as an administrator, click **Continue**. Otherwise, enter an administrator password, and click **OK**.

3. In the expanded dialog box, click **Settings**.

4. If you want, in the **Share media as** box in the **Media Sharing – Default Settings** dialog box, change the name of the collection of media files you are sharing.

5. Select or clear the check boxes under **Media types**, **Star ratings**, and **Parental ratings** to include only the specific media files you want to share. Then click **OK** in each of the open dialog boxes.

10 Managing Computer Security

To create a new user account, page 284

1. In **Control Panel**, under **User Accounts and Family Safety**, click the **Add or remove user accounts** task. In the **User Account Control** dialog box, if you are logged on as an administrator, click **Continue**. Otherwise, enter an administrator password, and click **OK**.

2. In the **Manage Accounts** window, click the **Create a new account** task. In the **New account name** box, type a name for your account. Select the **Administrator** option, and then click **Create Account**.

To change an account type, page 285

1. In **Control Panel**, under **User Accounts and Family Safety**, click the **Add or remove user accounts** task. In the **User Account Control** dialog box, if you are logged on as an administrator, click **Continue**. Otherwise, enter an administrator password, and click **OK**.

2. In the **Manage Accounts** window, on the **Choose the account you would like to change** page, click the account you want to change, and then click the **Change the account type** task.

3. On the **Choose a new account type for** page, select the option you want, and then click **Change Account Type**.

To create a password for an account, page 286

1. In **Control Panel**, under **User Accounts and Family Safety**, click the **Add or remove user accounts** task. In the **User Account Control** dialog box, if you are logged on as an administrator, click **Continue**. Otherwise, enter an administrator password, and click **OK**.

2. Click the account for which you want to create a password, and on the **Make changes to account** page, click the **Create a password** task.

3. On the **Create a password for account** page, in the **New password** box, type the password you want, and then press Tab to move to the next field. In the **Confirm new password** box, retype your password, and in the **Type a password hint** box, type something that will help you remember your password.

4. Click **Create password** to save the password.

To delete an account, page 287

1. In **Control Panel**, under **User Accounts and Family Safety**, click the **Add or remove user accounts** task. In the **User Account Control** dialog box, if you are logged on as an administrator, click **Continue**. Otherwise, enter an administrator password, and click **OK**.

2. Click the account you want to delete, and on the **Make changes to account** page, click the **Delete the account** task.

3. Choose whether to keep the content of selected personal folders. If you decide to delete files, click **Delete Files**. Then on the confirmation page, click **Delete Account**.

To change a user account picture, page 288

1. In **Control Panel**, click **User Accounts and Family Safety**.

2. Under **User Accounts**, click the **Change your account picture** task.

3. In the **Change Your Picture** window, click any picture that you like, and then click **Change Picture**; or, click **Browse for more pictures**, navigate to the picture you want to use, and click the picture.

To create a password reset disk, page 290

1. Insert a USB flash drive or floppy disk in your computer.

2. In **Control Panel**, click **User Accounts and Family Safety**, and then click **User Accounts**.

3. In the **Tasks** list, click the **Create a password reset disk** task.

4. On the **Welcome** page of the **Forgotten Password** wizard, click **Next**.

5. On the **Create a Password Reset Disk** page, select the USB flash drive or floppy disk drive you want to use, and then click **Next**.

6. On the **Current User Account Password** page, enter the password you use to log on to Windows Vista, and then click **Next**. When the **Progress** bar displays *100% complete*, click **Next**. Then click **Finish**.

To adjust parental controls for another user on your computer, page 291

1. Display **Control Panel**, and under **User Accounts and Family Safety**, click the **Set up parental controls for any user** task. In the **User Account Control** dialog box, if you are logged on as an administrator, click **Continue**. Otherwise, enter an administrator password, and click **OK**.

2. In the **Parental Controls** window, click the user for whom you want to set up parental controls.

3. In the **User Controls** window, under **Parental Controls**, select the **On, enforce current settings** option.

4. Under **Windows Settings**, adjust the parental controls as you want, and then click **OK**.

To view an activity report for a user account that has parental controls applied, page 293

1. Display **Control Panel**, and under **User Accounts and Family Safety**, click the **Set up parental controls for any user** task. In the **User Account Control** dialog box, if you are logged on as an administrator, click **Continue**. Otherwise, enter an administrator password, and click **OK**.

2. In the **Parental Controls** window, click the user for whom you want to view an activity report.

3. In the **User Controls** window, with the **On, collect information about computer usage** option selected under **Activity Reporting**, click **View activity reports**.

To change Windows Firewall setting options, page 296

1. In **Control Panel**, click **Security**, and then under **Security Center**, click the **Check firewall status** task. In the **User Account Control** dialog box, if you are logged on as an administrator, click **Continue**. Otherwise, enter an administrator password, and click **OK**.

2. Select the **On** option or the **Off** option. If you select **On** and will be connecting to a less-secure network, select the **Block all incoming connections** check box.

3. Click the **Exceptions** tab. Then in the **Program or port** list, select the programs or ports you want Windows Firewall to allow unlimited access.

4. Click the **Advanced** tab, and select each individual network connection you want protected by Windows Firewall. Then click **OK**.

To change Windows Defender setting options, page 300

1. On the **Start** menu, point to **All Programs**, and then click **Windows Defender**. Then on the Windows Defender toolbar, click **Tools**.

2. On the **Tools and Settings** page, set any options you want. Then in the **Settings** area, click **Options**. On the **Options** page, apply any settings you want.

3. In the **Automatic scanning** area, set the frequency and time for automatic scans to occur, select whether to perform a quick scan or full-system scan at that time, and click **Save**. In the **User Account Control** dialog box, if you are logged on as an administrator, click **Continue**. Otherwise, enter an administrator password, and click **OK**.

To check the security status of your computer, page 301

→ Display **Control Panel**, and then under **Security**, click the **Check this computer's security status** task. Make sure that all four settings are set to **On**. If any are not, click the corresponding **Find a program** button to locate and install the missing security application.

To set Internet Explorer security settings, page 304

1. In **Control Panel**, click **Security**, and then under **Internet Options**, click the **Change security settings** task.

2. In the **Internet Properties** dialog box, click **Default level** or slide the control to the level you want.

3. If you want to customize the security options, click **Custom level** to display the **Security Settings** dialog box for the currently selected Internet zone. Make any changes you want, and then click **OK**. In the **Warning** message box prompting you to confirm your changes, click **Yes**.

4. In the **Select a zone** area, click **Restricted sites**. Then click **Sites**.

5. In the **Add this website to the zone** box of the **Restricted sites** dialog box, type any sites you want to add, and click **Add**. Then close the **Restricted sites** dialog box, and click **OK** in the **Internet Properties** dialog box.

11   Optimizing Your Computer System

To adjust visual effects, page 314

1. In **Control Panel**, click **System and Maintenance**, and then click **Performance Information and Tools**.

2. In the **Tasks** list, click the **Adjust visual effects** task. In the **User Account Control** dialog box, if you are logged on as an administrator, click **Continue**. Otherwise, enter an administrator password, and click **OK**.

3. In the **Performance Options** dialog box, select the options you want, and then click **OK**.

To adjust power settings, page 316

1. In **Control Panel**, click **System and Maintenance**, and then click **Performance Information and Tools**.

2. In the **Tasks** list, click the **Adjust power settings** task.

3. In the **Power Options** window, under the **High Performance** option, click **Change plan settings**, and in the **Edit Plan Settings** window, change any settings you want.

4. Click **Change advanced power settings**, and in the **Power Options** dialog box, change any settings you want.

To turn Windows features on and off, page 318

1. In **Control Panel**, click **Programs**, and then under **Programs and Features**, click the **Turn Windows features on or off** task. In the **User Account Control** dialog box, if you are logged on as an administrator, click **Continue**. Otherwise, enter an administrator password, and click **OK**.

2. In the **Windows Features** dialog box, select the check box for any feature you want to install, or clear the check box for any feature you want to remove, and then click **OK**.

To view your temporary Internet files and associated settings, page 320

1. In **Control Panel**, click **Security**, and then under **Internet Options**, click the **Delete browsing history and cookies** task.

2. On the **General** tab of the **Internet Properties** dialog box, in the **Browsing history** area, click **Settings**. Then in the **Temporary Internet Files and History Settings** dialog box, click **View files** or **View objects**.

To run the Disk Cleanup utility, page 322

1. In **Control Panel**, click **System and Maintenance**, and then under **Administrative Tools**, click the **Free up disk space** task.

2. In the **Disk Cleanup Options** dialog box, click the option you want. In the **User Account Control** dialog box, if you are logged on as an administrator, click **Continue**. Otherwise, enter an administrator password, and click **OK**.

3. In the **Disk Cleanup** dialog box, select the check boxes of all the categories you want to delete, and click **OK**. Then click **Delete Files** to confirm that you want to delete the selected categories of files.

To schedule Disk Cleanup, page 325

1. In **Control Panel**, click **System and Maintenance**, and then under **Administrative Tools**, click the **Schedule tasks** task. In the **User Account Control** dialog box, if you are logged on as an administrator, click **Continue**. Otherwise, enter an administrator password, and click **OK**.

2. In the **Actions** pane, click **Create Basic Task**.

3. In the **Name** box of the **Create Basic Task** wizard, type a name for the task, and in the **Description** box, type a description. Then click **Next**.

4. On the **Trigger** page, select the frequency or condition that will cause the task to start, and then click **Next**.

5. If you selected the **Daily**, **Weekly**, **Monthly**, or **When a specific event is logged** option, enter the parameters associated with that option, and then click **Next**.

6. On the **Action** page, with the **Start a program** option selected, click **Next**.

7. On the **Start a Program** page, click **Browse**. Locate and select the program you want to schedule, and click **Open**. Then click **Next**.

8. On the **Summary** page, click **Finish** to create the new task and add it to your Windows schedule.

To schedule and then run Disk Defragmenter, page 327

1. In **Control Panel**, click **System and Maintenance**, and then under **Administrative Tools**, click the **Defragment your hard drive** task. In the **User Account Control** dialog box, if you are logged on as an administrator, click **Continue**. Otherwise, enter an administrator password, and click **OK**.

2. In the **Disk Defragmenter** dialog box, click **Modify schedule**.

3. In the **Disk Defragmenter: Modify Schedule** dialog box, click the **How often**, **What day**, and/or **What time** arrows, and in the respective lists, select the options you want. Then click **OK**.

4. Click **Defragment now**.

5. When the defragmentation process is complete, click **OK** to close the **Disk Defragmenter** window.

12   Identifying and Solving Problems

To open Windows Help And Support and enable Windows Online Help and Support, page 333

1. On the **Start** menu, click **Help and Support**.

2. In the **Windows Help and Support** window, at the right end of the toolbar, click **Options**, and then in the list, click **Settings**.

3. In the **Help Settings** dialog box, ensure that the **Include Windows Online Help and Support** check box is selected. Then click **OK**.

To browse Windows Help And Support, page 334

→ In the **Windows Help and Support** window, on the toolbar, click the **Browse Help** button, and then click any topic you wish to explore.

To search Windows Help And Support, page 335

1. In the **Windows Help and Support** window, type the topic you want to search for in the **Search Help** box, and then click the **Search Help** button.

2. Click any topic link that interests you. Move between visited topics by using the Back and Forward buttons.

To display the Problem Reports And Solutions window, page 336

→ In **Control Panel**, click **System and Maintenance**, and then click **Problem Reports and Solutions**.

To turn off automatic reporting, page 336

1. In **Control Panel**, click **System and Maintenance**, and then click **Problem Reports and Solutions**.

2. In the **Tasks** list, click the **Change settings** task.

3. On the **Choose how to check for solutions to computer problems** page, select the **Ask me to check if a problem occurs** option, and then click **OK**.

To manually submit problem reports, page 336

→ In **Control Panel**, click **System and Maintenance**, click **Problem Reports and Solutions**, and then click the **Check for new solutions** task.

To locate Windows Vista newsgroups, page 337

→ On the **Start** menu, click **Help and Support**. Then in the **Windows Help and Support** window, under **Ask someone**, click **Windows communities**.

To request remote assistance, page 339

1. On the **Start** menu, point to **All Programs**, click **Maintenance**, and then click **Windows Remote Assistance**.

2. On the **Windows Remote Assistance** page, click **Invite someone you trust to help you**.

3. If you have configured Windows Mail, Outlook, or another e-mail program on your Windows Vista computer, click **Use e-mail to send an invitation**, enter and confirm the password you want your remote assistant to use, and click **Next**; then skip to Step 6. Otherwise, click **Save this invitation as a file**.

4. In the **Password** box, type a string of six or more characters you want your remote assistant to enter in order to gain access to your computer. Then click **Finish**.

5. Start or switch to your e-mail program, and send the remote assistance invitation file to the person you want to assist you. Then contact him or her separately with the remote assistance password.

6. After the invitation is accepted, click **Yes** to allow your remote assistant to view your screen and chat with you.

7. In the **Windows Remote Assistance** window, on the toolbar, click the **Chat** button, and in the box at the bottom of the window, tell your remote assistant to take control of your computer.

8. When you receive a message asking if you would like to share control of your computer, click **Yes**.

9. When you decide that you no longer want to share control of your computer, on the toolbar, click the **Stop sharing** button.

10. When you finish the Remote Assistance session, click the **Disconnect** button.

To display the Remote Assistance settings, page 343

→ In **Control Panel**, click **System and Maintenance**. Then under **System**, click the **Allow remote access** task. In the **User Account Control** dialog box, if you are logged on as an administrator, click **Continue**. Otherwise, enter an administrator password, and click **OK**.

To completely disable Remote Assistance, page 343

1. In **Control Panel**, click **System and Maintenance**. Then under **System**, click the **Allow remote access** task. In the **User Account Control** dialog box, if you are logged on as an administrator, click **Continue**. Otherwise, enter an administrator password, and click **OK**.

2. In the **Remote Assistance** area of the **System Properties** dialog box, clear the **Allow Remote Assistance connections to this computer** check box, and then click **OK**.

To limit Remote Assistance access, page 343

1. In **Control Panel**, click **System and Maintenance**. Then under **System**, click the **Allow remote access** task. In the **User Account Control** dialog box, if you are logged on as an administrator, click **Continue**. Otherwise, enter an administrator password, and click **OK**.

2. In the **Remote Assistance** area of the **System Properties** dialog box, click **Advanced**.

3. In the **Remote Assistance Settings** dialog box, set the access level, invitation duration, and access type as you want, and then click **OK**.

To back up a document to a removable storage device and schedule future backups, page 345

1. Log on to your computer as an administrator.

2. Display **Control Panel**, and then under **System and Maintenance**, click **Back up your computer**.

3. In the **Backup and Restore Center**, under **Back up files or your entire computer**, click **Back up files**. Then in the **User Account Control** dialog box, click **Continue**.

4. Select the hard disk or other location where you want to save the backup, and then click **Next**.

5. In the **Back Up Files** wizard, select the categories you want to back up, and then click **Next**.

6. Adjust the **How often**, **What day**, and **What time** settings to the way you want them by clicking each one in turn and selecting from the list.

7. If you are backing up to a CD or DVD, insert a blank disk into your CD or DVD drive, and then click **Save settings and start backup**.

To restore files from a backup, page 349

1. In the **Backup and Restore Center**, under **Restore files or your entire computer**, click **Restore files**.

2. Select the restore option you want, and then click **Next**.

3. Click **Add files**. Navigate to the location of the file you want to restore, double-click its file name, and then click **Next**.

4. Select the options you want, and then click **Start restore**.

5. When Windows reports that the file has been successfully restored, click **Finish**, and close the **Backup and Restore Center**.

To create a manual restore point, page 352

1. In **Control Panel**, click **System and Maintenance**, and then click **System**.

2. In the **Tasks** list on the left side of the **System** window, click **System protection**. In the **User Account Control** dialog box, if you are logged on as an administrator, click **Continue**. Otherwise, enter an administrator password and click **OK**.

3. In the **System Properties** dialog box, click **Create**, and then in the **System Protection** box, type a name for the restore point.

4. In the **System Protection** box, click **Create**.

5. After Windows Vista creates the restore point, click **OK** in the **System Protection** box.

To restore your computer to a restore point, page 354

1. In **Control Panel**, click **System and Maintenance**, and then click **System**.

2. In the **Tasks** list, click **System protection**. In the **User Account Control** dialog box, if you are logged on as an administrator, click **Continue**. Otherwise, enter an administrator password, and click **OK**.

3. In the **System Properties** dialog box, click **System Restore**.

4. Select the **Choose a different restore point** option, and then click **Next**.

5. On the **Choose a restore point** page, click the restore point you want, and then click **Next**.

6. When asked to confirm your selected restore point, click **Finish**.

To transfer your files to another computer, page 355

1. Log on to your computer as an administrator.

2. On the **Start** menu, point to **All Programs**, click **Accessories**, click **System Tools**, and then click **Windows Easy Transfer**. Then in the **User Account Control** dialog box, click **Continue**.

3. Follow the instructions in the **Windows Easy Transfer** wizard to specify the transfer media or method, the information you want to transfer, and the password for recovering that information.

4. If you are transferring files and settings via removable media, start Windows Easy Transfer on the second computer, and then click **Continue transfer in progress**.

5. Provide the information requested by the wizard. When prompted to do so, insert the transfer disk into the second computer, select the destination drive, enter the password, and then follow the wizard's instructions to complete the transfer.

Chapter at a Glance

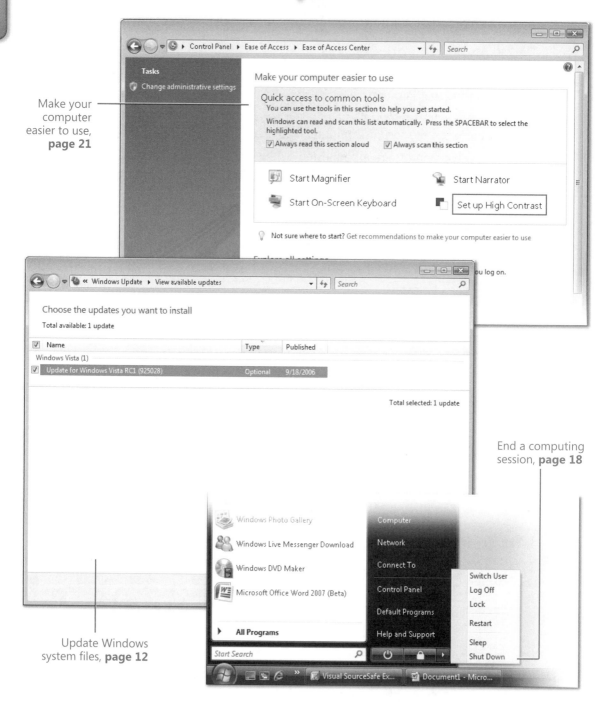

Make your computer easier to use, **page 21**

End a computing session, **page 18**

Update Windows system files, **page 12**

1 Getting Started with Windows Vista

In this chapter, you will learn to:

✔ Log on to Windows Vista.

✔ Activate Windows.

✔ Update Windows system files.

✔ End a computing session.

✔ Make your computer easier to use.

Each time you turn on your computer, it goes through a process of starting up (also called *booting*) during which it loads the system files necessary for you to interact with your computer and for your computer to interact with other devices. After the startup process completes, you *log on* to your Windows Vista user account—a package of permissions and preferences (recorded in a user profile) in accordance with which Windows Vista presents an individually tailored working environment (or *user interface*). If your computer is part of a domain, logging on to Windows Vista also logs you on to the domain. The process might sound somewhat complicated, but in actual practice, it is quite simple.

The first time you log on to Windows Vista, it is a very good idea to check for and install any available system updates. Then you can be sure that your computer system includes the most current features, tools, and security precautions by instructing Windows to update itself whenever necessary. You might also want to adapt Windows Vista to make its features easier for you to use or to make the on-screen elements easier to see.

When you finish working with your computer, you can either shut down the computer entirely, or you can leave it in running in various ways. For example, you can log off from Windows Vista, lock the computer, or put the computer into sleep mode to conserve resources.

In this chapter, you will log on to Windows Vista and if necessary, activate it. You will ensure that any available system updates are installed on your computer and that Windows Vista is configured to keep itself up to date by automatically checking for, downloading, and installing any available security and performance updates. Then you will explore different methods of logging off and shutting down your computer. We end with a discussion of the many accessibility features available as part of the Windows Vista operating system.

See Also Do you need only a quick refresher on the topics in this chapter? See the Quick Reference entries on pages xxxix–lxxiii.

Important No practice files are required to complete the exercises in this chapter. For more information about practice files, see "Using the Book's CD" on page xxix.

For all the exercises, Windows Vista must already be installed on your computer and you must know your user name and password (if your user account requires one).

Upgrading to Windows Vista

Upgrading is the process of updating your computer's operating system to a newer version, without disturbing the programs installed on your computer, your personal preferences and settings, or existing information, such as documents, spreadsheets, and data files. You can upgrade to Windows Vista from Microsoft Windows XP. You might be able to upgrade from a computer running an earlier version of Windows, but most computers purchased more than two years ago probably won't meet the Windows Vista hardware requirements.

Although upgrading to Windows Vista should not affect your personal files and settings, it is always a good policy to back up important files before upgrading. The time and effort it takes to back up files and settings will likely be far less than the time and effort required to re-create the same information.

See Also For information about backing up files and settings in Windows XP, refer to *Microsoft Windows XP Step by Step* (ISBN 0-7356-2114-4) by Online Training Solutions, Inc. (Microsoft Press, 2005) or consult Windows Help And Support.

If you have questions or concerns about whether you can upgrade your existing computer to Windows Vista, you can download the Windows Vista Upgrade Advisor from

www.microsoft.com/windowsvista/getready/upgradeadvisor/

After installing the program on your computer, you can run it to generate a list of any known compatibility issues with your computer and the peripheral devices connected to it. The Upgrade Advisor can recommend solutions for fixing some issues and also provides information about which edition of Windows Vista best fits the way you plan to use your computer.

Whether you have purchased a new computer with the Windows Vista operating system already installed on it or you have upgraded your computer's operating system from an earlier version of Microsoft Windows, this chapter will help you quickly get started doing useful work.

See Also For information about the different editions of the Windows Vista operating system and how they are addressed in this book, see "Introducing Windows Vista" earlier in this book.

Logging On to Windows Vista

Your computer might be used by only you, or it might be used by several people. If only you use your computer, it needs only one configuration, or *user account*. If other people use your computer, each person logs on with his or her own account. By using separate accounts, each person can set up the Windows Vista environment the way she or he wants it, without interfering with another person's computing experience. Each account is associated with a *user profile* that describes the way the computer environment looks and operates for that particular user. This information includes simple things such as the color scheme, desktop background, fonts, and program shortcuts, and personal information that you want to keep confidential, such as saved passwords, site-specific cookies, links to favorite sites and folders, and your Internet browsing history. Each user profile includes a personal folder not accessible by other people using the computer, in which you can store documents, pictures, media, and other files you want to keep private.

> **Important** In the high-tech world, people who use computers are referred to collectively as *users*. Although we use that rather impersonal term throughout this book, we never forget that users are people too!

Each user account is designated as either an administrator account or a standard account. The first user account created on your computer is automatically an administrator account—every computer must have at least one—so if you are the first person using the computer you are probably operating as an administrator.

See Also For information about standard and administrator accounts and why it is more secure to operate as a standard user, see "Administering Windows User Accounts" in Chapter 10, "Managing Computer Security."

The process of starting a computer session is called *logging on*. When you start the computer, Windows displays a *Welcome screen* containing links to each of the computer's active user accounts. (If your computer is part of a domain, you will need to press Ctrl+Alt+Delete to display the Welcome screen.) You select your user account and, if your account is password protected, enter your password to log on to the computer. When logging on to a computer that is part of a domain, you will always enter your domain credentials.

Networks, Domains, and Workgroups

A *network* is a physical group of computers that communicate with each other through a wired or wireless connection. A network can be as small as two computers connected by a cable, or as large as the Internet. For the purpose of simplifying the process of authorizing access to networked resources, computers on a network are grouped in one of two ways:

- A *domain* is a logical (rather than physical) group of *resources*—computers, servers, and other hardware devices—on a network, that are centrally administered through Microsoft Windows Server. Computers and users can connect to a domain—a computer connecting to the domain and validated by a *machine account* is visible as a domain resource; and a person logging on to the domain with a *user account* can access domain resources, from whatever computer she or he is working on. With the appropriate permissions, a domain user can connect to the computer of another domain user by entering the computer's *UNC (Universal Naming Convention)* address.

- A *workgroup* is a logical group of computers that is not centrally administered but communicates through a network. Individual users do not log on to a workgroup.

See Also For information about connecting your computer to a domain or workgroup, see Chapter 8, "Making Connections."

If you are not working on a domain and you enter your user account password incorrectly, Windows displays your password hint. If you still can't remember the password, all is not lost. If you have taken the time to create a *password reset disk*, you can reset the password by clicking the Reset Password link and then following the instructions given by the Password Reset wizard. If you are working on a domain and you experience password problems, you will have to seek the help of your network administrator.

See Also For information about password reset disks, see the sidebar "Backing Up Your Windows Password" in Chapter 10, "Managing Computer Security."

After you log on, Windows Vista loads your user profile and then displays your personalized working environment. The first time you log on to a computer, Windows also prepares your desktop, which takes a few extra seconds.

In this exercise, you will log on to a computer running Windows Vista. There are no practice files for this exercise.

See Also If you are new to computing, see the section "Information for New Computer Users" at the beginning of this book for an explanation of basic terminology you will encounter throughout this book.

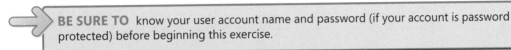

BE SURE TO know your user account name and password (if your account is password protected) before beginning this exercise.

1. Start your computer. Then if you see the message **Press CTRL+ALT+DELETE or use the Windows Security button to log on**, press [Ctrl]+[Alt]+[Del] to start the process of logging on to a domain.

   After the computer starts, the Welcome screen appears, displaying the names and pictures associated with all active user accounts.

   > **Troubleshooting** Certain editions of Windows Vista might bypass the Welcome screen when only one user account is active on your computer and that account is not password protected.

2. If multiple user accounts are available, point to each in turn.

   A glow effect enhances each picture as you point to it.

3. Click your user account name or the associated picture.

   See Also For information about changing your account picture, see "Managing Your Windows User Account" in Chapter 10, "Managing Computer Security."

Go

4. If your account is password protected, type your password in the **Password** box, and then click the **Go** button or press `Enter` to continue.

   Your Windows Vista desktop appears. The Welcome Center opens, and the Windows Sidebar appears at the right side of the screen.

Windows Sidebar

Quick Launch toolbar   Taskbar   Desktop   Notification area

Start button

Troubleshooting Some editions of Windows Vista do not automatically display the Windows Sidebar. For information about displaying and working with this useful and fun new feature, see "Using and Modifying Sidebar" in Chapter 7, "Working with Programs."

The manufacturer will probably have set a brand-specific desktop on any new computers you purchase with Windows Vista already installed. When you install Windows Vista yourself, you have the choice of several photographic desktop backgrounds. The default Windows Vista desktop background for new user accounts displays a picturesque scene of a lake and mountains. You can change this to one of the many beautiful photographs or artistic renderings that comes with Windows Vista, to a blank colored background, or to one of your own photos or graphics.

See Also For information about desktop background options, see "Changing the Desktop Background" in Chapter 4,"Personalizing Windows Vista."

Don't confuse the Welcome Center with the Welcome screen—they are similarly named, but completely different. The top section of the Welcome Center displays information specific to your computer; clicking Show More Details displays the System window and information about your computer hardware, network settings, and licensing. The middle section includes links to basic computer administration options, and the bottom section includes links to training, services, add-ins, and other offers from Microsoft. Clicking Show All in either of these two sections displays additional links. The Welcome Center opens each time you log on to a new Windows Vista session; if you would prefer not to see it, clear the Run At Startup check box in the lower-left corner of the Welcome Center.

See Also For detailed information about the elements of the Windows Vista desktop, see Chapter 2, "Working Efficiently in Windows Vista."

Activating Windows

When you upgrade your computer's operating system to Windows Vista, or the first time you start a new computer on which Windows Vista has been installed by the original equipment manufacturer (OEM), you are prompted to *activate* your copy of Windows.

Each copy of Windows Vista must be activated within 30 days of the first use. After that grace period expires, you will not be able to use all the functions of Windows. You can activate Windows over the Internet or by telephone, or it will activate itself after a few days, if you have an active Internet connection. You don't have to give any personal information about yourself or your computer during the activation process.

The goal of Windows Product Activation is to reduce a form of software piracy known as *casual copying* or *softlifting*, which is the sharing of software in a way that infringes on the software's *license terms*.

In this exercise, you will check whether Windows Vista has been activated, and manually activate it if necessary. There are no practice files for this exercise.

BE SURE TO log on to Windows before beginning this exercise.

1. At the left end of the taskbar, click the **Start** button.

   The Start menu opens.

Start

A link to your personal folder, labeled with your user name, appears in the upper-right corner of the menu. The appearance of the Start menu will vary depending on the programs installed on your computer and any previous computing activities.

2. On the **Start** menu, click **Control Panel**. Then in **Control Panel**, click **System and Maintenance**.

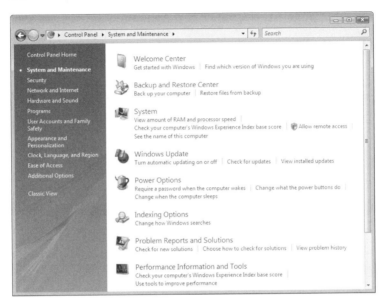

You can access all the Windows Vista tools and settings by navigating through the Control Panel feature groups.

See Also For information about navigating through Windows Vista, see "Finding Your Way Around Your Computer" in Chapter 2, "Working Efficiently in Windows Vista," and "Navigating to Folders and Files" in Chapter 3, "Working with Folders and Files."

3. In the **System and Maintenance** window, click **System**.

The System window provides current information about your computer system. If your copy of Windows has been activated, "Windows is activated" appears in the Windows Activation area at the bottom of the window. Otherwise, the time remaining in the grace period appears. A Windows security icon appears to the left of the activation information to indicate that the action requires administrator permission.

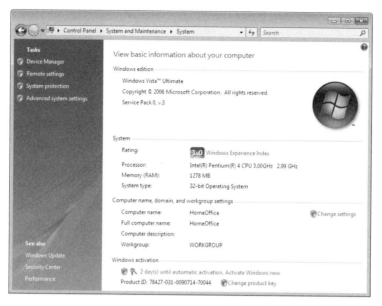

4. If Windows has not yet been activated, in the **Windows activation** area, click **Activate Windows now**.

5. In the **User Account Control** dialog box, if you are logged on as an administrator, click **Continue**. Otherwise, enter an administrator password and then click **OK**.

   See Also For information about User Account Control, see "Introducing Windows Vista" at the beginning of this book.

   The Windows Activation dialog box opens.

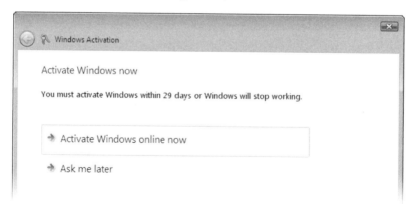

6. In the **Windows Activation** dialog box, click **Activate Windows online now**.

Windows Vista connects to the Internet, verifies that your copy of Windows is genuine, and activates it.

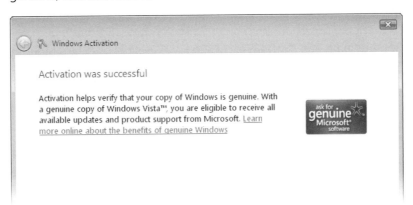

7. In the **Windows Activation** dialog box, click **Close**.

Identifying Genuine Windows Software

Counterfeit software floppy disks, CDs, DVDs, and packaging might look the same as or similar to the authentic software. A genuine individual copy of Windows Vista (one not acquired with the purchase of a computer or through the Microsoft Volume Licensing program) is distributed on a holographic CD. Each copy has a Certificate of Authenticity sticker on the top of the retail package and an orange product key label on the installation CD holder. The front of the CD features:

- A copper hologram with a clean, wavy outer edge.
- A high-resolution, three-dimensional hologram of the Windows logo, in which the flag appears to wave when you tilt the CD.
- A security patch located at the bottom of the CD, in which the word *Microsoft* changes to the word *GENUINE* when you tilt the CD.

The back of the CD features a detailed hologram on the inner mirror band, containing the words *Microsoft* and *GENUINE*.

See Also You can see samples of counterfeited software from around the world at ***www.microsoft.com/resources/howtotell/***. To verify whether your copy of Windows Vista is genuine, run the Windows Validation Assistant from that same location.

Pirated software is often distributed with re-bundled software or through auction Web sites, spam e-mail messages, and downloads from Web sites other than those located within the microsoft.com domain. The easiest way to avoid counterfeit software is to purchase it from a reputable reseller.

The Perils of Piracy

Windows Product Activation is a security measure instituted by Microsoft to help prevent the use of unlicensed copies of Windows. *Software piracy*—the illegal reproduction and distribution of software applications—is a multi-billion dollar industry. A recent Global Software Piracy Study commissioned by the Business Software Alliance (www.bsa.org) concluded that "thirty-five percent of the pack-aged software installed on personal computers worldwide in 2005 was illegal, amounting to $34 billion in global losses due to software piracy."

The counterfeit software manufacturing industry stifles the potential growth of the high-tech industry and contributes to loss of tax revenue. Software piracy is also harmful to its users, for these reasons:

- Unlicensed software is not eligible for technical support or product upgrades. When you attempt to install a product update, security patch, or service pack from the Microsoft Web site, your system or software is tested to verify whether it is licensed.

- Abuse of software licenses can result in financial penalties and legal costs, as well as a bad reputation for you or your company. Individual company executives can be held criminally and civilly liable for the copyright infringements of individuals within their organizations.

- Pirated software can contain harmful viruses with the potential to damage individual computers or entire networks.

Windows Vista has a built-in piracy protection system—if certain conditions alert it to the possibility that you are running a pirated copy, most Windows Vista function-ality will shut down, and you will be able to use only Windows Internet Explorer, for only one hour at a time. During that hour, you will be able to browse the Internet and receive security updates, but you won't be able to create or save any files until you activate your copy of Windows.

See Also For more information about software piracy, visit *www.microsoft.com/piracy/*.

Updating Windows System Files

When you first upgrade to Windows Vista or purchase a computer with Windows Vista already installed, the operating system files installed on your computer are the ones avail-able to the manufacturer when your installation media or computer was manufactured.

Over time, Microsoft will undoubtedly release Windows Vista updates, either to provide additional functionality or to protect your computer from new security threats. It's important to install these updates as soon as possible after they're released.

Microsoft Windows Update is a utility that scans your computer, confers with the Microsoft Update online database, and recommends or installs any updates that are available for your operating system, your software programs, or your hardware. Quite apart from knowing that you have the "latest and greatest," by using Windows Update, you can be sure that your computer is updated whenever necessary. You can access the Microsoft Update site at *windowsupdate.microsoft.com,* as well as from the Start menu, Control Panel, and Windows Help And Support.

During the update process, Windows Update collects the version numbers of your operating system, Web browser, and other installed software, as well as information about the hardware devices that are connected to your computer. It then compiles a list of updates that are available for your system. Updates are classified as follows:

- Critical updates are selected for installation by default. If you do not want to install a critical update, you can remove it from your list of selections.
- Optional updates are listed, but you must select the ones you want to install.

When the update process is complete, the version and ID information that was collected from your computer is discarded.

During the Windows Vista installation process, you are asked to indicate whether you want Windows to automatically update your system as updates become available on the Windows Update site. Automatic updating is very convenient if you don't want to bear the responsibility of remembering to manually update your system, or if you want to be sure you have updates as soon as they become available.

If you chose not to update automatically when Windows Vista was installed, you can change your selected update option at any time through Control Panel. The options are to have Windows Vista do one of the following:

- Download and install updates automatically.
- Download updates and notify you when they are ready to be installed.
- Simply notify you when an update is available.

> **Important** If your computer is part of a domain, your network administrator might control the installation of updates.

In this exercise, you will check your update settings, install any available updates, and make sure your computer is set to automatically install any available critical updates. There are no practice files for this exercise.

> **BE SURE TO** log on to Windows Vista before beginning this exercise.

Start

1. Click the **Start** button. Then on the **Start** menu, click **Control Panel**.

2. In the **Control Panel** window, click **Security**, and then click **Windows Update**.

   See Also For information about other Windows Vista security features, see Chapter 10, "Managing Computer Security."

   Windows Update displays information about your computer's update history and settings. Depending on the edition of Windows Vista installed on your computer, additional information about Windows components might also be shown here.

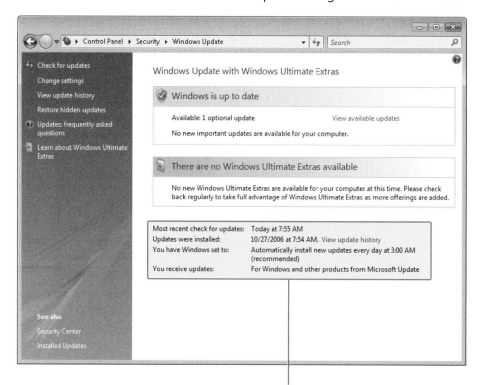

Your current update settings

3. If a **View available updates** link appears in the update status box, click it. (Otherwise, skip to Step 6.) Then in the list of available updates, select the check box for any update you want to install.

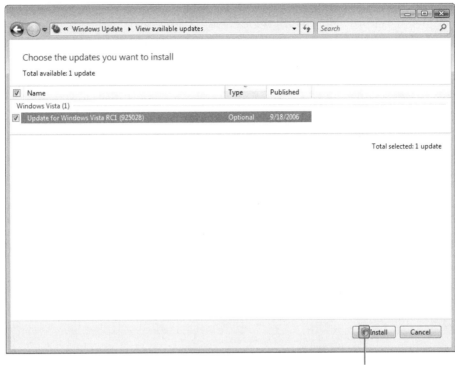

Windows Security icon

The Windows security icon on the Install button indicates that administrator permission is required to use that command.

4. Click **Install**. In the **User Account Control** dialog box, if you are logged on as an administrator, click **Continue**. Otherwise, enter an administrator password and then click **OK**.

A progress bar in the Windows Update window reports on the update activities as Windows downloads the selected update(s), creates a *restore point*, and then installs each update.

After installing the selected update(s), Windows Vista might prompt you to restart your computer. This is an indication that Windows is currently using some of the system files that need to be updated.

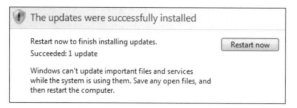

5. If Windows Vista prompts you to restart your computer, close any open files, and then click **Restart now**. After your computer restarts, log on and then repeat Steps 1 and 2 to return to Windows Update.

6. In the left pane, click the **Change settings** task.

   The Change Settings window opens. You can change the frequency, time, type, and scope of automatic updates.

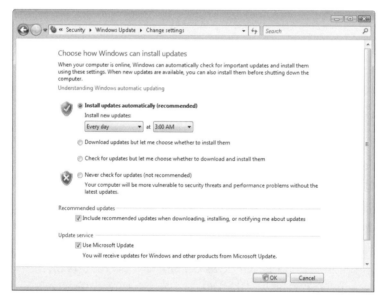

Microsoft recommends that you automatically install updates each day at 3:00 A.M. An obvious problem with this setting is that your computer might not be on in the middle of the night. You can change the update time and frequency by selecting from the lists.

7. If the **Install updates automatically** option is not already selected, select it now.

8. In the second **Install new updates** list, select a time at which your computer will usually be on and online.

   It's best to select a time outside your core work hours—say at the beginning or end of your workday—when connecting to the Internet and installing updates won't impact your ability to work by monopolizing your computer's resources.

> **Tip** If you prefer to have more control over the update process but still enjoy the benefit of automatic updates, select the Download Updates But Let Me Choose Whether To Install Them option. Windows Vista will then download available updates to your computer and displays a security icon in the notification area. You can click the icon to review and approve or reject the installation of each update.

9. With the **Include recommended updates** and **Use Microsoft Update** check boxes selected, click **OK**. In the **User Account Control** dialog box, if you are logged on as an administrator, click **Continue**. Otherwise, enter an administrator password, and then click **OK**.

Windows Update displays your selected settings.

 CLOSE the Windows Update window.

Switching Quickly Among Users

Fast User Switching makes it possible for multiple people to be logged on to their user accounts on a single computer at the same time. For example, if you want to read your e-mail or access a file stored in your *Documents* folder, but another person has been working on the computer you want to use, you can log on to your account without requiring that the other person close the programs and files she or he is working with. Fast User Switching was an optional feature in Windows XP but is always on in Windows Vista.

To log on to your user account while another account is active:

1. On the **Start** menu, click the **Shut Down Options** button, and click **Switch User**.

   The Welcome screen appears.

2. Click the user account you want to log on to, and enter the password if one is required.

Multiple user accounts can be logged on to a computer at one time without interfering with the activities of each other. If you want files to be available to all user accounts, store them in the Public folders rather than the folders within your user profile.

Ending a Computing Session

If you are going to stop working with your computer for any length of time, you can safeguard your information and save power in a number of ways:

● If you want to prevent passersby from seeing what you're working, you can *lock* the computer, which displays the Welcome screen and requires that you log on to your account to resume. Locking is most effective when your user account is protected by a password; otherwise anyone can click your user account picture to unlock the computer and access your information.

   You can have Windows lock itself by configuring a screen saver to start after a designated period of time and to display the logon screen when you resume your computing session.

   See Also For information about configuring a screen saver, see "Selecting and Managing a Screen Saver" in Chapter 4, "Personalizing Windows Vista."

● If you're finished working on a computer that you share with other people, you can end your Windows Vista session (but not affect other users' sessions) by *logging off.* You must save your files and shut down all running programs before you log off; if you don't, Windows Vista will close any open windows, losing unsaved data in the process.

● If you're going to be away from your computer, conserve power and protect your work by putting your computer into *Sleep mode*. This is one of the best features of Windows Vista—you simply click the Sleep button and within seconds, Windows Vista saves any open files, records their state and the state of any running programs in memory and on your hard disk, and then puts your computer into a power-saving mode. When you "wake" the computer, usually by pressing the Enter key or the power button, Windows Vista needs only a few seconds to restore your previous computer session exactly as it was when you left it. Now that we have Windows Vista, we realize just how Sleep-deprived we were with earlier versions of Windows!

   Putting your computer to sleep conserves power and keeps your work quickly available. When a desktop computer is sleeping, it uses approximately 10 percent of the power required to run normally. When a mobile computer is sleeping, it uses approximately 2 percent of its battery power per hour.

> **Troubleshooting** Some video card drivers do not support Sleep mode. If the Sleep option doesn't appear on the Shut Down Options menu, update your video driver or consult the video card manufacturer's Web site for driver information.

● If you need to turn off your computer entirely—for example, to install hardware or to move a desktop computer—you do so by *shutting down* the computer. Shutting down closes all your open applications and files, ends your computing session, closes network connections, stops system processes, stops the hard disk, and turns off the computer.

In this exercise, you will lock and unlock your computer, put it to sleep and wake it up, log off from Windows Vista, and then shut down the computer. There are no practice files for this exercise.

BE SURE TO log on to Windows Vista before beginning this exercise.

1. If no programs are currently running on your computer, click the **Launch Internet Explorer Browser** button on the **Quick Launch** toolbar or the **Internet Explorer** link in the upper-left corner of the **Start** menu.

Later in this exercise, having a program running will make the effect of the different shutdown options more apparent.

Lock

2. On the **Start** menu, click the **Lock** button.

Windows displays the Welcome screen with only your user account available. The word *Locked* appears under your user name.

3. If your account is password protected, enter your password in the **Password** box, and then press the [Enter] key. Otherwise, click your account picture.

Your previous computing session resumes.

Sleep

4. On the **Start** menu, click the **Sleep** button.

Windows saves your file and program information and then your computer goes into a power-saving state. The hard disk stops turning (the computer no longer makes any noise), but the power light on the computer itself is still on, either steadily or blinking slowly.

5. Depending on your specific hardware, either press [Enter] or press your computer's power button to wake up your computer.

> **Troubleshooting** If you don't know which method to use to wake up your computer, try pressing Enter first, and if that doesn't work, press the power button. If neither method works, consult the computer's manual or manufacturer's Web site.

The computer comes out of its power-saving state, and Windows Vista displays the Welcome screen.

6. If your account is password protected, enter your password in the **Password** box, and then press ⏎ Enter . Otherwise, click your account picture to resume your previous computer session.

Shut Down
Options

7. On the **Start** menu, click the **Shut Down Options** button to display a list of ways you can pause or end your computing session.

The Shut Down Options list will vary depending on your computer's hardware configuration.

8. In the **Shut Down Options** list, click **Log Off**.

If no programs are running on your computer, Windows Vista logs you off. Otherwise, Windows Vista displays a list of running programs and open files.

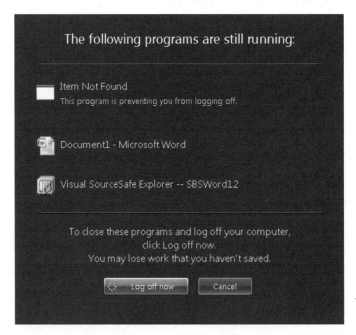

9. If you don't have any unsaved work, click **Log off now** to complete the process and display the Welcome screen. Otherwise, click **Cancel** to return to your computing session; then save and close open files, shut down running programs, and click **Log Off** in the **Shut Down Options** list to complete the process.

> **Troubleshooting** If you have unsaved files but don't click Cancel within 30 seconds, Windows Vista shuts down the running programs and logs you off.

Shut Down

10. In the lower-right corner of the Welcome screen, click the **Shut Down** button.

> **Troubleshooting** If any other user accounts are logged on to the computer, Windows Vista gives you the opportunity to cancel the Shut Down process. If you shut down a computer while people are logged on to it, they could lose data in open files or running programs.

Windows Vista shuts down all the computer processes and turns off your computer.

> **Troubleshooting** If your computer seems to be operating unusually slowly, or you're experiencing technical problems that seem related to the operating system rather than to an application, try restarting your computer. Restarting clears the *system cache*—an area in memory where Windows Vista stores information it might need to access quickly—and frequently resolves minor issues. To restart your computer, click Restart on the Shut Down Options menu.

Making Your Computer Easier to Use

Are the words on the screen too small to read easily? Do you wish the icons were larger? Does it take you a while to locate the insertion point because it is so skinny? Windows Vista includes these *utilities* (small programs) to assist people with visual or auditory disabilities:

- *Audio Description* narrates videos as they play, if this feature is available within the video file.

- *High Contrast* changes the display of your screen from the usual muted Windows Vista colors to a starker color scheme that makes individual items stand out on the screen.

- *Magnifier* opens a magnification panel in which the screen under the mouse pointer is displayed, magnified up to nine times. You can adjust the size and location of the magnification panel.

- *Narrator* is a text-to-speech tool that works with Windows setup, the Windows desktop, Control Panel programs, Windows Explorer, Notepad, and WordPad. It reads menu commands, dialog box options, and other screen features out loud, telling you what options are available and how to use them. It also reads your keystrokes to you as you type them and tells you the pointer location as you move the mouse around.

- *Sound Sentry* flashes the screen element you specify (your choices are the active caption bar, active window, or desktop) every time the system's built-in speaker plays a sound.

You can turn off unnecessary animations and background images; specify how long notifications stay open (the default is seven seconds); and change the size of text, icons, the focus rectangle, the cursor, and the mouse pointer. Windows Vista also supports text captions for spoken dialogue and text narratives for videos, if they are available for the content you are working with.

The traditional method of entering information into a computer document is by typing it using the keyboard. However, mobility problems can make typing difficult. Windows Vista includes a variety of tools to help with entering information, including the following:

- *On-Screen Keyboard* displays a visual representation of a keyboard from which you can select individual keys by using your mouse, pen, or other device.

- *Speech Recognition* allows you to control Windows, control open programs, and dictate text by speaking into a microphone.

- *Sticky Keys* makes it easier to use the keyboard with one hand by making the Ctrl, Shift, and Alt keys "stick" down until you press the next key.

- *Filter Keys* causes Windows to ignore brief or repeated keystrokes, or slows the repeat rate.

- *Mouse Keys* enables you to move the cursor around the screen by pressing the Arrow keys on the numeric keypad.

- *Toggle Keys* sounds an audio signal when you press the Caps Lock, Num Lock, or Scroll Lock key. A high-pitched sound plays when the keys are activated, and a low-pitched sound plays when the keys are deactivated.

You can also make the *keyboard shortcut* for a command more obvious by underlining the letter in the command name that corresponds to the shortcut key, and you can activate a window by pointing to it rather than clicking it. If your hardware supports handwriting recognition, you can write, draw, or otherwise record information within variety of programs, because Windows Vista includes the Tablet PC functions that were previously available only in Windows XP Tablet PC Edition.

See Also For information about using keyboard shortcuts, see "Information for New Computer Users" at the beginning of this book, and the "Keyboard Shortcuts" sections at the end of each chapter. For information about handwriting recognitions, see "Configuring Tablet PC Options" in Chapter 5, "Installing and Configuring Devices."

You can turn on the Narrator, Magnifier, High Contrast, On-Screen Keyboard, Sticky Keys, or Filter Keys features before logging on to Windows Vista by clicking the Ease Of Access icon in the lower-left corner of the Welcome screen (or by pressing Windows logo key+U), selecting the options you want, and then clicking Apply or OK.

After logging on to Windows Vista, you can control the accessibility settings from the Ease Of Access Center. To open the Ease Of Access Center:

1. On the **Start** menu, click **Control Panel**.
2. In **Control Panel**, click **Ease of Access**, and then click **Ease of Access Center**.

When you first open the Ease Of Access Center, an audio guide reads aloud the text at the top of the screen, and provides mouse-free access to the Magnifier, Narrator, and On-Screen Keyboard utilities, or to switch to a high-contrast display.

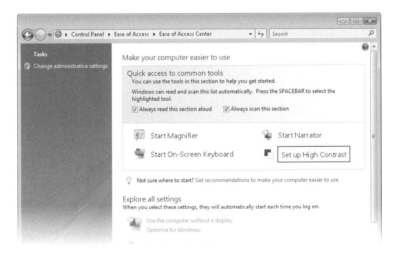

You can turn off the audio guide and/or scan functions if you don't need them.

To optimize a specific type of element, you can select from the groups of settings at the bottom of the Ease Of Access Center.

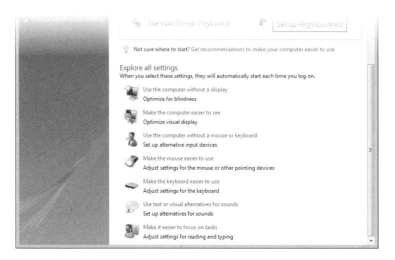

If you want Windows to help you determine what settings will improve your computing experience, click Get Recommendations To Make Your Computer Easier To Use near the center of the window to begin a simple, five-part questionnaire about your eyesight, dexterity, hearing, speech, and reasoning. (Don't worry; your results are private.) Based on the issues you indicate, Windows Vista recommends and describes adjustments that might be helpful. Some are accessibility features and others are simple adjustments to Windows settings.

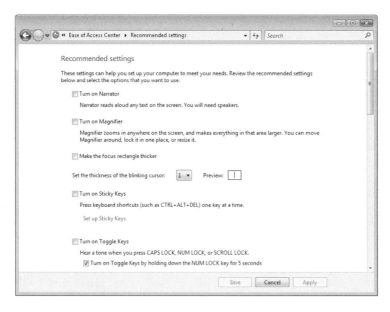

You can enact any suggested change by selecting its check box and clicking Apply or Save.

The tools available with Windows Vista provide only a minimum level of assistance for users with special needs. Most users with disabilities will need specialized programs with more advanced functionality for daily use.

Key Points

- You start a Windows Vista session by logging on, and end it by logging off. You can log off and leave the computer running, or you can log off as part of the process of shutting down.

- Each person who uses the computer logs on with his or her own user account. Your Windows Vista environment preferences are stored with your user account so that when you log on to Windows Vista, it looks and works the way you want.

- You must activate your copy of Windows Vista within 30 days of first use. After that period, you won't be able to create or save files until you activate Windows Vista.

- Windows Vista includes many alternative input and output options designed to make your computer more accessible.

- You can change the look of Windows Vista and the way your computer functions to make it easier for you to see or use the computer. You make these changes from the Ease Of Access Center as well as from the Welcome screen.

- It is important to keep your computer up to date with the most current upgrades and security updates. Windows Update makes it easy to do this automatically or manually.

- You can save power without closing files and quitting programs by putting your computer to sleep. This conserves more energy than shutting down the computer.

Keyboard Shortcuts

Press this	To do this
Ctrl+Esc or Windows logo key	Display the Start menu
Windows logo key+L	Lock your computer
Right Shift for eight seconds	Turn Filter Keys on or off
Left Alt+left Shift+Print Screen	Turn High Contrast on or off
Left Alt+left Shift+Num Lock	Turn Mouse Keys on or off
Shift five times	Turn Sticky Keys on or off
Num Lock for five seconds	Turn Toggle Keys on or off
Windows logo key+U	Open the Ease Of Access Center

Chapter at a Glance

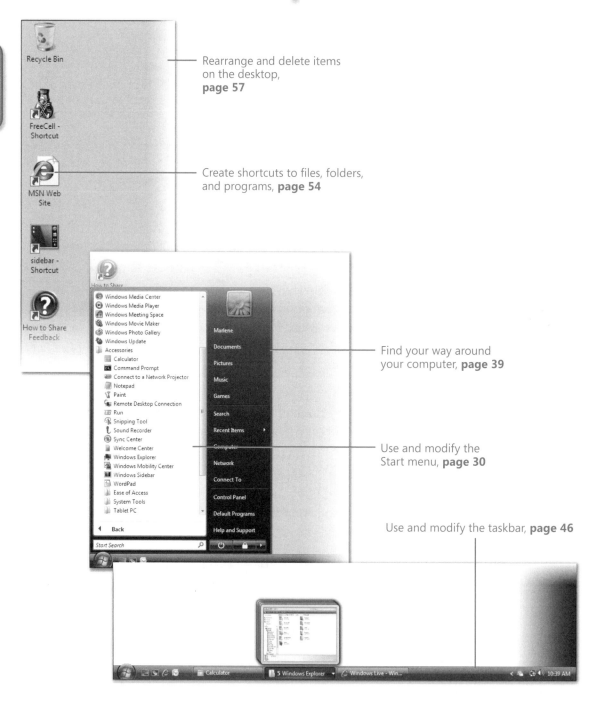

Rearrange and delete items on the desktop, **page 57**

Create shortcuts to files, folders, and programs, **page 54**

Find your way around your computer, **page 39**

Use and modify the Start menu, **page 30**

Use and modify the taskbar, **page 46**

2 Working Efficiently in Windows Vista

In this chapter, you will learn to:

✔ Find your way around the Windows desktop.

✔ Use and modify the Start menu.

✔ Find your way around your computer.

✔ Use and modify the taskbar.

✔ Create shortcuts to files, folders, and programs.

✔ Rearrange and delete items on the desktop.

Working in the Microsoft Windows environment is a lot like working in a real-world office environment. You have a desktop on which you can organize all your work tools, and you have folders in which to organize all your files. Windows incorporates all these elements into its user interface, which is the means by which you and your computer interact.

The most basic element of the Windows Vista user interface is a background screen called the *desktop*. All the programs you run on your computer open on top of this background screen. At the bottom of the screen, the *taskbar* displays buttons you can click to run programs, utilities, and commands, as well as buttons representing the windows of open programs and files. Depending on your edition of Windows Vista, the new *Windows Sidebar* might be open on the right side of the screen, displaying *gadgets* that provide constantly updated information, such as the time.

In this chapter, you will explore some of the elements of the Windows Vista user interface and the various ways in which you can look at the information on your computer. You will then see how to tailor some of these elements to suit the way you work.

See Also Do you need only a quick refresher on the topics in this chapter? See the Quick Reference entries on pages xxxix–lxxiii.

> **Important** No practice files are required to complete the exercises in this chapter. For more information about practice files, see "Using the Book's CD" on page xxix.

Finding Your Way Around the Windows Desktop

Windows Vista presents its tools, commands, and structure through a *graphical user interface (GUI)*. Graphical user interfaces include the following types of components:

- **Desktop.** The basic display area against which you can manipulate icons representing programs, folders, and files.

- **Icons.** Visual representations of programs, folders, files, or other objects or functions.

- **Pointing device.** A device such as a mouse that controls a pointer with which you can select objects displayed on the screen.

- **Windows.** A framework within which you can run a program or display a folder or file.

- **Menus.** Lists from which you can give instructions by running commands.

- **Dialog boxes.** Boxes in which you refine instructions by typing information or selecting from the available options.

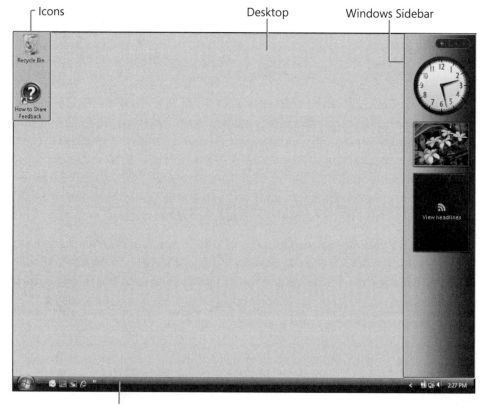

Icons   Desktop   Windows Sidebar

Taskbar

See Also For information about how to work with the components of a GUI, see the section "Information for New Computer Users" at the beginning of this book.

For information about Windows Sidebar, see "Using and Modifying Sidebar" in Chapter 7, "Working with Programs."

Depending on your Windows Vista settings and the programs installed on your computer, there might be one or more *icons* on your desktop, each representing a file, folder, link, or shortcut to a specific item. Windows Vista assigns an icon to every item you see on your computer. The icon might represent a file type (such as a document, a text file, or a database) or storage component (such as a folder, hard disk drive, or CD drive), or it might indicate the default program for opening a file. This visual representation can make it easier to find a file or program you're looking for. When an icon represents a *shortcut* to an item stored somewhere other than the folder you are viewing, an arrow appears in its lower-left corner.

You can save or move programs and files directly to your desktop, which is represented in your computer's storage hierarchy as a folder. For example, if you download a program or other file from the Internet that you will need to use only once, you might save it to your desktop so you can quickly find it, use it, and then delete it. When you install a program on your computer, a link to the program is added to the Start menu, and you usually have the option of creating a *desktop shortcut*. (Some installation programs automatically create a desktop shortcut, but others give you the courtesy of choice.) You can create your own shortcuts to programs, to specific folders or files, to network locations, or to Web sites, on the desktop or in any other folder. You delete an item from the desktop as you would from any other folder. When you delete a shortcut, however, you aren't actually deleting the program, folder, or file to which it points—only the pointer to that item.

When you purchase a new computer, the *original equipment manufacturer (OEM)* might already have installed programs—either trial or full versions—on it as part of a computer system. To make these programs discoverable, the manufacturer might place shortcuts to the programs on the desktop (in addition to those on the Start menu), along with links to "offers" (advertisements) for products and services you can purchase. It wouldn't be unusual to purchase a new computer and find 20 shortcuts already on its desktop the first time you start it up. If you upgrade to Windows Vista from a previous version of Windows, your existing desktop shortcuts and links will still be available.

One of the icons Windows places on the desktop is a link to the *Recycle Bin*, which is where Windows temporarily stores files you delete. When the Recycle Bin is empty, the icon depicts an empty trash can; when you delete items (but don't empty the Recycle Bin), the icon depicts pieces of paper in the trash can. You can recover deleted files from the Recycle Bin, or you can empty the Recycle Bin and permanently delete the files to free up space on your hard disk.

See Also For information about managing the Recycle Bin, see "Creating, Renaming, and Deleting Folders and Files" in Chapter 3, "Working with Folders and Files."

Below each icon on the desktop is the name of the element it represents. If the name is too long, it is truncated by an ellipsis (...) when not selected and displayed in full when you click it. Pointing to an icon (positioning the mouse pointer over it) displays a box, called a *ScreenTip*, containing identifying information. You can start a program, open a folder or file, or jump to a network location or Web site by double-clicking the associated icon or desktop shortcut.

At any time, you can click the Show Desktop button on the Quick Launch toolbar to minimize all open windows so that you can access your desktop icons and shortcuts.

Using and Modifying the Start Menu

The *Start menu* is a list of options that is your central link to all the programs installed on your computer, as well as to all the tasks you can carry out with Windows Vista. You open the Start menu by clicking the Start button at the left end of the taskbar, or by pressing the Windows logo key found to the left of the Spacebar on most keyboards. The menu looks similar to the Microsoft Windows XP version, but its functionality has been streamlined.

Pinned programs area

Recently opened
programs list

> **Tip** If you are accustomed to the *Windows Classic* Start menu found in Windows 2000 and earlier versions, you might find that the change takes a little getting used to. If you are unable to adjust, you have the option of changing back to the Classic version. However, the new menu is designed to increase efficiency, so we recommend that you at least give it a try!

You can quickly access your favorite programs by inserting shortcuts to them in a special area at the top of the left side of the Start menu called the *pinned programs area*. Links to your default Web browser and e-mail program are pinned here by default. You can rearrange pinned programs by dragging them into whatever order you want.

Below the first horizontal line (the menu separator) on the left side of the Start menu are links to the last nine programs you started. (You can adjust that number, or remove the list entirely.) When you first start Windows Vista, this *recently opened programs list* displays links to some of the programs that come with Windows Vista, including Windows Media Player, Windows Photo Gallery, and Windows Meeting Space, as well as links to a Web site from which you can download Windows Live Messenger (the replacement for Windows Messenger and MSN Messenger) and to other programs, depending on the edition of Windows Vista running on your computer.

Below the recently opened programs list, the All Programs link provides access to a list of most of the programs installed on your computer. You display the list by clicking or pointing to All Programs. You can find and start almost any installed program from this list. (Most program setup utilities put a link to the program on the Start menu.)

> **Tip** A right-pointing arrow next to a link or menu item indicates that clicking it, or simply pointing to it for a few seconds, will display a list of options.

The right side of the Start menu is divided by menu separators into three sections:

- The top section displays your user account picture and a link to your personal folder, as well as links to the folders where you are most likely to store your files.

- The middle section displays links to the Search Results window; to the 15 files you most recently opened; to a window that displays the contents of your computer; to a window that displays the computers, programs, folders, and files you can access on your network; and if you have created network connections, to those connections.

- The bottom section displays links to Control Panel, from which you can access all the Windows Vista settings; to the default settings for opening various types of files and media; and to Windows Help And Support, where you can find a variety of information and troubleshooting resources.

At the bottom of the Start menu are the Start Search box and the commands you use to log off from or shut down your computer.

You can customize the Start menu and change the way things work. For example, you can:

- Display or hide lists of recently used programs and files, and control the number of programs (up to 30, depending on your screen resolution) shown.

- Display or hide links to the Computer, Control Panel, and Games windows, as well as to your *Documents*, *Favorites*, *Personal*, and *Pictures* folders. By default, clicking a link displays the contents of the item in the associated window or folder. Alternatively, you can display its contents as a menu from which you can make a choice. (This can be more efficient than clicking items within windows.)

● Display or hide the Administrative Tools and Favorites menus.

● Display or hide links to the Connect To, Default Programs, Help, Network, Printers, and Search windows. These links aren't available as menus because they don't contain other groups or folders.

● Control the items and areas available for the Search function.

● Change the size of the icons that appear on the Start menu, activate the display of context menus when you right-click a Start menu item, rearrange Start menu items by dragging them, highlight newly installed programs, open submenus by pointing to them rather than clicking, and arrange the All Programs list in alphabetical order.

> **Tip** Don't worry if you don't understand what some of these customization options are right now. By the time you have worked your way through this book, you will know whether making adjustments to these options is appropriate for the way you work.

In this exercise, you will hide and redisplay the recently opened programs list and change the number of programs it shows. Then you will start a program from the Start menu. You will also add shortcuts to the pinned programs area, rearrange them, and remove them. There are no practice files for this exercise.

BE SURE TO log on to Windows before beginning this exercise, and if the Welcome Center is open, close it.

Start

1. Click the **Start** button to display the **Start** menu, and note the programs that appear in the recently opened programs list.

   > **Tip** If your recently opened programs list is empty, you can still follow along with this exercise so that you know how to clear the list later.

2. Right-click the **Start** button, and then click **Properties**.

   The Taskbar And Start Menu Properties dialog box opens, displaying the Start Menu tab.

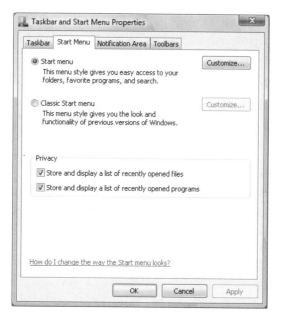

On this tab, you have the option to change to the Windows Classic Start menu, or to remove lists of recent files and programs from the Start menu.

3. With the **Start menu** option selected, click **Customize**.

The Customize Start Menu dialog box opens.

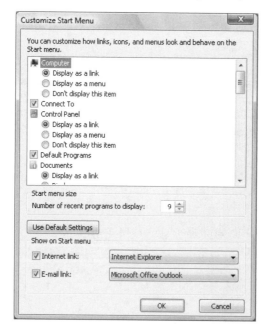

4. Scroll through the list to view the ways in which you can customize the menu, but don't change any of the default settings at this time.

5. In the **Start menu size** area, type or select (by clicking the arrows) 0 to clear the list of recently opened programs. Then click **OK**.

6. In the **Taskbar and Start Menu Properties** dialog box, click **Apply**.

7. Click the **Start** button.

   The recently opened programs list is empty, and the horizontal line separating it from the pinned programs area is no longer visible.

8. With the **Start** menu open, click the **Start** button to close the menu and return to the **Taskbar and Start Menu Properties** dialog box. Then click **Customize**.

9. In the **Start menu size** area, type or select 6 and then click **OK**.

10. In the **Taskbar and Start Menu Properties** dialog box, click **OK** to put your change into effect and close the dialog box. Then click the **Start** button.

   Six programs appear in the recently used programs list. Note that removing the list did not clear its contents; it only hid them.

11. On the **Start** menu, click **All Programs**.

   The All Programs list appears in the left pane of the Start menu, displaying your currently installed programs.

Programs you have recently installed might be highlighted.

12. In the **All Programs** list, click the **Accessories** folder.

The folder expands, pushing items at the top and bottom of the list out of view. All the programs in this folder come with Windows Vista.

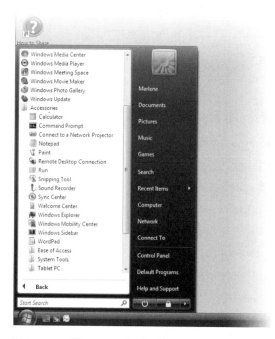

You can still access the hidden parts of the All Programs list by using the scroll bar on the right.

See Also   For information about scrolling, see "Information for New Computer Users" at the beginning of this book.

13. At the top of the **Accessories** list, click **Calculator**.

The Start menu closes, the Calculator program starts and displays a representation of a calculator on the screen, and a Calculator button appears on the taskbar.

14. Display the **Start** menu, and then on the right side, click **Games**.

> **Troubleshooting** In certain editions of Windows Vista, the Games link on the Start menu and the contents of the Games folder do not appear by default. You can complete this exercise by substituting any other window.
>
> If you want to add the Games link, follow Steps 2 and 3 of this exercise, and in the Customize Start Menu dialog box, under Games, click the Display As A Link option, and then click OK. To populate the Games folder, see "Turning Windows Features On and Off" in Chapter 11, "Optimizing Your Computer System."

When you point to *Games*, the icon at the top of the Start menu changes from your user account picture to a representation of a deck of cards. Then the Games window opens on top of the Calculator, and a Games button appears on the taskbar. The Games taskbar button appears pressed to indicate that it is the active window.

See Also For information about the performance ratings shown on the right side of the Games window, see "Improving Your Computer's Performance" in Chapter 11, "Optimizing Your Computer System."

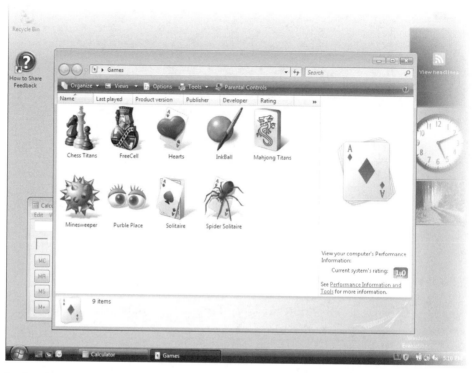

15. In the **Games** window, right-click **Solitaire**, and then click **Pin to Start Menu**.

16. Display the **Start** menu.

The pinned programs area now includes a link to the Solitaire game.

17. On the **Start** menu, drag **Calculator** from the recently opened programs list to the pinned programs area, and drop it above **Solitaire**.

> **Tip** You can also pin programs to the Start menu by dragging them from the All Programs list. You can delete a link from the pinned programs area by right-clicking the link and then clicking Remove From This List.

While you are dragging the link, a thick black line indicates where it will appear if you release the mouse button.

18. In the pinned programs area, right-click **Calculator**, and then click **Unpin from Start Menu** to return Calculator to the recently opened programs list.

19. In the pinned programs area, right-click **Solitaire**, and click **Unpin from Start Menu**.

    The Solitaire link disappears from the pinned programs area and (because it was never on the recently opened programs list) from the Start menu.

20. Click away from the **Start** menu to close it.

21. On the Windows taskbar, click the **Games** taskbar button to minimize the Games window, and then click the **Calculator** taskbar button to minimize the Calculator.

    You will learn more about windows and taskbar buttons later in this chapter.

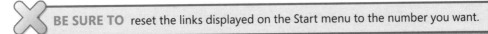

BE SURE TO reset the links displayed on the Start menu to the number you want.

Finding Your Way Around Your Computer

Programs, tools, and information are available on your computer in a hierarchical structure. Information is stored in files that are organized in folders on hard disk drives and other storage devices (such as a CD, DVD, or USB flash drive). You can look at a representation of this storage structure by displaying the contents of the disks in the available drives.

The tools available to you in each folder window vary based on the folder's contents, but all include these basic features:

- The *Address bar* reflects your navigation *path*, beginning with the Windows symbol representing the overall Windows storage structure. The arrow after each folder name links to a list of its subfolders.

> **Tip** The path of a folder or file gives the address where the folder or file is stored on your hard disk. A typical path starts with the drive letter and lists the folders and subfolders, separated by backslashes (\), you have to navigate through to get to the folder or file.

● The *toolbar* presents menus and buttons specific to the content of the current window. When more buttons are available than can be shown, chevrons (>>) appear at the right end of the toolbar; clicking the chevrons displays a list of other commands.

● The *Navigation pane* displays your personal folders and (when you expand the Folders list) displays a hierarchical view of the entire storage structure of your computer. To display the contents of a personal folder, click the folder name. To expand a folder in the Folders list, point to the folder, and then click the white arrow that appears to its left. (Click the black arrow to hide the subfolders.)

● The *Content pane* displays files and folders stored in the currently selected folder or storage device.

Each drive is identified by a letter, and in some cases by a description. Your computer's primary hard drive (the one where the operating system is installed) is almost always identified by the letter C. (By tradition, the letters A and B are reserved for floppy disk drives, which have been superseded by higher capacity storage media and are rarely installed in computers these days.) If your computer has additional hard drives, they are assigned the next sequential letters, followed by any drives for removable media. You can navigate through the folder hierarchy on each drive, displaying the contents of folders within folders until you find the file you want. This navigation process is called *browsing*.

> **Tip** You can assign a drive letter to a specific computer or shared folder on your network by *mapping a drive* to that folder. This is commonly done to create a constant connection to a *network share* (a folder on a different computer on your network) but can also be used to maintain a connection to an Internet location.

However, you don't have to browse to find the programs, tools, and information you need in your daily work. You don't even have to know precisely where things are stored, because Windows Vista provides a system of links that you can use to navigate directly to Windows Vista settings and tools, to programs, and to certain "buckets" of information. You have already seen evidence of this link system with the icons on the desktop and the links on the Start menu, but it is also used in other key components of Windows Vista, which we will explore here and in other topics of this book.

See Also For more information about browsing drives and networks, see "Navigating to Folders and Files" in Chapter 3, "Working with Folders and Files."

When Windows Vista was installed on your computer, it created three *system folders*:

- **Program Files.** Most programs (including the programs and tools that come with Windows Vista) install the files they need in subfolders of the Program Files folder. During installation, you are given the opportunity to designate a different folder. Thereafter, you shouldn't move, copy, rename, or delete the folders and files; if you do, the program will probably not run, nor will you be able to uninstall it.

- **Users.** The first time a user logs on to the computer, Windows Vista creates a user profile containing 12 subfolders: AppData, Contacts, Desktop, Documents, Downloads, Favorites, Links, Music, Pictures, Saved Games, Searches, and Videos. All but one of these folders is available from your *personal folder*, which you open by clicking your user name at the top of the Start menu. You can save documents, spreadsheets, graphics, and other files in your personal folder. As you work on your computer and personalize Windows, it saves information and settings specific to your individual user profile in this folder.

> **Tip** If you log on to your computer with more than one user name, Windows creates a user profile folder for each name. If you want to make files on the computer available regardless of how you log in, save them in the Public profile folder.

The Users folder also contains a Public profile folder, the contents of which are accessible to anyone logged on to the computer. By default, the Public folder contains five subfolders: Public Documents, Public Downloads, Public Music, Public Pictures, and Public Videos. Computers running Windows Vista editions that support Windows Media Center also have a Recorded TV folder.

> **Tip** You can make the Public folder available to other computers on your network by selecting that option in the Network And Sharing Center. For more information, see "Sharing Drives and Folders" in Chapter 8, "Making Connections."

- **Windows.** Most of the critical operating system files are stored in this folder. You can look, but unless you really know what you are doing, don't touch! Most Windows Vista users will never need to access the files in the Windows folder.

> **Troubleshooting** If you upgraded your computer from an earlier version of Windows, the Windows folder from the earlier version might still remain on your computer. However, it will have been renamed to Windows.old during the upgrade process to avoid confusion.

In this exercise, you will explore the storage structure of your computer, and locate basic Windows Vista settings and tools, while learning different ways of getting to the information stored on your computer. There are no practice files for this exercise.

> **BE SURE TO** log on to Windows before beginning this exercise.

Start

1. Click the **Start** button, and then on the right side of the **Start** menu, click **Computer**.

   When you point to *Computer*, the Start menu icon changes from your user account picture to a representation of a computer system. Then when you click *Computer*, the Computer window opens.

Address bar   Toolbar

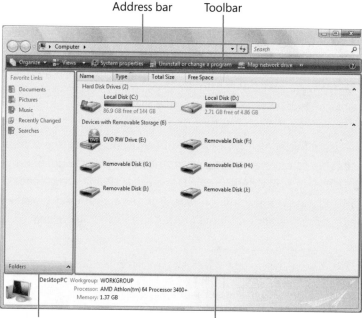

Navigation pane   Content pane

> **Troubleshooting** The contents of your Computer window will correspond with the number and types of drives your computer can access, and will probably not be identical to those shown here. If you have used the Computer window before, the Folders list might be expanded. If the items you see in your Computer window are represented by words or icons in a different way than shown here, take a minute to adjust the view. On the toolbar, click the Views arrow, and then in the list, click Tiles. If the Folders list is expanded, click the Folders header to hide the list.

2. In the **Computer** window, double-click **Local Disk (C:)** to display the contents of drive C.

   Icons identify each item in the window. For example, the icon on the hard disk drive with the Windows logo above it identifies the drive on which Windows Vista is installed.

3. At the bottom of the **Navigation** pane, click **Folders** to display the Folders list.

> **Troubleshooting** If your Folders list is already displayed, skip Step 3.

Personal folders

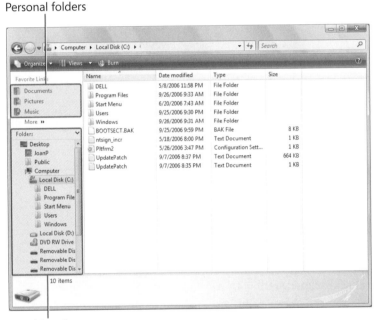

Folders list

From this window, you can navigate through the storage structure of the selected drive in three ways: by double-clicking folders in the Content pane, by expanding folders in the Folders list, or by clicking locations in the Address bar.

> **Important** The folders and files stored directly on a drive are said to be stored in that drive's *root directory*. The root directory often contains system files that should not be modified or moved in any way.

4. In the **Folders list**, under **Local Disk (C:)**, point to the **Users** folder, and then click the arrow that appears to the left of the folder name.

The folder expands to display a list of user accounts on the computer.

5. In the **Folders list**, under the **Users** folder, click your own user name.

Your personal folders appear in the window.

6. In the **Address** bar, click the arrow to the right of **Users**, and then in the list, click **Public**.

The folders available to all users appear in the window.

Minimize, Maximize, and Close buttons

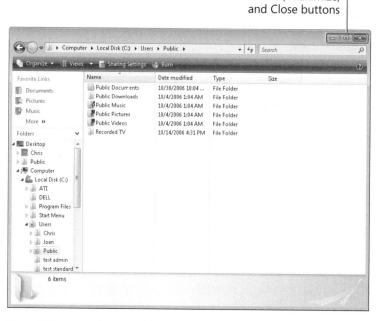

Maximize

7. To quickly experiment with window-management techniques, click the **Maximize** button in the upper-right corner of the open window.

The window expands to completely fill your screen, and if your display is set to Windows Aero, the title bar changes from gray to black to provide a quick visual indicator of the window size. A Restore Down button replaces the Maximize button; clicking this button will return the window to its previous size.

> **Tip** You can manually resize a window by positioning the mouse pointer over the window's frame and, when the pointer changes to a double-headed arrow, dragging the frame to make the window smaller or larger. You cannot manually resize a maximized window; you must first restore the window to its non-maximized state.

Minimize

8. In the upper-right corner of the window, click the **Minimize** button.

   The folder disappears behind its taskbar button.

Close

9. Click the **Public** taskbar button once to redisplay the window. Then click its **Close** button.

10. On the **Start** menu, click **Control Panel**.

    When you point to Control Panel, your user account picture changes to a representation of a touch-screen. Then the Control Panel window opens.

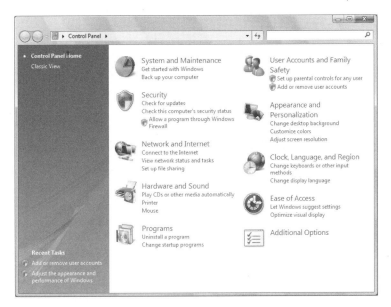

You can access almost all the Windows Vista settings and tools by clicking links within Control Panel. If you know the specific setting or tool you're looking for, you can type it in the Search box in the upper-right corner. Control Panel then displays only the settings and tools containing or tagged with your search term. We discuss the features available from Control Panel throughout this book.

See Also For information about Windows Vista's excellent search features, see "Finding Specific Information" in Chapter 3, "Working with Folders and Files."

Using and Modifying the Taskbar

The taskbar that appears across the bottom of your screen (your primary display, if you have more than one) is your link to current information about what is happening on your Windows Vista computer. In addition to the Start button, the taskbar displays the Quick Launch toolbar, taskbar buttons, and notifications. You can hide the Quick Launch toolbar and the notifications, but not the Start button and taskbar buttons.

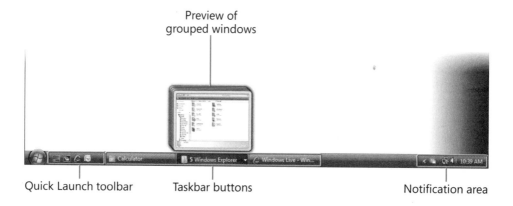

Preview of grouped windows

Quick Launch toolbar   Taskbar buttons   Notification area

> **Troubleshooting** If the Quick Launch toolbar is not visible, right-click an empty area of the taskbar, point to Toolbars, and then click Quick Launch.

The *Quick Launch toolbar* displays single-click links to programs and commands. Windows Vista installs links to Windows Internet Explorer and to the Show Desktop and Switch Between Windows commands on the Quick Launch toolbar. You can add more program links at any time by dragging a program icon or shortcut icon onto the toolbar. You can also adjust its width or remove it from the taskbar entirely. When the toolbar contains more links than can be shown in the space allocated to the toolbar, chevrons appear at its right end. Clicking the chevrons displays a list of the hidden links, in which you can click the one you want.

A *taskbar button* represents each open window, file, or program (but not dialog boxes, message boxes, warnings, or the Windows Sidebar). When more than one file is open in a program, Windows might group the taskbar buttons by program to avoid taking up space on the taskbar with a button for each window. When windows are grouped, a number following the *program icon* on the button indicates the number of open windows represented by the button.

Pointing to a taskbar button displays a thumbnail of the window (or windows) it represents. Clicking the button activates the window. When multiple windows are grouped under one taskbar button, you can:

- Display one window by clicking the taskbar button and then in the list, clicking the window you want to display.
- Display all the windows in the group by right-clicking the taskbar button and then clicking the arrangement you want:
- Cascade displays the windows on top of each other, with the title bar of each window visible and the contents of only the top window visible.
- Show Windows Stacked displays the content of all the windows arranged in a grid, with more windows stacked vertically than horizontally. For example, eight windows are arranged in two columns of four.
- Show Windows Side By Side displays the content of all the windows arranged in a grid, with more windows stacked horizontally than vertically. For example, eight windows are arranged in four columns of two.

In every arrangement, the open windows are the same or similarly sized, regardless of their size before you minimized them.

- Minimize all the windows in the group by right-clicking the taskbar button and then clicking Minimize Group.
- Close all the windows in the group by right-clicking the taskbar button and then clicking Close Group. Windows Vista will prompt you to save or discard any unsaved changes.

Taskbar buttons change size so that they fit on the taskbar as you open and close programs. The maximum number of buttons that can fit on the taskbar varies depending on your monitor and display settings. When you exceed the maximum, Windows either tiles the buttons or displays a scroll bar, depending on the current taskbar configuration.

The *notification area* displays information about the status of programs, including those running in the background (programs you don't need to interact with), as well as links to certain system commands. Some notification icons are hidden by default, and you can choose to hide others that you don't actively want to monitor.

When the Show Hidden Icons button appears at the left end of the notification area, you can click it to temporarily display all the notifications. Icons appear temporarily in the notification area when activities such as the following take place:

- The printer icon appears when you send a document to the printer.
- A message icon appears when you receive a new e-mail message.
- The Windows Security icon appears if you need to install an update, or if an element of your security system (such as antivirus software) is missing or fails.
- Network connections and Windows Live Messenger icons appear when those features are in use. (Inactive connections are indicated by the presence of a red X on the icon.)

A digital clock at the right end of the notification area displays the current system time. You can display more date and time information by pointing to the clock or by increasing the space available.

The taskbar displays one row of buttons and is *docked* at the bottom of the desktop, but you can control its size and position:

- You can dock the taskbar at the top, bottom, or on either side of the desktop by dragging it to the edge of the screen against which you want to dock it.
- When the taskbar is docked at the top or bottom, you can expand it to be up to half the height of your screen by dragging its border down or up.
- When the taskbar is docked on the left or right, you can expand it to be up to half the width of your screen by dragging its border right or left.
- You can stipulate that the taskbar should be hidden when you're not using it, or that it should always stay on top of other windows so that its tools are always available.

> **Troubleshooting** By default, the taskbar is locked so that you can't move it or change its properties. To unlock the taskbar, right-click an empty area of the taskbar, and then click Lock The Taskbar. A check mark indicates when this option is selected.

In this exercise, you will display, hide, and move between multiple windows by using the taskbar. You will then change the taskbar appearance and the links that appear on it.

> **USE** the Calculator and Games windows you opened earlier in this chapter. If you didn't complete that exercise or closed the windows, open and minimize them now.

Launch Internet Explorer Browser

1. On the **Quick Launch** toolbar, click the **Launch Internet Explorer Browser** button.

   Internet Explorer starts, and a button appears on the taskbar. The button label is preceded by an Internet Explorer icon to indicate what type of window it represents.

2. Repeat Step 1 nine times so that ten browser windows are open.

> **Troubleshooting** If your screen resolution is so high that opening ten windows doesn't cause their taskbar buttons to group, continue opening browser windows until they do.

   The number to the left of the Internet Explorer icon on the taskbar button indicates the number of windows represented by that button.

3. Click the **Games** taskbar button, and then the **Calculator** taskbar button.

   The Games and Calculator windows open on top of the browser windows.

4. Click the **Internet Explorer** taskbar button, and then in the list, click the first (from the bottom) **Windows Internet Explorer** link.

   The first browser window you opened comes to the top of the stack.

Switch between windows

5. On the **Quick Launch** toolbar, click the **Switch between windows** button.

   A visual representation of the open windows appears.

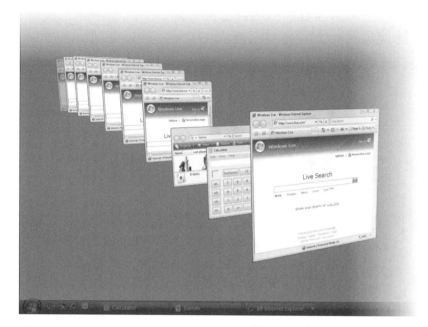

What you see at this point will vary depending on the video card installed in your computer and your display settings. Each window might be represented by a three-dimensional version displaying its exact content, with all the windows stacked on top of each other. Or it might be represented by its program icon in a box on top of the current display.

6. Press the → and ← keys to move through the display of windows. Then click the representation of any browser window.

   The selected window comes to the front and the display returns to normal.

Show desktop

7. On the **Quick Launch** toolbar, click the **Show desktop** button.

   All the open windows minimize.

8. Right-click the **Internet Explorer** taskbar button, and then click **Show Windows Stacked**.

   The ten Internet Explorer windows appear, arranged in a grid.

9. Click the **Close** buttons of any three of the visible Internet Explorer windows. Then repeat Step 8 to display the windows first stacked, and then side by side.

10. Investigate other arrangements, and then click the **Show desktop** button to minimize all the open windows.

11. Right-click an empty area of the taskbar, and then, if a check mark appears to the left of **Lock the Taskbar**, click it.

   Three columns of dotted lines appear at each end of the Quick Launch toolbar to indicate that the taskbar is unlocked. You can now change the size and location of the taskbar, and the size of the Quick Launch toolbar.

12. Point to the top border of the taskbar. When the pointer changes to a double-headed arrow, drag the border up until the taskbar is three rows high.

   Notice that although there is enough space for all the buttons to display individually, they remain grouped.

13. Right-click an empty area of the taskbar, and then click **Properties**.

   The Taskbar And Start Menu Properties dialog box opens, displaying the Taskbar tab.

14. Review the options for customizing the appearance of the taskbar. Then clear the **Group similar taskbar buttons** and **Show Quick Launch** check boxes.

The taskbar preview above the list of options reflects your change.

15. Click the **Notification Area** tab.

16. Review the options for modifying the notification area. Then in the **System icons** area, clear the **Clock** check box, and click **Apply**.

The taskbar reflects your changes, and the dialog box remains open. You can individually hide or display notification icons by clicking the Customize button, clicking the behavior for the icon you want to change, and then selecting the behavior you want (Hide When Inactive, Hide, or Show) from the list.

17. In the **Taskbar and Start Menu Properties** dialog box, click the **Toolbars** tab.

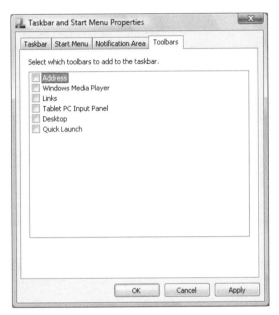

You can display the Quick Launch toolbar from this tab, as well as from the Taskbar tab and from the context menu that appears when you right-click the taskbar. You can also display a number of useful toolbars that might help streamline your computing activities.

18. Select the **Address** check box, and then click **OK**.

The Address bar appears on the taskbar, and the dialog box closes.

You can type a folder path or a *Uniform Resource Locator (URL)* in the Address bar and then press Enter to open the target destination in a new window.

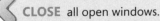

CLOSE all open windows.

BE SURE TO return the taskbar to its original state by displaying the Quick Launch toolbar, grouping similar taskbar buttons, displaying the clock, hiding the Address bar, reducing the height of the taskbar to one row, and then locking it before continuing.

Creating Shortcuts to Files, Folders, and Programs

Shortcuts are icons on your desktop or the Quick Launch toolbar that are linked to programs, folders, and files in other locations. Many programs give you the option of creating one or more shortcuts during installation, or in some cases, they create the shortcuts without asking.

You can create your own shortcuts on the desktop, and you can add a shortcut to the Quick Launch toolbar by dragging it from the desktop to the toolbar. You can also delete any shortcut you don't want. Deleting a shortcut does not delete the program, folder, or file that the shortcut is linked to.

In this exercise, you will create one desktop shortcut to a program and another to a Web site. There are no practice files for this exercise.

> **BE SURE TO** minimize any open windows before beginning this exercise.

1. Right-click an open area near the center of the desktop, point to **New**, and then click **Shortcut**.

   The Create Shortcut wizard starts.

   > **Tip** *Wizards* consist of a series of pages (similar to dialog boxes) that walk you through the steps necessary to accomplish a particular task. In this case, the wizard will prompt you for the information necessary to create a desktop shortcut.

2. Click **Browse**. In the **Browse for Files or Folders** dialog box, click the arrow to the left of **Compute**r to expand the folder. Then expand **Local Disk (C:)** and **Program Files**.

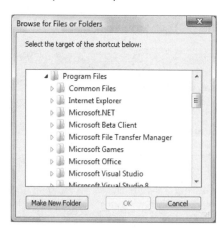

Most programs create their own subfolder in the Program Files folder and then install most of the files they need to run in that subfolder.

3. In the **Select the target** box, expand the **Windows Sidebar** folder, click the **sidebar** file, and then click **OK**.

The path to the selected file appears in the Type The Location Of The Item box.

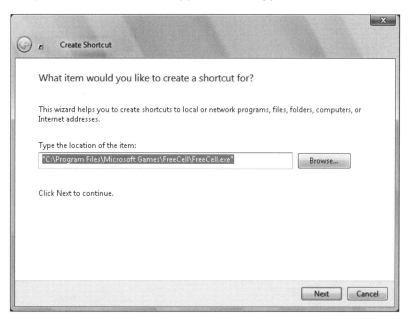

4. In the **Create Shortcut** wizard, click **Next**. On the wizard's second (and final) page, click **Finish** to create a shortcut with the same name as the selected file.

> **Tip** You can change the name that appears below the shortcut by replacing the text in the Type A Name box with the name you want. After you create the shortcut, you can change its name by clicking its icon, clicking its name to select it for editing, and then typing the new name.

A shortcut to the Windows Sidebar appears on the desktop in approximately the place you originally right-clicked. The shortcut icon matches the Windows Sidebar program icon.

> **Tip** You can change the size of your desktop icons by right-clicking the desktop, pointing to View, and then clicking Large Icons or Classic Icons. (The default selection is Medium Icons.)

5. If the Windows Sidebar is displayed on the right side of your screen, right-click it (don't right-click a gadget), and click **Close Sidebar**. Then double-click the **sidebar** shortcut to test that it works.

   The Windows Sidebar opens.

6. If you want, close the Windows Sidebar again. Then right-click another open area near the center of the desktop, point to **New**, and click **Shortcut**.

7. In the **Create Shortcut** wizard, in the **Type the location of the item** box, type http://www.msn.com. Then click **Next**.

8. In the **Type a name for this shortcut** box, replace *New Internet Shortcut* with MSN Web Site. Then click **Finish** to close the dialog box and create another shortcut.

   The Internet Explorer icon represents the Web site shortcut.

9. Double-click the **MSN Web Site** shortcut to open the MSN Web site in your default Web browser.

10. Click the Web browser window's **Close** button to close the window.

 BE SURE TO retain the two shortcuts for use in the next exercise.

Rearranging and Deleting Items on the Desktop

After you have installed several programs and created shortcuts to put the programs, folders, and files you use most often at your fingertips, your desktop might start to get pretty messy. To cope with the clutter, some people like to line up their icons and shortcuts in regimented rows, some like to arrange them as a sort of frame around the perimeter of their screen, and others like to group them by type in various discrete locations. You can organize your icons and shortcuts manually, or if you are happy with simple arrangements, you can have Windows Vista arrange them for you.

In this exercise, you will rearrange the items on your desktop, and then delete a shortcut from your desktop.

 USE the desktop shortcuts you created in the previous exercise. If you did not complete that exercise you can do so now, or use any desktop shortcuts of your own.

1. Drag your desktop shortcuts to random positions on the desktop.

   Notice that as you drop the desktop shortcuts, they align to an invisible grid.

2. Right-click an empty area of the desktop, point to **View**, and then click **Auto Arrange**.

   > **Tip** A check mark indicates when the Auto Arrange option is selected.

   Windows Vista neatly arranges your shortcuts and icons on the left side of the desktop.

3. Now try to drag a shortcut to a different position on the desktop.

   You can move the shortcuts up and down, but not away from the left edge of the screen.

4. If you don't like the Auto Arrange feature, right-click an open area of the desktop, point to **View**, and then click **Auto Arrange** to turn it off.

5. Right-click the **MSN Web Site** shortcut, click **Delete**, and then in the confirmation message box, click **Yes**.

Key Points

- The Windows Vista user interface is designed to provide simple and intuitive access to the tools and information you need to do useful work.

- Files are organized on your computer in a folder structure. You can locate files by navigating through folders, or by entering file information in the Start Search box.

- You can locate Windows Vista settings and tools by clicking links in Control Panel or by entering search terms in the Control Panel Search box.

- The Start menu tracks recently opened files and programs so that you can easily reopen them.

- You can create and rearrange shortcuts to programs, folders, and files so that you can open them directly from the Start menu, desktop, or Quick Launch toolbar.

- You can customize the Windows desktop, including the Start menu, taskbar, and Quick Launch toolbar, to help you work most efficiently.

Keyboard Shortcuts

Press this	To do this
Ctrl+Esc or Windows logo key	Open or close the Start menu
Windows logo key+D	Display the desktop
Windows logo key+M	Minimize all windows
Windows logo key+Shift+M	Restore all minimized windows
Windows logo key+E	Open the Computer window
Alt+Tab	Switch between open items
Windows logo key+Tab	Cycle through programs by using Windows Flip 3-D
Alt+Esc	Cycle through items in the order in which they were opened

Chapter at a Glance

Navigate to folders and files, **page 62**

Chris ▸ Documents ▸ MSP ▸ SBS_Vista ▸ Chapter03 ▸

Search

Organize ▾   Views ▾   Open   E-mail   Share   Burn

Name   Date modified   Type   Size   Tags

05_Photographs
File Folder

New Folder

01_AlbumSlides
Microsoft Office PowerPoin...
935 KB

01_ColorSlides
Microsoft Office PowerPoin...
117 KB

01_FabricSpecial
Microsoft Office Word Docu...
13.4 KB

01_FengShuiSlides
Microsoft Office PowerPoin...
157 KB

01_JournalSlides
Microsoft Office PowerPoin...

01_LoanPayment
Microsoft Office Excel Work...

01_OrgSlides
Microsoft Office PowerPoin...

Create, rename and delete folders and files, **page 82**

03_Costs Properties

General | Security | Details | Previous Versions

Property	Value
Description	
Title	Disorganization
Subject	Organization
Tags	
Categories	Workshop
Comments	Copyright (c) 2006 Online Training S...
Origin	
Authors	Joyce Cox
Last saved by	Joyce
Revision number	
Version number	
Program name	Microsoft Excel
Company	Online Training Solutions, Inc.
Manager	
Content created	10/2/2006 12:06 PM

View information about a folder or file, **page 78**

Find specific information, **page 90**

Search Results in Indexed Locations

tag

Show only: All E-mail Document Picture Music Other

Advanced Search

Organize ▾   Views ▾   Open ▾   Save Search   Search Tools ▾   Print   Share   Burn

Favorite Links

Documents
Pictures
Music
More »

Folders

Desktop
Chris
Public
Computer
Network
Control Panel
Recycle Bin
Search Results in Inc

Name	Date modified	Type	Fo
06_BookBeat	10/11/2006 12:57 ...	Microsoft Office ...	Ch
06_Welcome	10/11/2006 11:19 ...	Microsoft Office ...	Ch
06_TagIntroduce	10/11/2006 10:50 ...	Microsoft Office ...	Ch
06_TagAnnounce	10/11/2006 10:50 ...	Microsoft Office ...	Ch
06_TagSlides	10/11/2006 10:49 ...	Microsoft Office P...	Ch
06_BookSales	10/11/2006 10:47 ...	Microsoft Office E...	Ch
01_TagTemplate	10/11/2006 9:05 AM	Microsoft Office P...	02
05_Sales	10/11/2006 8:13 AM	Microsoft Office E...	Ch

Did you find what you were searching for?
Advanced Search

View folders and files in different ways, **page 70**

L U C E R N E
P U B L I S H I

Boo
Bea

*A bi-monthly
newsletter for
booksellers*

Author Meet

ncel   Apply

06_BookBeat   Title: Newsletter Announcem...   Date modified: 10/11/2006 12:57 PM
Microsoft Office Word Document   Authors: Susie Bayers; Joyce Cox   Tags: newsletter; Taguien
Size: 11.9 KB

3 Working with Folders and Files

In this chapter, you will learn to:

✔ Navigate to folders and files.

✔ View folders and files in different ways.

✔ View information about a folder or file.

✔ Create, rename, and delete folders and files.

✔ Move and copy folders and files.

✔ Find specific information.

To simplify the way you work with files on your computer, the Windows Vista interface uses a hierarchical storage concept that resembles information storage in an office. Instead of organizing paper files in paper folders in filing cabinets, you organize electronic files in electronic folders on the storage disks accessible to your computer.

There are many different types of files, but they fall into these two basic categories:

- **Files used to run programs or created by programs.** These include *executable files* and *dynamic-link libraries (DLLs)*. These files are sometimes hidden (not shown in a standard folder view) to protect them—hidden files can't be selected or deleted. You can unhide files from the Folder Options dialog box discussed in "Viewing Folders and Files in Different Ways" later in this chapter.

- **Files created by you.** These include documents, spreadsheets, graphics, text files, slide shows, audio clips, video clips, and other things that you can open, look at, and change using one or more applications.

The files needed to run a program and those it creates for its own use are organized the way the program expects to find them, and you shouldn't move them. However, you control the organization of the files you create (such as documents and spreadsheets), and knowing how to manage these files is essential if you want to be able to use your computer efficiently.

No matter how organized you are, there will be times when you can't remember where you stored a particular file. No problem! Windows Vista includes a powerful new search feature that can help you almost instantly locate any file on your computer.

In this chapter, you will use the Windows Vista navigation tools to explore the file storage structure on your computer. You will experiment with different ways of displaying information and learn how to find information. You will also create, edit, delete, move, and rename files, as well as search for files in various ways.

See Also Do you need only a quick refresher on the topics in this chapter? See the Quick Reference entries on pages xxxix–lxxiii.

> **Important** Before you can use the practice files in this chapter, you need to install them from the book's companion CD to their default location. See "Using the Book's CD" on page xxix for more information.

Navigating to Folders and Files

You view all the drives, folders, files, and peripherals that are part of your computer system, as well as those on any computers you are connected to through a network, in Microsoft Windows Explorer. There are several ways to do this. For example, you can:

- Click a folder link on the Start menu to open that folder. You can:
    - Click Computer or Network to display an overview of all the hard disk drives and storage devices accessible to your computer.
    - Click your user name to open your personal folder, or click Documents, Pictures, or Music to open those subfolders directly.
- Point to All Programs on the Start menu, click Accessories, and then click Windows Explorer (or press Windows logo key+E) to display the contents of your Documents folder.
- Right-click a folder on the Start menu or desktop and then click Explore.

The latter two options display the folder contents with the Folders list expanded in the Navigation pane.

Windows Explorer provides the means to manipulate folders and files in a variety of ways. For now, we will focus on the elements of the window that you use to navigate through the folder structure on your computer. In addition to the Address bar, Navigation pane, and Content pane discussed earlier in the book, these elements include the following:

● **Back button and Forward button.** Click these to display the contents of folders you have already viewed in the Content pane.

● **Recent Pages button.** Click this button to see a list of folders you have viewed so that you can select the one you want to display.

Back and Forward buttons
Recent Pages button

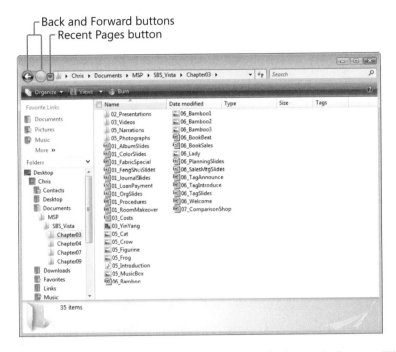

See Also For an introduction to the Windows Explorer window, see "Finding Your Way Around Your Computer" in Chapter 2, "Working Efficiently in Windows Vista."

In this exercise, you will navigate among folders in various ways.

BE SURE TO log on to Windows before beginning this exercise.

USE the practice folders and files located in the *Chapter03* subfolder under *SBS_WindowsVista*.

Start

1. Click the **Start** button, and then click **Computer**.

In the window that opens, the Content pane displays information about the storage devices and locations accessible to your computer.

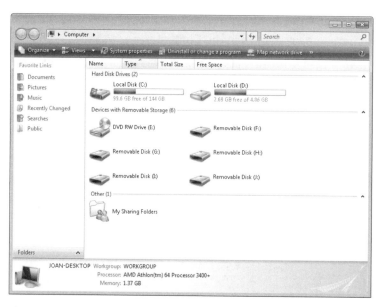

2. If your Folders list is closed as shown above, at the bottom of the **Navigation** pane, click **Folders**.

The Folders list expands, displaying a hierarchical view (also called a *tree view*) of disks and folders. You can also access network resources (if any), Control Panel tools, and the Recycle Bin from the Folders list.

> **Tip** Your Windows Explorer display depends on the storage structure of your computer and whether you have explored its contents before. As a result, it will be different than the one shown in our graphics, but you will still be able to follow the steps in this exercise.

3. In the **Content** pane, double-click the icon for your drive **C** (called *Local Disk (C:)* in the preceding graphic).

The Content pane displays the folders and files stored on this disk. The Address bar reflects the fact that you are now looking at the contents of one of the drives accessible to your computer.

4. In the **Content** pane, double-click **Users**.

The Content pane displays all the user profile folders currently set up on your computer.

5. In the **Content** pane, double-click your user profile folder.

The Content pane displays your 11 personal content folders.

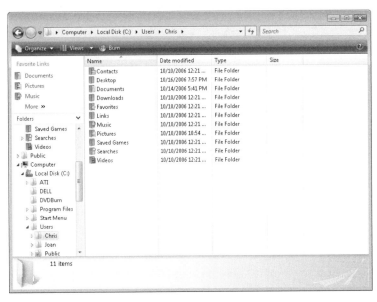

The currently displayed folder is also selected in the Folders list so that you can see your position within the overall storage hierarchy.

In some of these folders, such as Documents, you will store files; others, such as Contacts, will contain information you save through Windows Vista or Windows Internet Explorer.

See Also For information about Windows Contacts, see "Using the Programs That Come with Windows Vista" in Chapter 7, "Working with Programs."

6. In the **Favorite Links** list, click **Documents**.

> **Tip** You can add any folder to the Favorite Links list by selecting it in the Content pane and dragging it to the list. A black bar indicates where the new link will appear when you release the mouse button.

The Address bar indicates that the contents of your *Documents* folder are currently displayed in the Content pane. At the top of the hierarchy in the Folders list, the link to the *Documents* folder within your personal folder is selected. You can use the links in Favorite Links and the links at the top of the Folders list to jump quickly to the folders you will probably use most, without having to navigate through the storage structure to find them.

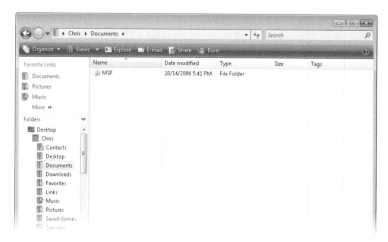

> **Troubleshooting** The *MSP* folder will appear in your *Documents* folder only if you installed the practice files for this book in the default location. You can follow the steps in this exercise and the other exercises in this chapter using your own files, but to see the results shown, you need to install the practice files. Refer to "Using the Book's CD" on page xxix for more information.

7. In the **Folders** list, point to **Documents**, and then click the white arrow to the left of the folder name. In the list of subfolders, click the white arrow to the left of *MSP*. Then click the white arrow to the left of *SBS_WindowsVista*.

Each time you click, the arrow turns black and the folder expands to show its contents. As the structure indents to the right with each click, the Folders list adjusts itself in the Navigation pane, scrolling up or down or to the left or right to give you the best view of the current items. By clicking the arrows in the Folders list rather than the folders in the Content pane, you expose the hierarchical structure without changing the display in the Content pane or the path in the Address bar.

8. In the **Folders** list, click *Chapter03* to display that folder's contents in the Content pane.

The Address bar changes to reflect the path of the displayed files.

9. In the **Address** bar, click the arrow to the right of *Chapter03*.

A list shows the subfolders within the *Chapter03* folder.

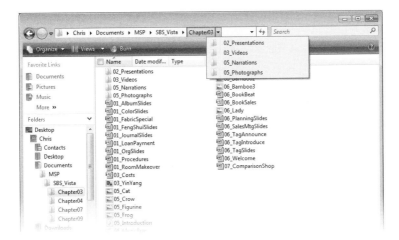

10. In the list, click *02_Presentations* to display the files stored in that folder.

> **Tip** To close a list without making a selection, press the Esc key.

11. In the **Address** bar, click the arrow between *Chapter03* and *02_Presentations*, and then in the subfolder list, click *03_Videos*.

By clicking the arrows between folders you can easily navigate to other folders in the same folder path.

Back

12. In the upper-left corner of the window, click the **Back** button to return to the most recently displayed folder, *02_Presentations*.

Notice that the Back button takes you back through your browsing history rather than back up the folder path.

13. In the **Folders** list, point to **Documents**, and then click its black arrow to collapse the hierarchical structure without changing the Content pane.

> **Tip** You might have to wait until *Documents* moves to the right in the Folders list to see its arrow.

Forward

14. Point to the **Forward** button to display a ScreenTip telling you where clicking the button will take you. Then click the **Forward** button to redisplay the *03_Videos* folder.

Recent Pages

15. To the right of the **Back** and **Forward** buttons, click the **Recent Pages** button.

The Recent Pages list displays the folders you have opened since opening the Computer window, in reverse order.

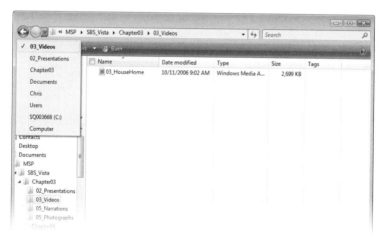

16. In the **Recent Pages** list, click **Computer** to return to your starting point.

17. Experiment with the Windows Explorer navigation features until you feel comfortable moving through your computer's storage structure in various ways.

Close

18. In the upper-right corner of the window, click the **Close** button to close Windows Explorer.

Accessing Your Entire Network

If you are connected to a network, you can use Windows Explorer to navigate not only to drives and resources on your own computer, but also to drives and resources across your entire network. To display an overview of your network resources, click Network on the Start menu.

If you want to access a particular network drive or resource on a regular basis—for example, if you regularly connect to a specific server—you can *map* the drive in Windows Explorer to make it more easily available. When you map a drive, you assign it a *local* drive letter so that it appears along with other available storage devices and locations when you view the contents of your computer. You can map a drive temporarily or instruct Windows to reconnect to that drive every time you log on.

To map a drive:

1. On the **Start** menu, click **Computer**.

2. On the toolbar above the Content pane, click **Map network drive**.

3. In the **Map Network Drive** window, specify the drive letter you want to use for this drive.

4. Click **Browse**, navigate to the drive or folder you want to map, and then click **OK** to return to the Map Network Drive window with the path entered in the Folder box.

5. If you want to connect to this location only until the end of the current Windows session, clear the **Reconnect at logon** check box.

6. Click **Finish**.

   The network drive opens in a new window.

To disconnect from a mapped drive or folder, right-click it, and then click Disconnect.

Viewing Folders and Files in Different Ways

The Windows Explorer window is dynamic and changes to reflect the content you are viewing. You can also customize the window to suit the way you work. The Back and Forward buttons, the Address bar, the Search box, the toolbar, and the Content pane are always displayed, but you can display or hide other elements by clicking Organize on the toolbar, clicking Layout, and then clicking the element. These optional elements include the following:

- **Navigation pane.** When you become accustomed to navigating from the Address bar, you might want to turn off the Navigation pane to provide more space for the Content pane.

- **Details pane.** This pane at the bottom of the window provides information about the displayed content, such as the number of items in a folder, or the file type of a selected file. This information might or might not be useful, depending on the Content pane view.

- **Menu bar.** If you prefer working with menus and commands rather than toolbar buttons, you can display the Menu bar above the toolbar.

- **Preview pane.** This pane on the right side of the window displays a preview of the content of a selected file so that you can see what it contains.

- **Search pane.** When you search for information on your computer, you can display this pane above the toolbar to refine the search.

In the Content pane, you can view folders and files in different ways by making a selection from the Views list on the toolbar. You can set the view for each folder, or you can set a default view for all folders. Available views include the following:

- **Icons.** The four Icon views (Extra Large, Large, Medium, and Small) display an icon and file name for each file or folder in the current folder. In all but Small Icons view, the icons display either the file type, or in the case of graphic files (including PowerPoint slides) the actual file content. Folder icons display the contents of the folder.

- **List.** This view is similar to Small Icons view in that it shows the names of the files and folders accompanied by a small icon representing the file type.

- **Details.** This view displays a list of files or folders and their properties. The properties shown by default for each file or folder are Name, Date Modified, Type, Size, and Tags. You can hide any of these properties, and you can display a variety of other properties that might be pertinent to specific types of files, including Author and Title.

> **Tip** Although the Content pane always displays column headings, they are pertinent only to Details view.

● **Tiles.** This view displays a medium-size icon and the name, type, and size of each file or folder in the selected folder.

You can display the properties of a folder or file in the Details pane by selecting the folder or file in any view. You can further refine the display of files and folders by changing the settings in the Folder Options dialog box, which you can display by clicking Organize on the toolbar and then clicking Folder And Search Options. You can also change how you browse folders and whether you click or double-click to navigate in this dialog box.

For example, you can specify whether Windows Explorer and all Windows programs should display file name extensions, which are hidden by default. All file names have an extension, separated from the name itself by a period, that designates the file's type or the program in which it was created. If you often need to know the type of a file, it might be easier to turn on the display of file name extensions so that they are visible in all views than to have to constantly switch to Tiles or Details view to see the file type.

> **Tip** When discussing file types, people often refer to files by their extensions. For example, when talking about documents with the file name extension *.doc*, they might say "I'm going to send some docs for your review."

In this exercise, you will adjust the display of the Windows Explorer window and view the contents of a folder in different ways. You will also explore the Folder Options dialog box.

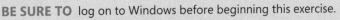

BE SURE TO log on to Windows before beginning this exercise.

USE the *02_Presentations* folder and the practice files located in the *Chapter03* subfolder under *SBS_WindowsVista*.

1. On the **Start** menu, click **Computer**.

   The Computer window opens.

2. On the toolbar, click **Organize**, point to **Layout**, and then in the list, click **Details Pane** to hide the pane.

   > **Troubleshooting** If Details Pane does not have a blue border around it on the Organize list, it is already hidden, and you can skip Step 2; otherwise, clicking Details Pane will display the pane instead of hiding it.

3. Display the **Organize** menu, point to **Layout**, and then click **Navigation Pane** to hide the pane.

The Content pane now occupies the entire area below the toolbar.

> **Tip** If you have changed the default folder view, your window might look different from this one.

4. In the **Address** bar, click the arrow to the left of **Computer**, and then click your personal folder.

5. In the **Content** pane, double-click **Documents**, double-click *MSP*, double-click *SBS_WindowsVista*, double-click *Chapter03*, and then double-click *02_Presentations*.

The *02_Presentations* folder contains two files, which are currently displayed in Details view.

6. On the toolbar, click the **Views** button (not the arrow) four times to cycle through the four most common views: Tiles, Large Icons, List, and Details.

7. In the **Address** bar, click *Chapter03* to display the contents of that folder. Then if the folder is not displayed in Details view, click the **Views** button to switch to that view.

8. On the toolbar, click the **Views** arrow.

A list appears, showing the available view options. The slider on the left indicates which view is currently selected.

9. In the list, drag the slider up and down without releasing the mouse button, pausing to see the effect on the display in the Content pane.

10. Release the button when the slider is to the left of **Medium Icons**.

> **Tip** You can also switch views by clicking the view you want in the list.

Notice that the graphic files are represented by thumbnails, and the folders and other files are represented by type icons.

11. Display the **Views** list, and then click **Details**.

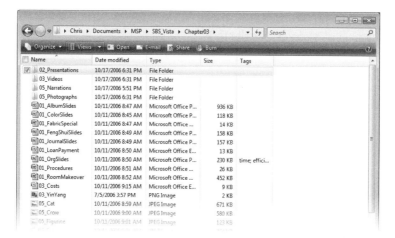

12. Point to each of the five column headings in turn (*Name, Date Modified, Type, Size,* and *Tags*).

    As the pointer passes over each heading, the heading changes color to indicate that it is selected, and an arrow appears at the heading's right end. You can click the arrow to filter the contents in various ways.

13. Click the **Size** heading (not its arrow).

    The files are sorted in descending order by file size, as indicated by the downward-pointing arrow above the *Size* heading.

14. Click **Size** again.

    The files are re-sorted in ascending order by file size, and the arrow changes direction to indicate the change of order.

15. Right-click anywhere in the column headings.

    A list of attributes that might be attached to a file or folder appears; those currently displayed in Details view are indicated by check marks. *Name* is unavailable (gray) because the file name must be displayed.

16. In the attributes list, click **Authors**.

A new *Authors* column is displayed, and the names of the people who created the files are listed.

17. Right-click anywhere in the column headings, and then in the attributes list, click **More**.

The Choose Details dialog box opens. The currently displayed properties appear at the top of the list.

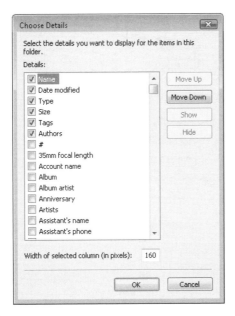

18. Scroll through the list to see the approximately 240 file attributes you can display in Details view. Then clear the **Authors** check box, and click **OK**.

The *Authors* column disappears from the window.

19. Click the **Name** column header to return to the default order. Then in the **Views** list, click **Tiles**.

Tiles view displays a thumbnail or icon for each item, along with its name, file type, and file size.

20. On the **Organize** menu, click **Folder and Search Options**.

The Folder Options dialog box opens, displaying the General tab. On this tab, you can change the basic way that Windows Explorer works.

Important If you change any of the settings on this tab, the instructions in this book will not work for your computer. We recommend that you wait until you are an experienced user of Windows Explorer before changing these options.

21. In the **Folder Options** dialog box, click the **View** tab.

On this tab, you can set the default view for all folders, and you can change specific view settings.

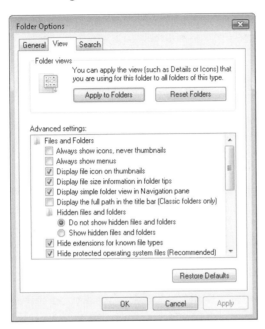

> **Tip** When you first start working in Windows Vista, the default view for each folder is determined by its type. If you apply the current folder view to all folders and then change your mind, you can click Reset Folders to restore the type-based default views. For information about folder types, see "Viewing Information About a Folder or File" later in this chapter.

22. Scroll the **Advanced settings** list, and note the ways you can change the Windows Explorer display.

Notice that by default, Windows Vista system folders and files that have been assigned a hidden attribute are not shown. Also notice that extensions for known file types are hidden.

If you don't want to view files in Details or Tiles view to ascertain their file types, you can clear the Hide Extensions For Known File Types check box to display file names with their extensions; for example, *01_cat.jpg*. Then the file name identifies the type of each file.

23. Click **Cancel** to close the dialog box without changing any settings.

> **BE SURE TO** redisplay the Navigation pane if you want to be able to use it to move around your computer.
>
> **CLOSE** the Chapter03 window.

Viewing Information About a Folder or File

Every file or folder has a variety of information associated with it, including its name, size, and author. You can view this information in several ways:

- Display the files and folders in Details view.
- Select a specific file or folder, and view some items of information in the Details pane.
- Point to a file to display a ScreenTip with some items of information.
- Right-click a file or folder, and click Properties to view all the available information in the Properties dialog box.

You can add a title to a file in the Details pane, and you can add and edit other information in the Properties dialog box.

In this exercise, you will view file information in the Details pane and add a title to a file. Then you'll display the Properties dialog box and add other information.

> **BE SURE TO** display your Documents folder before beginning this exercise.
>
> **USE** the *03_Videos* folder and the practice files located in the *Chapter03* subfolder under *SBS_WindowsVista*. It may be necessary to clear the read-only attribute in the sample file's Property box in order to complete the following steps.

1. Navigate to the *MSP\SBS_WindowsVista\Chapter03* subfolder, and display the contents in **Tiles** view.

2. If the **Details** pane isn't open, point to **Layout** on the **Organize** menu, and then in the list, click **Details Pane**.

The Details pane indicates that there are 35 items in the *Chapter03* folder.

3. In the **Content** pane, click the *03_Costs* worksheet.

The Details pane displays the file's icon, name, type, authors, size, and date modified, with placeholders to a title and tags.

4. In the **Details** pane, click **Add a title**.

The Title box becomes editable.

5. In the **Title** box, type Disorganization, and then click **Save**.

After Windows Vista updates the file properties, the title appears in the Details pane.

6. In the **Content** pane, point to *03_Costs*.

A ScreenTip displays several items of information about the file, including the title you just created. The modification date and time given reflect the date and time you added the title to the file properties.

7. Right-click *03_Costs*, and then click **Properties**.

> **Tip** You can also display a file's properties by selecting the file and then clicking Properties on the Organize menu.

The 03_Costs Properties dialog box opens. The General tab gives overview information about the file; the Security tab gives information about who can use the file; and the Previous Versions tab lists previous versions that you can restore if you need to.

> **Tip** As long as a file is stored in a subfolder of your personal folder, other people cannot access it unless they know your user account credentials. However, if you work on a network with shared folders, or if you need to store a file in the Public folder so that it is accessible to other users of your computer, you might want to limit who can do what with the file. You cannot set a password for a file or folder in Windows but you can assign permissions to specific users or groups of users on the Security tab of the file's Properties dialog box. On that tab, you can click the Learn About Access Control And Permissions link to display a detailed Help topic.

8. In the **03_Costs Properties** dialog box, click the **Details** tab.

This tab displays all the file's properties. If you can change a property, pointing to its right displays a box where you can enter or edit the information.

9. On the **Details** tab, point to the right of **Tags**, click the box that appears, and then type e. Then wait a few seconds.

   A list appears, displaying tags beginning with the letter *e* that are assigned to files in this folder (in this case, there are two—*efficiency* and *Excel*).

10. Select the *efficiency* check box to insert that tag.

    Now when you search for all files associated with *efficiency*, this file will be part of the search results, even though that word doesn't appear in the file.

    See Also For information about searching for files, see "Finding Specific Information" later in this chapter.

11. Click **OK** to close the dialog box.

12. In the **Content** pane, double-click the *03_Videos* folder.

    The folder contents appear in Details view. The Type column indicates that the one item in this folder is a Microsoft Windows Media Audio/Video file.

13. Right-click a blank area of the **Content** pane, and then click **Properties**.

    The 03_Videos Properties dialog box opens. The General, Security, and Previous Versions tabs provide the same information as the corresponding tabs in a file's

Properties dialog box. You can use the options on the Sharing tab to share this folder with colleagues on a network.

See Also For information about sharing folders, see "Sharing Drives and Folders" in Chapter 8, "Making Connections."

14. In the **03_Videos Properties** dialog box, click the **Customize** tab.

This folder is assigned the Documents type.

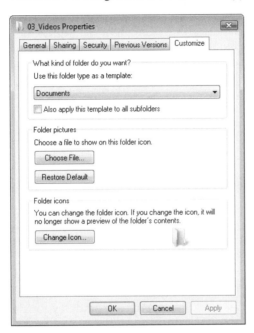

15. Click the **Use this folder type as a template** arrow, and in the list, click **Pictures and Videos**. Then click **OK**.

The folder contents now appear in Large Icons view, because that view is more suited to quickly identifying pictures and videos. The toolbar now has a Slide Show button, which you can click to see a full-screen view of the files in the folder.

 CLOSE the 03_Videos window.

Tip You can quickly remove the properties from a file you have created (but not from a folder) by selecting the file and then clicking Remove Properties on the Organize menu. In the Remove Properties dialog box, you can then select the properties you want to remove.

Creating, Renaming, and Deleting Folders and Files

With each program you use on your computer, you create files of a particular type. For example, with Microsoft Office Word 2007, you create documents (*.docx* files); with Microsoft Office Excel 2007, you create worksheets (*.xlsx* files); and with Microsoft Office PowerPoint 2007, you create presentations (*.pptx* files). You can also create and edit simple text documents and graphics using the tools that come with Windows Vista.

As you create files, you will want to create folders in which to organize the files for easy retrieval. Often you will need to rename a folder or file to accurately reflect its content. And periodically you will want to delete folders and files you no longer need. For safety reasons, removing a file from your computer is a two-step process: You first delete the file, which moves it to the Recycle Bin—a holding area on your hard drive from which is it possible to restore an item if you realize you need it. Then you periodically empty the Recycle Bin, which permanently erases its contents.

> **Tip** The contents of the Recycle Bin take up space on your hard disk. If you need this space, and are absolutely positive you will never need to restore a deleted file, you can instruct Windows to erase items immediately when you delete them. To do so, right-click the Recycle Bin, click Properties, and select the Do Not Move Files To The Recycle Bin option.

When you buy a computer these days, it likely comes with a hard disk that will store several *gigabytes (GB)* of information. A gigabyte is 1 billion *bytes*, and a byte is a unit of information that is the equivalent of one character. Some of your files will be very small—1 to 2 *kilobytes (KB)*, or 1000 to 2000 characters—and others might be quite large—several *megabytes (MB)*, or several million characters. The small ones are easy to copy and move around, but large files or large groups of files are easier to copy and move from one place to another, or to send by e-mail, if you *compress* them. You can compress files you created, program files, or even other folders into a compressed folder that is identified by a zipper on its folder icon.

In this exercise, you will create a new folder and two new files: a text document and a picture. After renaming one of the files, you will compress the two files and then delete all the files and folders you created in the exercise. There are no practice files for this exercise.

> **BE SURE TO** display your Documents folder and the Details pane before beginning this exercise.

1. Navigate to your *Documents\MSP\SBS_WindowsVista\Chapter03* folder, and display its contents in **Tiles** view.

2. On the **Organize** menu, click **New Folder**.

A new folder appears in the Content pane, with the name *New Folder* selected so that you can change it.

3. Press the [Home] key, type My followed by a space, and then press [Enter].

4. Press [Enter] again to open the empty folder.

5. Right-click anywhere in the **Content** pane, point to **New**, and then click **Text Document**.

A new text document is created, with the name *New Text Document* selected so that you can change it.

6. Double-click **New**, type My followed by a space, and then press [Enter].

The file name, date, type, and size are displayed to the right of the file's icon. Because the file is empty, the size is 0 KB.

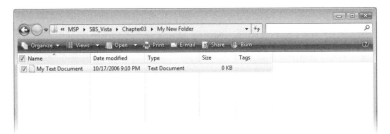

7. Press [Enter] again to open the file.

The text document opens in the Microsoft Notepad program, a text-editing program that comes with Windows Vista.

> **Troubleshooting** If the document opens in a different program, that program has been designated as your default text editor. You can follow the next two steps in that program.

8. Type This is a text file.

Close

9. Click the **Close** button to close the file, and click **Save** when prompted to save your changes.

The file size reported in the Content pane is 1 KB because the size is rounded up to the nearest whole kilobyte. However, the size reported in the Details pane is the actual size of 20 bytes.

File size rounded to nearest kilobyte

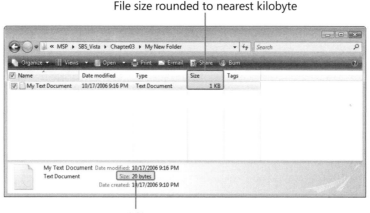

Actual file size

10. Right-click a blank area of the **Content** pane, point to **New**, and then click **Bitmap Image**.

A new graphic file is created, with the name *New Bitmap Image* selected so that you can change it.

11. Change the name of the file to My Bitmap Image, and then press `Enter`.

When you rename the file, it moves to the top of the file list to maintain the alphabetical sort order.

> **Tip** *Bitmap* images represent images as dots, or *pixels*, on the screen and are saved in the bitmap (*.bmp*) format.

12. Right-click the graphic file, and then click **Edit**.

The blank graphic file opens in the Microsoft *Paint* program, a simple graphics program that comes with Windows Vista.

> **Troubleshooting** If the file opens in a different program, that program has been designated as your default graphics editor. You can follow the next step in that program.

13. Experiment with the Paint tools while creating a picture of any kind. (Click a tool, move the pointer over the blank canvas, and drag the pointer to use the tool.) When you're done, click the **Close** button to close the file, and click **Save** when prompted to save your changes.

    In the Content pane, the Size column reflects the size of the graphic. The Details pane displays a thumbnail of the graphic you created, and reports the file's dimensions as well as its size. If you want, you can switch to an icon view to see an image of the graphic.

14. With *My Bitmap Image* selected, point to *My Text Document*, and then add it to the selection by selecting the check box that appears to its left.

    > **Troubleshooting** If you don't see a check box when you point to a file or folder in the Content pane, display the View tab of the Folder Options dialog box, select the Use Check Boxes To Select Items check box in the Advanced Settings list, and then click OK.

    The Details pane indicates that two items are selected and reports the total size of the selection. Because the file sizes in the Content pane are rounded up, the total in the Details pane might be less than the sum of the individual file sizes.

15. Right-click the selection, point to **Send To**, and then click **Compressed (zipped) Folder**.

    A compressed folder named for one of the selected files is created. The folder name is selected so that you can change it.

16. Type My Compressed Folder, and then press Enter .

17. Double-click the compressed folder to open it.

    The Content pane now displays the files that have been compressed into the zipped folder. The Extract All Files button on the toolbar and the zipped folder icon in the Details pane indicate that you are viewing a compressed folder rather than a standard folder.

18. Point to the right border of the Name column heading, and when the pointer changes to a bar with opposing arrows, double-click. Then double-click the right borders of the other column headings to see all the information available in Details view.

File-compression information

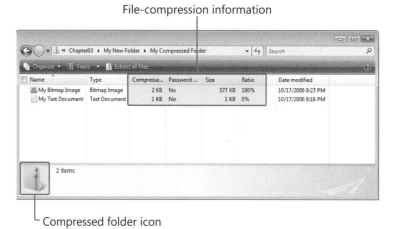

Compressed folder icon

Back

19. In the upper-left corner of the window, click the **Back** button to redisplay the contents of the *My New Folder* folder.

Because you created a graphic in this folder, it has been assigned the Pictures And Video type, with a default view of Large Icons.

20. Click *My Bitmap Image* to select it, hold down the ⌃Ctrl key, and click *My Text Document* to add it to the selection. Then press the Del key, and click **Yes** to confirm the deletion.

> **Tip** You can also delete a file or folder by selecting it and then clicking Delete on the Organize menu. You cannot delete a file by pressing the Backspace key.

21. If the **Navigation** pane is not displayed, point to **Layout** on the **Organize** menu, and then click **Navigation Pane**. Scroll to the bottom of the **Navigation** pane, and then click **Recycle Bin**.

The Recycle Bin contains all the files you have deleted. The toolbar displays the Empty The Recycle Bin and Restore All Items buttons so that you can quickly perform those tasks.

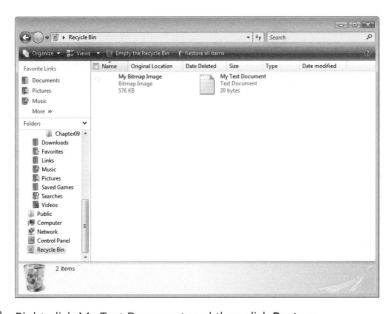

22. Right-click *My Text Document*, and then click **Restore**.

The file is moved from the Recycle Bin back to the location from which it was deleted.

23. Scroll up in the **Navigation** pane, and click the *My New Folder* subfolder of the *Chapter03* folder to see the restored file.

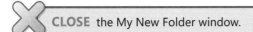

CLOSE the My New Folder window.

Moving and Copying Folders and Files

When you have accumulated enough files that you need to organize them in some way, you can easily move files and folders from one location to another. The methods of copying, pasting, moving, and renaming are the same for both files and folders.

One of the ways you might want to organize your files is by type. As you saw in "Viewing Information About a Folder or File" earlier in this chapter, Windows Vista includes four types of folders that are designed to hold files of a certain type: Documents, Pictures and Videos, Music Details, and Music Icons. When you display the contents of the folder, buttons on the toolbar provide easy access to features appropriate for that type of file, such as playing music or viewing photographs.

> **Tip** If more than one person uses your computer, you might want to move files into subfolders of the Public folder, to make them available for all users.

In this exercise, you will make copies of files and folders and then move files between folders.

BE SURE TO display your Documents folder, the Details pane, and the Navigation pane before beginning this exercise.

USE the *05_Narrations* and *05_Photographs* folders and the practice files located in the *Chapter03* subfolder under *SBS_WindowsVista*.

1. Navigate to the *MSP\SBS_WindowsVista\Chapter03* subfolder.

2. With the contents of the *Chapter03* folder displayed in the Content pane in **Details** view, click the *05_Introduction* audio file to select it. Then on the **Organize** menu, click **Copy**.

   Nothing seems to happen.

3. Right-click the *05_Narrations* folder, and then click **Paste**.

   The folder's modification date changes to reflect when the folder was modified.

4. Double-click the *05_Narrations* folder to verify that it now contains a copy of the *05_Introduction* file.

   A Play All button appears on the toolbar so that you can play the audio file if you want.

5. Click the **Back** button, select the *05_Introduction* file, and delete it, clicking **Yes** when prompted to confirm the deletion.

6. In the **Content** pane, right-click *05_Cat*, and click **Cut**. Then right-click the *05_Photographs* folder, and click **Paste**.

   The *05_Cat* image moves to the *05_Photographs* folder.

7. Click the **Type** column heading to sort the files by type.

8. Click *05_Crow* (the first JPEG Image file in the list), hold down the ⎡Shift⎦ key, and click *05_Frog*. Then on the **Organize** menu, click **Cut**.

9. Right-click the *05_Photographs* folder, and then click **Paste**.

   The selected JPEG image files move to the folder.

10. In the **Content** pane, drag the *05_MusicBox* file to the *05_Photographs* folder, but don't release the mouse button.

Back

The *05_Photographs* folder is highlighted, and a ScreenTip appears with the instruction *Move to 05_Photographs*.

11. Release the mouse button to move the file.

> **Tip** To copy a file by dragging it, point to the file, hold down the Ctrl key, and then drag the copy to its new location, releasing first the mouse button and then the Ctrl key.

12. In the **Navigation** pane, click *05_Photographs* to display its contents in the Content pane.

Because this folder has been designated as a Picture And Video folder, the toolbar includes a Slide Show button.

13. Click the first image in the file (*05_Cat*), and on the toolbar, click **Slide Show**.

The *05_Cat* graphic is displayed full-screen. After a few seconds, the next graphic appears.

14. After the slide show has cycled through all the graphics in the folder, press the Esc key to end the slide show.

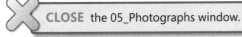

CLOSE the 05_Photographs window.

Finding Specific Information

As far as we are concerned, the awesome new search capabilities of Windows Vista are one of its three best features. (The others are Sleep mode and the amazing graphic capabilities—for those people with video cards capable of supporting them.)

With Windows Vista, you can find files, messages, and message attachments on your computer almost instantly. You don't need to know the name of the file or item you want to find; simply type a word or phrase in the Start Search box on the Start menu or the Search box in the upper-right corner of a Windows Explorer window to display a list of matching items. If you want to find information on the Internet, click the Search The Internet link that appears above the Start Search box on the Start menu to open the Windows Live Search site displaying links to sites related to the term you typed.

How does Windows Vista find items so quickly? Behind the scenes, Windows Vista maintains an index of all the key words in and associated with the data files on your computer—documents, music, videos, graphics, local copies of e-mail messages, Web pages stored in your recent history or Favorites list, and so on. (It does not include the system or program files; such an index would be huge and would slow down the search process.) When you type a search term, Windows looks for it in the index instead of searching your hard disk. You shouldn't ever need to worry about the index, but after you have some experience with searching, you might want to check Windows Help And Support for information about index locations and settings.

> **Tip** After a lot of file moving or renaming, your search results might seem inaccurate because the index is out of date. Just be patient. If you have a lot of files stored on your computer, it can take Windows several hours to update its index. If you need to force Windows Vista to update the index, you can open Control Panel, click System And Maintenance, and then click Indexing Options. In the Indexing Options dialog box, click Advanced, and then in the Advanced Options dialog box, click Rebuild.

If a simple search in the Start Search or Search box doesn't locate the item you are looking for, you can perform more advanced searches in the Search Results folder. Your search criteria can include the date a file was created, its size, part of its name or title, its author, and any tags you might have listed as properties of the file.

In this exercise, you will quickly locate items on your computer and on the Internet. You will then use advanced criteria in the Search Results folder to look for other files and will open the Preview pane to help identify the correct file.

USE the practice files located in the *Chapter03* subfolder under *SBS_WindowsVista*.

Start

1. Click the **Start** button.

   The Start menu opens with the insertion point blinking in the Start Search box at the bottom.

2. In the **Start Search** box, type bamboo.

   As you type, Windows filters the programs, files, folders, and e-mail messages stored on your computer and displays a list of items (only as many as will fit on the Start menu) related to your search term.

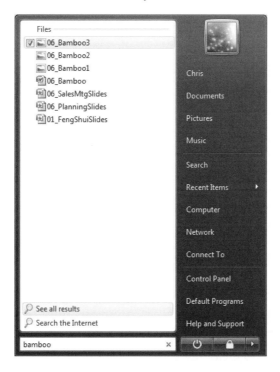

> **Tip** If your search returns more results than can be shown, you can display the entire list in the Search Results window by clicking See All Results.

3. Point to each file in the search results in turn to display a ScreenTip with the file's properties.

   If you get in the habit of entering properties for your files, this handy trick can help you quickly identify the file you want.

4. At the bottom of the **Start** menu, click the **Search the Internet** link.

Your Web browser starts, displaying the results of a Windows Live Search for *bamboo*.

5. Close your Web browser.

6. On the **Start** menu, click **Search**.

The Search Results folder opens in a window.

7. In the upper-right corner of the window, in the **Search** box, type bamboo.

The Search Results window displays the files that match the search term. You can change the view and sort the files the same way you would with any folder.

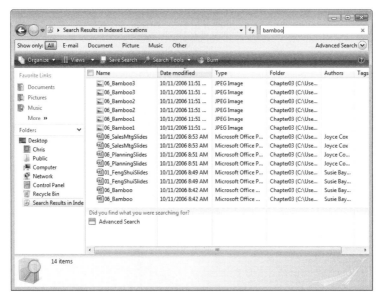

See Also For information about changing views and sorting files, see "Viewing Folders and Files in Different Ways" earlier in this chapter.

8. On the **Search** toolbar, to the right of **Show only**, click **Picture**.

The Picture filter hides any file in the search results that is not a graphic, and the view switches to Large Icons so that you can see thumbnails of the graphics.

9. Double-click the word **bamboo** in the **Search** box, and type statue.

No items match this search term.

10. At the right end of the **Search** toolbar, click the **Advanced Search** arrow.

The Search pane opens at the top of the window.

When a simple search term fails to find the file you are looking for, you can use the options in this pane to supply more information about the file.

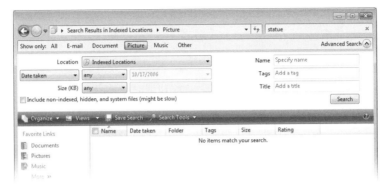

11. Click the **any** box to the right of **Date taken**, and then in the list, click **is before**. Then click the date box to the right, and use the calendar to set the date to **December 31, 2006**.

12. Delete the word **statue** from the **Search** box. Then in the **Tag** box, type statue*, and click **Search**.

    You have specified that you want to find a picture created before December 31, 2006 that has some variation of the word *statue* (perhaps *statues* or *statuette*) in the title. The Search Results window displays two files that match these criteria.

    > **Tip** In searches, the asterisk (*) is a *wildcard character* that represents any number of characters (including zero). The question mark (?) represents one character. For example, enter *.txt to search for any text file; enter s*.txt to search for any text file with a file name that begins with the letter s; and enter s??.txt to search for any text file that has a three-letter file name beginning with the letter s.

13. Click the **is before** box to the right of **Date taken**, and then in the list, click **any**. Then click the **Advanced Search** arrow to close the Search pane.

    > **Troubleshooting** If you don't reset the date criteria, the date setting will be applied to future searches.

14. To the right of **Show only** on the **Search** toolbar, click **All**. Then select the contents of the **Search** box, and type tag.

    The Search Results window displays any file that has *tag* in its file name or in its text. In this case, you are looking for a file containing an announcement from Lucerne Publishing about a new book series called *The Taguien Cycle*.

15. On the **Organize** menu, point to **Layout**, and then click **Preview Pane**.

The Preview pane opens on the right side of the window.

16. Click the first file in the search results to view its contents in the Preview pane.

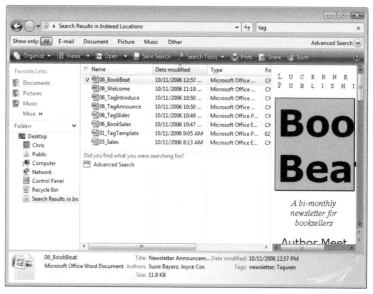

17. Press the ↓ key to preview each file in turn.

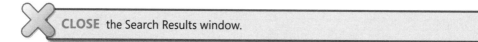

CLOSE the Search Results window.

Key Points

- Windows Explorer provides several ways to move around your computer. Becoming familiar with them will increase your ability to quickly find specific files.

- Displaying the folders and files in different ways can help you identify them more easily.

- Windows Vista displays graphic representations of the files and folders on your computer. Different file types are represented by different graphic icons, so you can differentiate between them at a glance.

- In addition to its name, properties such as size, author, and date of creation or modification are stored with each file. You can view and change this information in the file's Properties dialog box.

- To organize folders and files in a logical structure, you can rename, move, copy, and delete them.

- You can quickly locate information on your computer by using a search term, or you can use the Search pane to set up search criteria with whatever information you have available.

Keyboard Shortcuts

Press this	To do this
Ctrl+C	Copy the selection
Ctrl+X	Cut the selection
Ctrl+V	Paste the selection
Delete	Delete the selected item and move it to the Recycle Bin
Shift+Delete	Delete the selected item without moving it to the Recycle Bin first
F2	Rename the selected item
Shift+Arrow key	Select more than one item in a window
Ctrl+A	Select all items in a window
F3 or Windows logo key+F	Search for a file or folder
Alt+Enter	Display properties for the selected item
F4	Display the Address bar list in Windows Explorer
Alt+Up Arrow	View the folder one level up in Windows Explorer
Windows logo key+E	Open Computer
Ctrl+Windows logo key+F	Search for computers on a network
End	Display the bottom of the active window
Home	Display the top of the active window
Left Arrow	Collapse the current selection (if it is expanded), or select the parent folder
Alt+Left Arrow	View the previous folder
Right Arrow	Display the current selection (if it is collapsed), or select the first subfolder
Alt+Right Arrow	View the next folder

Chapter at a Glance

Change the desktop
background, **page 108**

Optimize visual effects,
page 101

Manage your system
date and time, **page 115**

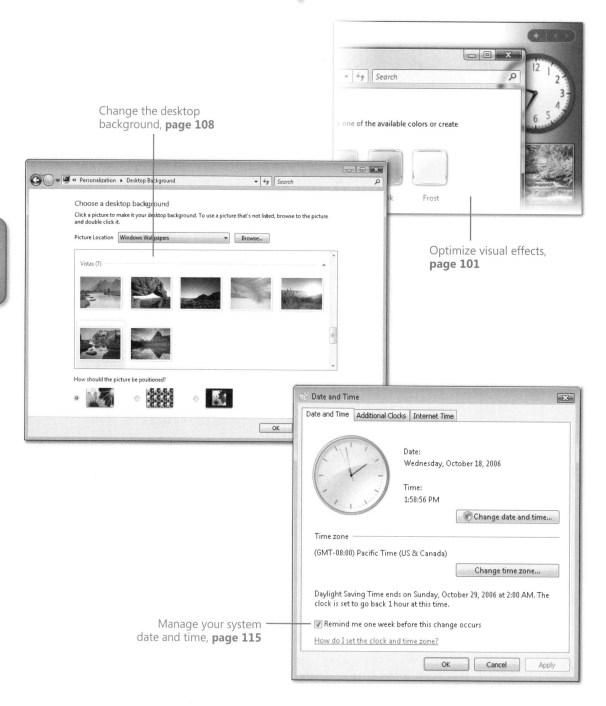

4 Personalizing Windows Vista

In this chapter, you will learn to:

- ✔ Change the the look of Windows Vista on your screen.
- ✔ Optimize visual effects.
- ✔ Change the desktop background.
- ✔ Select and manage a screen saver.
- ✔ Manage your system date and time.
- ✔ Change your computer's name.

The way programs look on your computer screen and the way you use them are to a large extent determined by the Windows Vista user interface. Some elements of the interface, such as the graphics, fonts, and colors, might seem merely cosmetic but they can affect the way you work. You can personalize almost any aspect of your computer's appearance and functionality to suit your needs.

In this chapter, you will change the appearance of Windows Vista by working with themes, color schemes, and backgrounds. You will also select a screen saver, update the system date and time, and change the name by which your computer is identified on a network.

See Also Do you need only a quick refresher on the topics in this chapter? See the Quick Reference entries on pages xxxix–lxxiii.

> **Important** Before you can use the practice files in this chapter, you need to install them from the book's companion CD to their default location. See "Using the Book's CD" on page xxix for more information.

Changing the Look of Windows Vista on Your Screen

You can easily change the look of the Windows interface by applying a different *theme*. A theme usually includes a desktop background color or picture; a color scheme that affects title bars and labels; specific fonts that are used on title bars, labels, and buttons; sounds that are associated with specific actions; and other elements. Previous versions of Windows came with a long list of available themes, and additional themes could be downloaded from the Internet. Windows Vista has simplified the theme-selection process by offering only two themes—Windows Vista and Windows Classic. You can search for other themes online, or possibly purchase theme packs from software retailers.

In this exercise, you will switch between the Windows Vista and Windows Classic themes. If you want, you can explore the online options on your own at a later time. There are no practice files for this exercise.

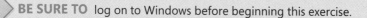

> **BE SURE TO** log on to Windows before beginning this exercise.

Start

1. Click the **Start** button, click **Control Panel**, and then in Control Panel, click **Appearance and Personalization**.

The Appearance And Personalization window opens.

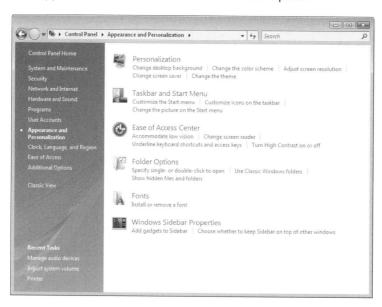

2. Under **Personalization**, click the **Change the theme** task.

The Theme Settings dialog box opens, displaying a preview of the current theme.

3. Click the **Theme** arrow, and then in the list, click **Windows Classic**.

   The Sample box changes to reflect your selection. You might recognize this theme if you previously used a computer running Microsoft Windows 2000.

4. Click **OK** to close the dialog box and apply your settings.

   The left pane of the Appearance And Personalization window now has a white background. The font, title bar, and buttons have changed, and if you were displaying the Windows Aero interface, you'll notice even more changes, such as the absence of transparency in the window frames.

5. In the **Appearance and Personalization** window, point to **Personalization** to view the Windows Classic item selection indicator.

Minimize

6. In the upper-right corner of the **Appearance and Personalization** window, click the **Minimize** button.

The solid blue Windows Classic desktop looks quite dull compared to the Windows Vista desktop. The taskbar has changed from blue to gray; the Start button from round to rectangular; and Windows Sidebar, if it is displayed, from translucent to solid gray.

7. On the taskbar, click the **Control Panel\Appearance and Personalization** taskbar button to redisplay the window.

8. Under **Personalization**, click the **Change the theme** task to redisplay the Theme Settings dialog box.

9. In the **Theme** list, click **Windows Vista**.

The Sample box displays the Windows Vista default desktop. Regardless of the desktop background you were displaying before beginning this exercise, the default desktop depicting a lake and mountain scene is shown.

10. In the **Theme Settings** dialog box, click **OK**.

Your desktop, Start button, taskbar, Sidebar, and open windows now have the default Windows Vista look and feel.

> **Tip** You'll be working with the desktop background in the next exercise, so there is no need to reset your desktop background before continuing.

 CLOSE the Appearance And Personalization window.

Optimizing Visual Effects

In the previous exercise, you set the desktop theme, which selected the Windows Vista background, sounds, icons, buttons, windows shape, and so on. These options provide a pleasant user interface and are available on any computer running Windows Vista. However, the pinnacle of the Windows Vista visual experience is Windows Aero, which is identified within Windows Vista as a color scheme, but is so much more than simply colors. It is truly a thing of beauty, incorporating soft edges, shadows, transparent window frames, animated window transitions, active previews of hidden windows from the taskbar, and a three-dimensional rotating stack display. In short, all the bells and whistles! Unfortunately, Windows Aero works only on systems that have the necessary hardware configuration, which includes:

- 1 GHz 32-bit (x86) or 64-bit (x64) processor
- 1 GB of RAM
- 128 MB graphics adapter
- DirectX 9-class graphics processor that supports a Windows Display Driver Model Driver, Pixel Shader 2.0, and 32 bits per pixel

If you purchased your computer before 2006, it is unlikely that it meets these requirements (unless your computer is set up for gaming or professional graphics production). You might be able to upgrade your system by purchasing more RAM and a new graphics card. If your hardware does meet the minimum requirements, you will have the pleasure of the Windows Aero experience when running these Windows Vista editions:

- Windows Vista Home Premium
- Windows Vista Ultimate
- Windows Vista Business
- Windows Vista Enterprise

> **Tip** Don't know which edition of Windows Vista is installed on your computer? Click System And Maintenance in Control Panel, and then click Welcome Center. The edition is reported at the top of the Welcome Center window.

If you purchased a Windows Aero-qualified computer system with Windows Vista already installed, Windows Aero was probably turned on when you first started the computer. If you upgraded your hardware or upgraded to Windows Vista from a previous version of Windows, you might need to make some adjustments.

In this exercise, you will check your hardware configuration to see whether it meets Windows Aero requirements, set the monitor colors and refresh rate to the levels necessary to support Windows Aero, and then configure the Windows Aero color scheme, including window frame transparency. There are no practice files for this exercise.

> **Tip** The screens shown in other exercises in this book are captured with Windows Aero and font smoothing turned off, because those features do not present as clearly on the printed page.

OPEN Control Panel.

1. In **Control Panel**, click **System and Maintenance**, and then click **System**.

   The System window opens.

Processor speed

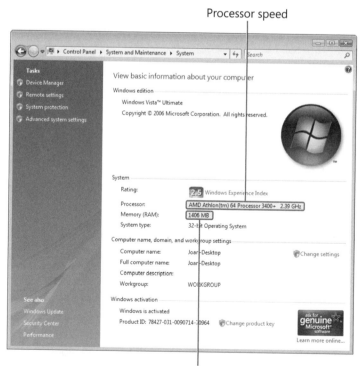

RAM

Your processor speed and installed RAM are shown under System. You need a processor speed of at least 1.0 GHz, and at least 1 GB (1024 MB) of RAM to display Windows Aero features.

2. In the **Address** bar, click the arrow to the right of **Control Panel**, and then in the list, click **Appearance and Personalization**.

3. In the **Appearance and Personalization** window, click **Personalization**.

The Personalization window opens. From this window, you can customize any aspect of the Windows Vista user interface.

> **Tip** You can display the Personalization window by right-clicking the desktop and then clicking Personalize.

4. In the **Personalization** window, click **Display Settings**. Then in the **Display Settings** dialog box, click **Advanced Settings** to display information about your graphics adapter.

Graphics adapter memory

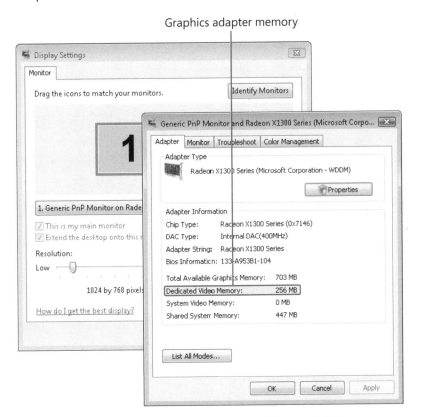

Windows Aero features require 128 MB of dedicated video memory.

5. In the **Advanced Settings** dialog box, click the **Monitor** tab. In the **Monitor Settings** area, click the **Screen refresh rate** arrow to display a list of valid refresh rates for the selected monitor.

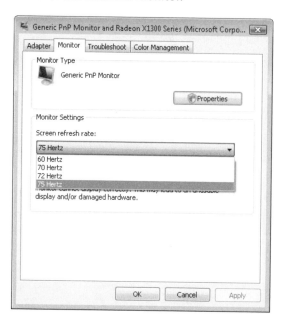

Tip The screen refresh rate, which varies from monitor to monitor, determines the number of times per second your monitor redraws the image. At lower refresh rates, the monitor may appear to be flickering rather than displaying a constant picture, and this can lead to eyestrain. A refresh rate of 70 Hertz (Hz) or above is considered to be flicker-free.

6. Select a screen refresh rate of at least 10 Hertz, preferably 70 or over. Then click **OK**.

7. If your computer system includes multiple monitors on the same graphics adapter or multiple enabled graphics adapters, select the other monitors in turn, click **Advanced Settings**, confirm the available graphics memory, select an appropriate refresh rate, and click **OK**.

8. In the **Display Settings** dialog box, click the **Colors** arrow to display the available color qualities.

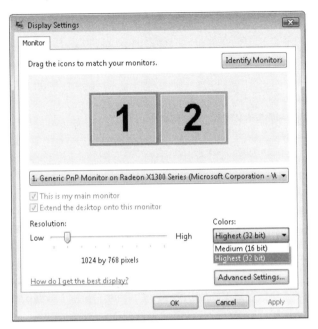

9. Set the color quality to at least **32 bit**. Then click **OK**.

10. In the **Personalization** window, click **Window Color and Appearance**.

   If the Window Color And Appearance page opens, then Windows Aero is already selected as your color scheme; skip to Step 15 to continue. Otherwise, the Appearance Settings dialog box opens.

11. In the **Color scheme** list, click **Windows Aero**. Then click **Effects**.

> **Troubleshooting** The Windows Aero option appears only if your hardware supports it.

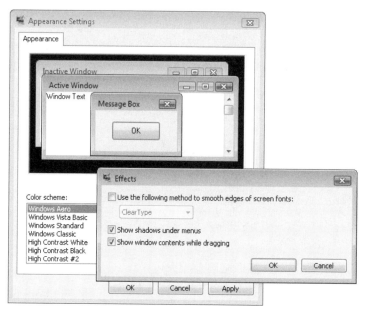

12. In the **Effects** dialog box, select the **Use the following method to smooth edges of screen fonts** check box if it is not already selected, and in the list, click **ClearType**. Then click **OK** in each of the two open dialog boxes.

Windows Vista applies the Windows Aero interface. One effect you might imme-diately notice regardless of other settings is the change in the appearance of the Personalization window; the title bar takes on a subtle pattern, and if transparency is already enabled, you can see right through the window frame to whatever is behind the window.

> **Troubleshooting** Screens shown in the remainder of this exercise depict the full Windows Aero user interface; this interface is beautiful on screen, but might not display as well on the printed grayscale page of this book, so you'll need to rely on what you see on screen for a true representation.

13. Point to the **Personalization** taskbar button.

A thumbnail representation of the window appears. This is another effect of Windows Aero.

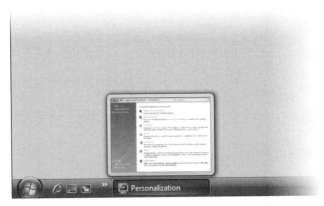

14. In the **Personalization** window, click **Window Color and Appearance**.

When the Windows Aero color scheme is in effect, clicking this link opens the Window Color And Appearance page.

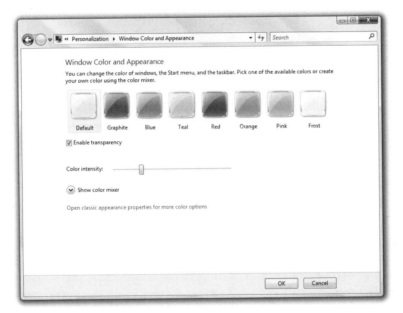

15. Click each of the eight color icons at the top of the page in turn.

The current selection is immediately previewed in the frame of the Window Color And Appearance page. The subtle pattern in the window frame might be more apparent against darker colors. You can tailor any of the colors to your liking by clicking Show Color Mixer and then adjusting the Hue, Saturation, and Brightness.

16. Select the **Enable transparency** check box, or if it is already selected, clear it and then reselect it.

Notice the subtle change between the transparent and solid window frames.

17. With the **Enable transparency** check box selected, drag the active window around the screen so that its title bar passes over another screen element such as a picture on the desktop background, the Sidebar, or a desktop icon.

You can see through the top, bottom, and both sides of the window frame, although the transparency is most noticeable in the title bar. The Default color provides the most transparency.

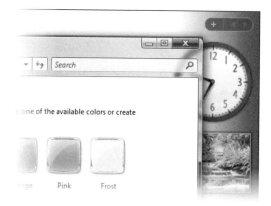

18. On the **Window Color and Appearance** page, click **OK**.

CLOSE the Personalization window.

Changing the Desktop Background

If the default Windows Vista desktop background doesn't appeal to you or if you want to change the background for another reason, you can do so at any time. Your choice of background usually reflects your personal taste—what you like to see when your program windows are minimized or closed. Some people prefer simple backgrounds that don't interfere with their desktop icons, and others like photos of family members, pets, or favorite places.

Windows Vista comes with over 35 desktop backgrounds to choose from, including photographs, paintings, and computer art. You can preview each background on your desktop before actually applying it. If you prefer, you can opt for a plain background and then set its color. You can also choose from the 15 sample photos that come with Windows Vista or any digital image of your own.

In this exercise, you will preview the available desktop background options, and display a photograph as your background. Then you will switch to a plain, solid color background.

USE the series of images beginning with *00_Arizona* located in the *Chapter04* subfolder under *SBS_WindowsVista*.

OPEN Control Panel.

1. In **Control Panel**, under **Appearance and Personalization**, click the **Change desktop background** task.

   The Desktop Background page opens, with Windows Wallpapers selected in the Picture Location list, and thumbnails of the available wallpapers grouped in categories in the box below, scrolled to the category containing your current desktop.

   Troubleshooting If your desktop background is currently set to something other than one of the Windows Wallpapers, that category is selected in the Picture Location list and shown in the box.

   Tip If Use Check Boxes To Select Items is selected in your Folder Options dialog box, a check box with a check mark appears in the corner of the current desktop background thumbnail. Otherwise, the current background is indicated by a gray box. For more information, see "Moving and Copying Folders and Files" in Chapter 3, "Working with Folders and Files."

2. With **Windows Wallpapers** selected in the **Picture Location** list, scroll through the available wallpapers, and click any thumbnails that interest you.

   When you click a thumbnail, a preview of the wallpaper appears on the desktop behind the window.

3. Click the **Picture Location** arrow, and then in the list, click **Sample Pictures**.

   The 15 sample pictures displayed come with Windows Vista. These pictures are stored in the *Public Pictures\Sample Pictures* folder. (You can also find a link to that folder in your personal *Pictures* folder.) They are also displayed by default in other Windows Vista features such as the Photos screen saver and the Sidebar slide show.

4. In the **Picture Location** list, click **Pictures**.

   The Picture Location box displays the contents of your *Pictures* folder.

5. Click **Browse**. Then in the **Browse** dialog box, navigate to your *Documents\MSP\SBS_WindowsVista\Chapter04* folder, and double-click the *00_Arizona02* image.

   The selected picture appears as your desktop background, the Picture Location list shows the path to the practice file folder, and the entire contents of the folder appear in the Picture Location box.

6. Below the **Picture Location** box, select the **Center** option.

On your desktop, the picture changes to its actual dimensions. If your monitor is set to a screen resolution of 1024×768, this might result in blank space above and below the picture; a higher resolution might display blank space on all four sides.

> **Troubleshooting** Results can vary depending on your hardware.

7. Click **Change background color**. In the **Color** dialog box that opens, click any color you like, and then click **OK**.

   The blank space around the picture changes to the selected color.

8. In the **Picture Location** list, click **Solid Colors**.

   The window now displays 39 thumbnails of plain, solid colors.

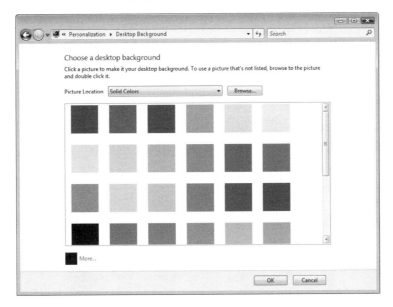

> **Tip** If none of these suit your needs, you can click the More link to display the Color dialog box from which you can select any color.

9. Click the light gray color (third row of the second column, when the window is sized to display six thumbnails across), and then click **OK** to apply your background selection.

CLOSE Control Panel.

BE SURE TO adjust the desktop background to suit your preferences before moving on. We retained the pale gray background to make the graphics in this book easier to see.

Selecting and Managing a Screen Saver

Screen savers are static or moving images that are displayed on your computer after some period of inactivity. The original concept behind screen savers was that they prevented your computer's monitor from being permanently "imprinted" with a specific pattern when it was left on for too long without changing. Modern monitors are not as susceptible to this kind of damage, but it is still a good idea to use a screen saver or to have your monitor automatically use power-saver mode after a period of inactivity.

Another reason for using a screen saver is to protect your computer from prying eyes when you are away from your desk. To further protect your data, you can require that your password be entered to unlock the screen saver after it is set in motion.

The default screen saver is a Windows Vista logo that moves around on a black background. Windows Vista comes with eight additional animated screen savers. You can choose any of these, display a slide show of the images and/or videos in a specific folder as a screen saver, download other animated screen savers from the Internet, or display no screen saver at all.

> **Tip** To quickly locate additional screen savers online, visit *search.microsoft.com*, type screen savers in the Search Microsoft.com For box, and then click the Search button.

In this exercise, you will preview available screen savers and then select a screen saver that consists of a slide show of photographs.

> **USE** the practice files located in the *Chapter04* subfolder under *SBS_WindowsVista*.
> **OPEN** Control Panel, and then click Appearance And Personalization.

1. Under **Personalization**, click the **Change screen saver** task.

   The Screen Saver Settings dialog box opens

2. Click the **Screen saver** arrow, and then in the list, click **Photos**.

The preview screen displays a slide show of the 15 pictures in the *Public Pictures\ Sample Pictures* folder.

> **Troubleshooting** If you have pictures in your own *Pictures* folder, you might see those pictures instead of the samples in the public *Sample Pictures* folder.

3. Click **Settings**.

The Photo Screen Saver Settings dialog box opens.

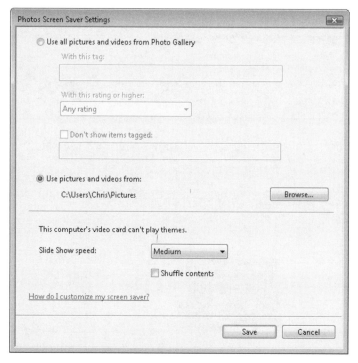

4. To the right of **Use pictures and videos from**, click **Browse**.

5. In the **Browse For Folder** dialog box that opens, browse to your *Documents\MSP\ SBS_WindowsVista\Chapter04* folder, and then click **OK**.

> **Tip** If you have a folder of your own favorite photos on your computer, feel free to browse to that folder instead.

6. Adjust the slide show speed if you want, and then click **Save**.

In the Screen Saver Settings dialog box, the slide show preview cycles through the pictures in the selected folder. You can click Preview to see the full-screen slide show as it will appear when in action; move the mouse or press the Esc key to return to the dialog box.

> **Tip** To use a password to return to your regular desktop in Windows Vista, select the On Resume, Display Logon Screen.

7. Choose the screen saver option you want to use on your computer, and then click **OK**.

 CLOSE the Appearance And Personalization window.

Managing Your System Date and Time

Your computer has an internal clock that keeps track of the date and time, even when it is turned off. By default, Windows Vista displays the *system time* in the notification area at the right end of the taskbar. When you point to the time, the *system date* is displayed as a ScreenTip. The system time controls a number of behind-the-scenes settings and is also used by Windows and your programs to maintain an accurate record of happenings on your computer.

> **Tip** If you prefer to not display the time, right-click a blank area of the taskbar, click Properties, click the Notification Area tab, and then clear the Clock check box in the System Icons area of the Taskbar And Start Menu Properties dialog box.

You can set the system date, system time, and time zone manually, or, if your computer is connected to the Internet, you can synchronize your system date and time with an Internet-based *time server*. If you have a continuous Internet connection, you can program your computer to synchronize itself on a regular schedule. If your computer is on a domain, the time is centrally controlled from the domain server and you can change it only temporarily (until the next time the server synchronizes the domain clock).

In this exercise, you will manually reset your system time and then connect to an Internet time server for an automatic update. There are no practice files for this exercise.

> **Troubleshooting** If your computer is on a domain, you will not be able to complete Steps 8 through 10 of this exercise.

> **BE SURE TO** have an active Internet connection available before beginning this exercise.

1. Close any open programs to display the Windows desktop.

The notification area displays the current system time.

> **Tip** If your taskbar is vertical, or is more than one row high, the notification area displays the time and the date. For information about changing the taskbar, see "Using and Modifying the Taskbar" in Chapter 2, "Working Efficiently in Windows Vista."

2. Point to the clock to display the current system date as a ScreenTip. Then click the clock to display the date, a calendar, and the time in both analog and digital formats.

3. Click **Change date and time settings**.

The Date And Time dialog box opens, displaying the Date And Time tab. This tab displays your current system date, time, and time zone. The system time appears in both analog and digital formats, with both clocks changing in one-second increments.

> **Tip** If you want to keep track of the time in a different time zone, you can activate up to two additional clocks. On the Additional Clocks tab of the Date And Time dialog box, select a Show This Clock check box, select the time zone, enter a display name, and click OK. The additional clock is displayed in the ScreenTip that appears when you point to the clock in the notification area.

4. Click **Change date and time**. In the **User Account Control** dialog box, if you are logged on as an administrator, click **Continue**. Otherwise, enter an administrator password, and then click **OK**.

5. In the **Date and Time Settings** dialog box, position the insertion point in the hours (or drag the mouse pointer over the hour displayed in the digital clock to select it), and then click the up arrow to the right of the clock once, to change the hour.

The analog clock reflects your change, and both clocks stop advancing. You can also use this technique to change the minutes, seconds, and AM/PM setting.

6. In the **Date and Time Settings** dialog box, click **OK**.

The clock on the taskbar changes to reflect the new time.

7. In the **Date and Time** dialog box, click the **Internet Time** tab.

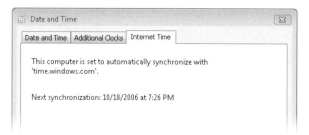

> **Troubleshooting** If the contents of the tab are dimmed, the Internet Time Synchronization feature is not currently available, and you are done with this exercise.

8. Click **Change settings**. In the **User Account Control** dialog box, if you are logged on as an administrator, click **Continue**. Otherwise, enter an administrator password, and then click **OK**.

The Internet Time Settings dialog box opens.

9. With the **Synchronize with an Internet time server** check box selected, click the **Server** arrow. In the list, click the server you want to use, and then click **Update now**.

> **Tip** The four servers in the list with *nist* in their names are maintained by the National Institute of Standards and Technology at various locations around the U.S. The time.nist.gov server is at the National Center for Atmospheric Research in Boulder, Colorado; time-nw.nist.gov is at Microsoft in Redmond, Washington; and time-a.nist.gov and time-b.nist.gov are at NIST in Gaithersburg, Maryland.

Your computer connects to the selected time server via the Internet, and updates your system time.

 CLOSE the Internet Time Settings dialog box and the Date And Time dialog box.

Changing Your Computer's Name

When Windows Vista was installed on your computer, the person doing the installation provided a name by which the computer is identified. If you installed Windows Vista yourself, you might have chosen a name that was meaningful or helpful to you, such as *TabletPC* or *Accounting1*. If you purchased the computer with Windows Vista already installed, the name might be only a series of numbers and characters. If you have administrator permissions, you can change the computer name.

To view the computer name:

→ On the **Start** menu, click **Computer**.

The Computer folder name appears in the Address bar, and the name assigned to your computer appears in the Details pane at the bottom of the window.

To change the computer name:

1. On the **Start** menu, right-click **Computer**, and then click **Properties**.

The System window opens.

2. Under **Computer name, domain, and workgroup settings**, click **Change settings**. In the **User Account Control** dialog box, if you're logged on as an administrator, click **Continue**. Otherwise, enter an administrator password, and then click **OK**.

3. On the **Computer Name** tab of the **System Properties** dialog box, click **Change**.

4. In the **Computer Name/Domain Changes** dialog box, replace the existing computer name with the name you want, and then click **OK**.

5. Click **OK** to acknowledge that the name change won't take effect until you restart your computer, and then close the **System Properties** dialog box.

6. In the **Microsoft Windows** message box, click **Restart Now**, or if it isn't convenient to restart your computer at this time, click **Restart Later**.

Changing the Name of the Computer Folder

By default, the link to your Computer folder is called *Computer*. If you want, you can change this name to match your computer name (or any other name, but that might be confusing). To change the link name:

1. On the **Start** menu, right-click **Computer**, and then click **Rename**.

2. With *Computer* selected for editing, type the name you want to appear, and then press [Enter].

   The link name can't contain a slash (/ or \), colon (:), asterisk (*), question mark (?), double quotation mark ("), less than sign (<), greater than sign (>), or pipe (|). Some symbols, such as an exclamation point (!), at symbol (@), pound sign (#), dollar sign ($), percent symbol (%), caret (^), ampersand (&), and underscore (_) are valid, as are uppercase and lowercase letters, numbers, spaces, commas, periods, and parentheses. Windows displays up to two lines of characters (if separated by a space) on the Start menu.

Key Points

- You can easily personalize Windows Vista interface elements such as colors, fonts, and the desktop background.
- If your computer hardware meets the minimum requirements, you can enjoy the ultimate Windows Vista visual experience by implementing the Windows Aero color scheme.
- You can choose from a number of screen savers that come with Windows Vista, download others from the Web, and display your own pictures as a screen saver.
- The date and time shown on your computer can be automatically updated from an Internet time server.
- If your computer was assigned an impersonal string of letters and numbers as its name, you can easily change it. In no time, *SQ003GG8* can become *Heidis-Helper*.

Keyboard Shortcuts

Press this	To do this
Windows logo key+D	Display the desktop
Ctrl+Esc	Open the Start menu
Windows logo key	Open or close the Start menu

Press this	To do this in a dialog box or task pane
Spacebar	Select or clear the check box if the active option is a check box
Arrow keys	Select a button if the active option is a group of option buttons
Ctrl+Tab	Move forward through tabs
Ctrl+Shift+Tab	Move back through tabs
Tab	Move forward through options
Shift+Tab	Move back through options

Chapter at a Glance

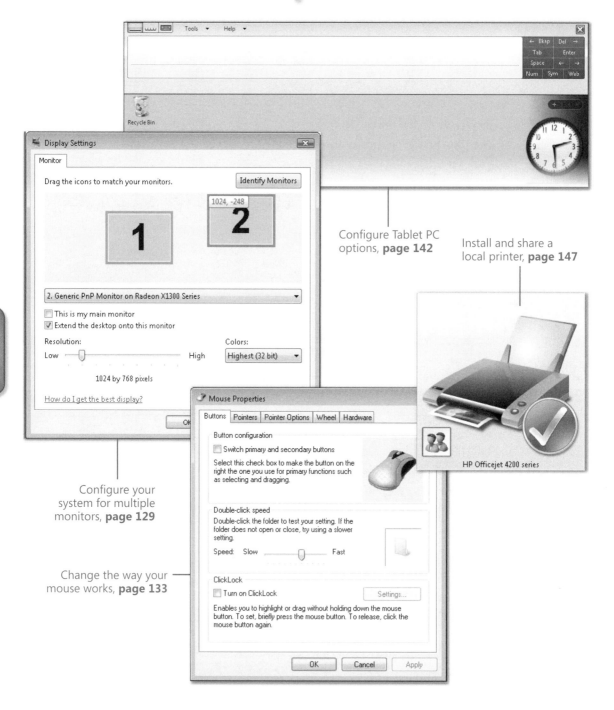

Configure Tablet PC options, **page 142**

Install and share a local printer, **page 147**

HP Officejet 4200 series

Configure your system for multiple monitors, **page 129**

Change the way your mouse works, **page 133**

5 Installing and Configuring Devices

In this chapter, you will learn to:

✔ Display more on your monitor.

✔ Configure your system for multiple monitors.

✔ Change the keyboard input language.

✔ Change the way your mouse works.

✔ Configure Tablet PC options.

✔ Install and share a local printer.

✔ Connect to a remote printer.

✔ Set up speakers and a microphone.

People discuss computers in terms of *hardware* and *software*. As you probably know, physical items such as computers and monitors are hardware, and all the programs that you use to do things with that hardware are collectively known as software.

Whether you're working in an office or at home, you will eventually want to install one or more bits of extra hardware, called *peripheral devices*, on your computer. Some devices, such as the keyboard, monitor, and mouse, usually come with the computer, but you will purchase others separately. The most common devices are speakers and a printer. Other popular devices include scanners, storage devices such as Zip drives, and fax machines. Depending on your interests and use of the computer, you might also have a microphone, camera, biometric identification device, joystick, or drawing tablet.

The hardware devices fall into two categories:

● *External peripherals.* You can install these devices by connecting them to ports without having to open up your computer. Examples are your computer's monitor, keyboard, mouse, and speakers.

Many external peripherals that connect to your computer through a USB port fall into a category called *Plug and Play*, which quite literally means that you can plug them in and use them. When you connect such a device to your computer, Windows Vista communicates with it and configures the necessary settings. Other external peripherals might require a specific *device driver* in order to work properly. Device drivers are bits of code that enable peripheral devices to "talk" to your computer, but they are unfortunately not universal. To hook up a printer, for example, you might need a driver that is not only specific to the printer but also specific to Windows Vista. If you purchased the peripheral before the release of Windows Vista, you might need to download updated drivers for it.

Some devices come with software you can install to take full advantage of its capabilities. For example, you might connect an all-in-one printer/scanner/fax/copy machine to your computer and be able to print, fax, scan to a file, and copy without installing additional software, but to be able to send scanned pages as e-mail messages or to edit them as text files, you will need to install the software provided with the machine.

● *Internal peripherals*. You have to install these devices inside your computer's case. The internal component might be in the form of a card that provides a new connection at the back of the computer, or it might be a new hard disk drive, DVD drive, or tape backup drive that is accessed from the front of the computer. Probably the most common internal devices people install themselves are RAM (random access memory) sticks, because increasing the RAM in a computer increases its speed and performance.

See Also For information about increasing the speed of your computer, see "Improving Your Computer's Performance" in Chapter 11, "Optimizing Your Computer System."

To install an internal device, you need to remove the cover from your computer and delve into its innards. Be sure to shut down the computer and disconnect it from its power source before attempting to install any internal component. Then follow the installation instructions provided by the manufacturer of the device.

The point of all these devices, of course, is to make your computing experience more productive, more enjoyable, and hopefully, simpler (although it might not seem that way when you need to use a half dozen hardware devices in order to write a letter).

In this chapter, you will work with a computer's most common external peripherals—the monitor, keyboard, mouse, printer, speakers, and microphone. You will adjust your screen resolution to provide the largest possible working area, and if your computer supports dual monitors, configure the primary and secondary displays as you want them. You will change keyboard and mouse settings and see how to configure Tablet PC options. You will install a printer for your own use and make it available for other people to connect to, and then you will learn how to locate and connect to printers on your network. You will also set up speakers and a microphone.

See Also Do you need only a quick refresher on the topics in this chapter? See the Quick Reference entries on pages xxxix–lxxiii.

Important No practice files are required to complete the exercises in this chapter. For more information about practice files, see "Using the Book's CD" on page xxix.

Need More Ports?

Most computers come equipped with a standard set of *ports* with which you connect a keyboard, mouse, monitor, or printer. If your computer has a sound card and a network card, you also have audio and network ports. All modern desktop and laptop computers have *Universal Serial Bus (USB)* ports through which many peripheral devices connect. (A USB connection provides both power and data transfer capabilities to a peripheral device.) Many computers also have *IEEE 1394* ports for the high-speed transfer of audio and video data.

If you want to install several peripheral devices on the same computer, you might find that you don't have enough ports to connect them all. All is not lost! Here are three options for expanding your connection capacity:

- **Install extra ports.** You can purchase a card with more ports in almost any computer store. After turning off your desktop computer and removing its cover, you insert the card into one of the available *expansion slots*. When you turn the power back on, Windows Vista detects and installs the new ports without further ado.

- **Daisy-chain multiple devices.** Many devices that connect to the computer via its *parallel port* can be "daisy-chained" together to form a linked network of devices. For example, you might connect a Zip drive to your computer's parallel port and then connect a printer to the parallel port on the Zip drive. Data you send to the printer will pass through the Zip drive.

- **Use a hub or switch box.** You can connect a single multi-port *hub* to your computer and then connect multiple devices to the hub, enabling all the devices to share that single connection. Hubs are available for network, parallel, and USB devices. If you want to physically connect multiple peripheral devices but you don't need to use more than one at a time, you can use a *switch box*, which looks similar to a hub but allows only one active connection at a time.

Displaying More on Your Monitor

When you purchase a computer monitor, one of the things you consider is its size, or display area, which is measured like a television screen: diagonally in inches. More important than the physical size, though, is the *screen resolution* it supports, which is measured in *pixels* and is expressed as the number of pixels wide by the number of pixels high. Pixels are the individual dots that make up the picture displayed on your screen. Each pixel displays one color; depending on your screen resolution, the images you see on screen might consist of 500,000 to 1,000,000 individual dots of color.

When personal computers first became popular, most computer monitors were capable of displaying only 640 pixels horizontally and 480 pixels vertically (a screen resolution of 640×480). Now most display at 800 × 600 pixels and 1024×768 pixels, and some can display at 2048×1536 pixels (or perhaps by the time this book is published, even higher). In effect, as the screen resolution increases, the size of each pixel decreases, and more information can be shown in the same display area. The graphics in this book were captured on a monitor set to a screen resolution of 1024×768.

> **Tip** The maximum resolution is the lower of the resolution supported by your monitor or the resolution supported by the graphics card installed in your computer. As you change the screen resolution, the Colors setting might also change. Lower resolutions might support higher color quality.

Most computer users have a choice of at least two different screen resolutions, but you might have many more choices. Some people prefer to work at 800×600 because everything on their screen appears larger; others prefer to fit more information on their screen with a 1024×768 (or higher) display. Recent statistics indicate that approximately 79 percent of Internet users have their screen resolution set to 1024×768 or greater—up from 60 percent in 2004 and 42 percent in 2001.

Many mobile PCs have widescreen displays, intended to improve the experience of viewing movies on the computer by displaying them at the correct *aspect ratio*. You might find that your computer offers screen resolutions designed specifically for widescreen displays.

In this exercise, you will change your screen resolution to the maximum and minimum sizes supported by your computer. There are no practice files for this exercise.

> **Troubleshooting** Screen resolution capabilities are specific to your monitor. The settings shown or specified in this exercise might not be available on your computer.

BE SURE TO log on to Windows Vista and open Control Panel before beginning this exercise.

1. In the **Control Panel** window, click **Appearance and Personalization**, and then click **Personalization**.

   > **Tip** You can open the Personalization window directly by right-clicking the Windows Vista desktop and then clicking Personalize.

2. In the **Personalization** window, click **Display Settings**.

   The Display Settings dialog box opens.

   Resolution setting markers

Display Settings
Monitor
Drag the icons to match your monitors.   Identify Monitors
1   **2**
1. Generic PnP Monitor on Radeon X1300 Series
☑ This is my main monitor
☑ Extend the desktop onto this monitor
Resolution: Colors:
Low ——◻—— High   Highest (32 bit)
1024 by 768 pixels
How do I get the best display?   Advanced Settings...
OK   Cancel   Apply

   Selected screen resolution

3. If you have more than one monitor installed, select the monitor you want to change. Then drag the **Resolution** slider all the way to the left to switch to the minimum resolution.

   > **Tip** You can easily tell which monitor is which by clicking the Identify Monitors button. A large number corresponding to the icons in the preview pane flashes on each monitor.

The change is reflected in the preview area, but not on your screen.

4. In the **Display Settings** dialog box, click **Apply**. Then in the **Display Settings** message box that appears, click **Yes**.

> **Tip** You have 15 seconds to decide whether to retain the changed resolution. If you click Yes, the resolution is retained; if you click No or don't click either button, the resolution returns to its previous setting.

Your display changes to the lowest resolution supported by your system. Unless your monitor was already set to the minimum resolution, everything shown on the screen—the taskbar, Personalization window, Display Settings dialog box, and any other open windows and dialog boxes—appears much larger.

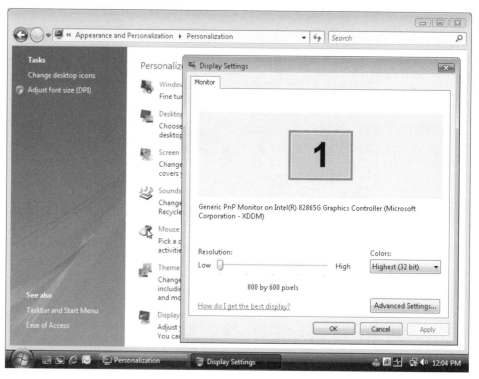

5. In the **Display Settings** dialog box, click the slider bar above the right-most resolution marker to change to the maximum resolution supported by the selected monitor.

You can either drag the slider to a marker or click above the marker you want.

6. Click **Apply**, and then in the **Display Settings** message box, click **Yes**.

Your screen resolution changes to the maximum supported by your system.

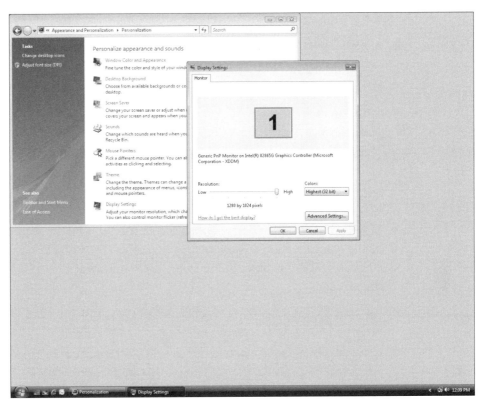

7. Experiment with the available screen resolutions. Apply the one you like best, and then in the **Display Settings** window, click **OK**.

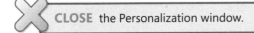

CLOSE the Personalization window.

Configuring Your System for Multiple Monitors

If you often work with multiple programs or with large-format files (such as spreadsheets) that are difficult to see on your monitor because of their width, you might want to extend your desktop by adding one or more monitors. Or if you deliver presentations through a projector attached to your computer, you might find it convenient to configure your desktop to display on two screens so that you can work privately on your computer screen while displaying information publicly through the projector. Windows Vista makes it easy to configure up to 10 display devices attached to your computer.

To add a second monitor, you must have one of the following:

- A video card that supports multiple monitors. If you do, there will be two video ports on the back of your computer for connecting your monitors.
- More than one video card.
- A dual monitor adaptor.

After connecting your monitors and restarting your computer, you might be prompted to install additional video drivers, as directed in the instructions that came with your monitor.

When you connect your computer to a secondary display, Windows Vista detects the device and prompts you to specify how you want to display information on it:

- **Mirrored.** The same content appears on both displays. This is useful when you are giving a presentation and are not facing the screen (for example, when standing at a podium facing an audience) or want to have a closer view of the content you are displaying.
- **Extended.** Your desktop expands to cover both displays. The Windows taskbar appears only on the screen you designate as the primary display.
- **External display only.** Content appears only on the second display. This is useful if you are working on a mobile PC running on battery power. When connected to a second display, you can conserve battery power by turning off the mobile PC screen.

To configure your computer to display your Windows desktop across two monitors:

1. Open the **Display Settings** dialog box by right-clicking the desktop, clicking **Personalize**, and then clicking **Display Settings** in the Personalization window.

   If a second monitor is connected to your computer but not active, it appears in the preview area but is screened.

2. In the preview area, click Monitor **2**, select the **Extend the desktop onto this monitor** check box, and then click **Apply**.

   Your desktop expands across both display devices.

When working on a computer connected to two display devices, Windows appoints one the *primary display* and the other the *secondary display*. The Welcome screen and taskbar always appear on the primary display, as do most application windows when they first open. You can then drag selected windows to the secondary screen.

> **Troubleshooting** You can't move a maximized window between screens; you must first reduce the size of the window either by clicking the Restore Down button on the window's title bar or by double-clicking the title bar.

To ascertain which monitor or other display device is the primary display, point to either monitor representation in the Display Settings dialog box. A ScreenTip appears, displaying the monitor's role (primary or secondary) and in the case of the secondary monitor, its position in relation to the primary monitor.

To change the primary monitor:

1. In the preview area of the **Display Settings** dialog box, click the secondary display.

2. Select the **This is my main monitor** check box, and then click **Apply**.

By default, Monitor 2 appears immediately to the right of Monitor 1. When you move the cursor horizontally from screen to screen, it should leave the right edge of the left screen and enter the left edge of the right screen at vertically the same point. If your monitors are not physically the same size, are set to different screen resolutions, or are not placed level with each other, you can change the alignment of the displays so that the cursor moves cleanly between them.

To adjust the relationship of the displays to each other:

→ In the preview area of the **Display Settings** dialog box, drag Monitor **2** to the location you want it to be in relationship to Monitor **1**.

As you move the monitor representation, a ScreenTip displays the position in pixels of the upper-left corner of Monitor 2 in relation to the upper-left corner of Monitor 1. Monitor 1 is always at 0,0.

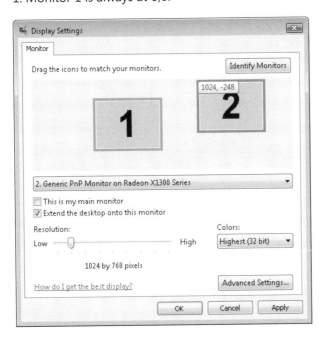

Expanding Your Laptop with Peripheral Devices

Laptop computers are useful when you want to be able to move around with your computer—from room to room, from work to home, or from city to city. Although laptops can offer fast computing and large hard-disk storage and many now offer a widescreen display, you usually have to deal with a smaller monitor, a smaller keyboard, and a touchpad or joystick mouse instead of a standard mouse. It is also possible that your laptop computer came without an internal CD or DVD drive.

In addition to the frustration caused by these basic differences between laptop and desktop computing, you might find that your wrists become tired because you can't rest them on the keyboard, or you accidentally tap the touchpad when you're typing and move the insertion point without realizing it—which can result in inadvertent errors in your documents.

Although carrying a full-size monitor, keyboard, and mouse when you travel with your laptop is not convenient, expanding your laptop computer with full-size peripherals is a great way to improve your computing experience whether you're in your office or at home. If you use a laptop because you need it both at home and at work, you can set up a monitor, keyboard, and mouse at each location for a relatively small sum of money. You then have the best of both worlds—portable computing and a full-size setup.

You connect peripheral devices to your laptop in the same manner that you would connect them to a standard desktop computer. You might find that your laptop has a limited number of ports, or that it has only a USB port and not a parallel port; inexpensive adaptors are available to help you increase the available ports as required. Some newer USB keyboards also incorporate a USB port into the keyboard, so you can plug the keyboard into the laptop and the mouse into the keyboard.

If you attach a full-size monitor to your laptop, you might at first see the same display on both monitors, or the display might appear only on the laptop. To change the monitor displaying your desktop, look at the function keys at the top of the laptop's keyboard—one of them (usually F5, sometimes F4) includes a graphic representation of a monitor. Hold down the Alt key, and then press the appropriate function key to switch among three options: laptop display and external display, external display only, and laptop display only.

> **Tip** If the monitor-switching key is not obvious, consult your laptop manual or the manufacturer's Web site for further information.

Changing the Way Your Mouse Works

In the beginning, a computer mouse consisted of a shell with one button to click with and a rubber ball on the bottom that correlated your mouse movements with a pointer on the screen. Nowadays, mice come in many shapes and sizes, employing a variety of functions, buttons, wheels, and connection methods.

Windows Vista offers enhanced wheel support that allows for smooth scrolling both vertically (as is traditional) and horizontally (on the newer mice that support this). Check the manufacturer's documentation to see if your mouse is able to take advantage of this technology. But even if your mouse is not of the latest generation, you can still customize your mouse settings in various ways to optimize the way it works with Windows.

To change the way the mouse buttons work:

1. In the **Control Panel** window, under **Hardware and Sound**, click **Mouse**.

   The Mouse Properties dialog box opens, displaying the Buttons tab.

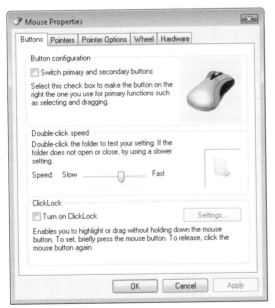

2. On the **Buttons** tab, in the **Button configuration** section, select the **Switch primary and secondary buttons** check box to change the default primary button from left to right.

   This setting is useful if you are left-handed, you injure your right hand, or switch mousing hands to decrease wrist strain.

3. In the **Double-click speed** area, drag the slider to the speed you want. Explore and change the other options on this page, and then click **OK**.

To change how the mouse pointer looks and works:

1. Open the **Mouse Properties** dialog box, and then click the **Pointers** tab.

2. In the **Scheme** list, click one of the 21 available system schemes to change the pointer set.

    Experiment with some of the more-interesting system schemes, such as Conductor, Dinosaur, and Hands. The Customize list displays the pointers associated with that scheme.

3. In the **Customize** list, click any pointer, and then click **Browse**.

4. In the **Browse** dialog box displaying the contents of the Cursors folder, double-click any cursor to replace the selected pointer.

> **Tip** Feel free to experiment with the shapes of pointers; you can restore the pointers to the original scheme defaults at any time by clicking Use Default.

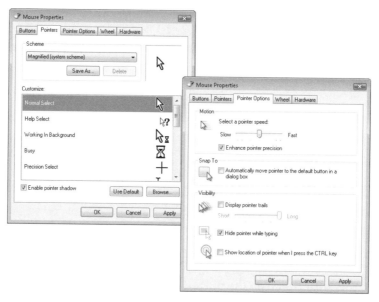

5. Click the **Pointer Options** tab, set the pointer speed, movement, and visibility options, and then click **OK**.

To change how the mouse wheel works:

1. Open the **Mouse Properties** dialog box, and then click the **Wheel** tab.

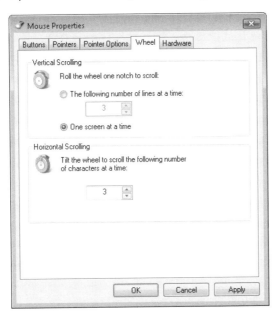

2. To control how much of the screen scrolls as you turn the mouse wheel, in the **Vertical Scrolling** area, either select the **The following number of lines at a time** option and then type or click the arrow keys to set the number of lines you want to scroll, or select the **One screen at a time** option.

   The default setting is to scroll three lines at a time, but if you frequently use the mouse to scroll through lengthy documents or Web pages, you might find it more convenient to scroll by screen rather than by line. Windows Vista sets the scrolling distance based on the size of the window you are scrolling in.

   > **Tip** You can move forward and backward between visited Web pages by holding down the Shift key and then scrolling the wheel vertically.

3. If your mouse supports horizontal scrolling, in the **Tilt the wheel to scroll the following number of characters at a time** box, enter the number of characters you want to scroll horizontally when you tilt the mouse wheel to the left or right.

Changing the Keyboard Input Language

Keyboards come in a variety of language-specific versions that incorporate special alphabet characters used in those languages. Your desktop or laptop computer might have a keyboard configured for American English, UK English, French, Canadian French, German, Swedish, Danish, Belgian, Dutch, Spanish, Italian, Portuguese, Arabic, Chinese, Hebrew, Russian... the list goes on, and includes some specialized languages such as Gaelic, Inuktitut, and Maori. Some keyboards, such as the Japanese keyboard, depict two alphabets.

When you first set up your Windows Vista computer, you choose an *input language* that matches your keyboard, and Windows Vista programs itself to correctly recognize the keys that you press to match the letters, numbers, characters, or commands depicted on each key.

Under some circumstances, you might want to use a keyboard configured for a different language, or you might want to instruct Windows to treat your keystrokes on your existing keyboard as if you were using a different-language keyboard. For example, if your computer is set up to recognize a US English keyboard and you frequently correspond with customers in a language—such as French, German, or Swedish—that uses characters not included in the English alphabet—such as ç, ä, or å—you will need to enter letters that don't exist on the US English keyboard. You can enter those characters in a Microsoft Office Word document by selecting them from the Symbol dialog box, and in most programs by pressing Alt and then a specific number combination on the numeric keypad, if you have one. (The symbol is inserted when you release the Alt key.) Or to save yourself that trouble, you can connect a language-specific keyboard to your computer. All the letters of that language appear on the keyboard and you simply press the keys to enter them.

> **Tip** When you attach a different-language keyboard to your laptop, both keyboards are available to you.

If you are familiar with the layout of a language-specific keyboard but don't want to physically switch keyboards to enter the keystrokes in that language, you can configure your computer to recognize keystrokes as though you were using the different-language keyboard. You switch between input languages by using the tools on the Language bar that appears on the Windows taskbar.

In this exercise, you will configure your computer to enter keystrokes as though you are typing on a Swedish keyboard. There are no practice files for this exercise.

> **Tip** If you are already working with a Swedish keyboard, substitute another language in this exercise.

OPEN Control Panel.

1. In the **Control Panel** window, click **Clock, Language, and Region**. Then under **Regional and Language Options**, click the **Change keyboards or other input methods** task.

   The Regional And Language Options dialog box opens, displaying the Keyboards And Languages tab.

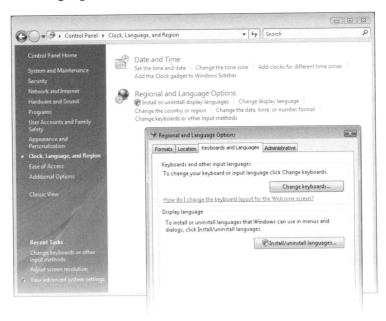

2. Click **Change keyboards**.

The Text Services And Input Languages dialog box opens, displaying your current input language and the input devices configured for that language, as well as any other languages you have installed.

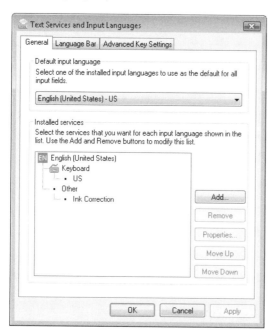

3. Click the **Default input language** arrow to expand the list of available languages.

Only the original input language appears in the list. To accept input from another language-specific keyboard, you must first install the language.

4. In the **Installed services** area, click **Add**.

The Add Input Language dialog box opens.

5. Browse through this dialog box, noting the available languages. Expand a few of the languages and their Keyboard lists.

Notice that each language does not have its own keyboard, but some have more than one associated keyboard.

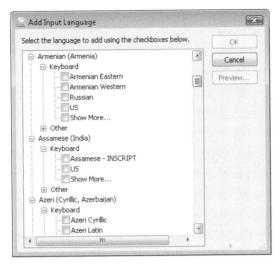

6. In the list, click the **Expand** button to the left of **Swedish (Sweden)**, and then click the **Expand** button to the left of **Keyboard**.

   The standard keyboard options for this language are Swedish and US.

7. In the **Keyboard** list, select the **Show More** check box.

   The list expands to include all the available language keyboards.

8. Scroll the list to see the amazing variety of available keyboards.

   Some languages have up to six available keyboards, each with different keyboard layouts or alphabets. You can enter the selected language (Swedish) from any of these keyboards.

9. In the expanded **Keyboard** list, select the check box of the keyboard that is connected to your computer. Then click **Preview**.

> **Troubleshooting** If you are working on a standard US English keyboard, you will notice that there are six layouts available. If you don't know which yours is, select US.

   A diagram of the selected keyboard appears.

10. Click **Close**. Then in the **Keyboard** list, select the **Swedish** check box, and click **Preview**.

   A diagram of the Swedish keyboard appears.

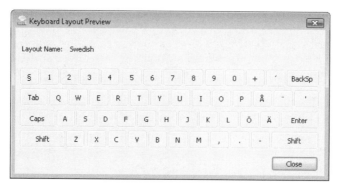

Notice the three Swedish letters to the left of the Enter key: Å, Ä, and Ö. These are the last three letters of the Swedish alphabet. The characters in these three positions on your own keyboard have been rearranged to make room for them.

11. Close the **Keyboard Layout Preview** window and, provided the first keyboard preview displayed a keyboard layout matching your own, click **OK** in the **Add Input Language** dialog box.

> **Troubleshooting** If the US keyboard did not match your own keyboard, repeat Step 9 until you locate one that does match.

The Default Input Language list and Installed Services area now include both your original keyboard language and keyboard layout, and Swedish with two keyboard layouts. Your original language is still selected as the default, as indicated in the Default Input Language list.

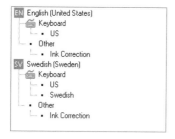

Note that each language in the Installed services box is represented by a specific two-letter combination in a small blue square. The two-letter abbreviation for Swedish is SV, short for *Svensk—Swedish* in Swedish.

12. In the **Text Services and Input Languages** dialog box, click **OK**.

To the left of the notification area on the Windows taskbar, the Language bar appears, displaying the two-letter abbreviation of the default input language.

> **Tip** The contents of the Language bar vary depending on what language-specific capabilities are configured. You can change the location and appearance of the Language bar from the Language Bar tab of the Text Services And Input Languages dialog box.

13. On the **Language** bar, click the input language button. Then in the input language list, click **Swedish (Sweden)**.

The input language button label changes to SV, and a keyboard button appears to its right.

14. Click the keyboard button.

The keyboard list displays the two keyboards you chose for Swedish input: Swedish and your own.

Keyboard list

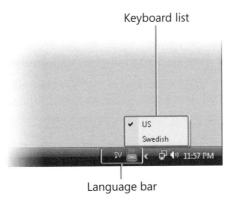

Language bar

15. In the keyboard list, click **Swedish**.

Start

16. To confirm that the input language has changed, click the **Start** button, and then with the insertion point in the **Start Search** box, press the single quote (') key to the left of the Enter key.

The letter ä, which appears to the left of the Enter key on the Swedish keyboard, appears in the Search box.

17. Experiment with the input languages if you want. Then redisplay the **Keyboards and Languages** tab of the **Regional and Language Options** dialog box, and click **Change keyboards**.

18. In the **Installed services** area, click **Swedish (Sweden)**, and then click **Remove**.

 CLOSE the Regional And Language Options dialog box and the Clock, Language, And Region window.

Configuring Tablet PC Options

A variety of new and improved features for working with a Tablet PC are built in to Windows Vista—you don't have to purchase a different edition of the operating system for a laptop than you would for a desktop PC. The most visible improvement is the updated Input Panel, which is readily available as a tab at the edge of the screen. Tap the tab, and the Input Panel opens, ready to receive your written input. This input is more likely to be interpreted accurately if you take a little time to train the handwriting recognition program.

You can enter information into a Tablet PC with a pen and, if your computer supports touch input, with your finger. You can configure options to support pen and finger flicks as a means of navigating in documents and other files.

In this exercise, you will explore the Tablet PC configuration options, as well as those for your pen and the Input Panel. There are no practice files for this exercise.

> **Troubleshooting** The instructions in this exercise assume you are working on a Tablet PC. You can work through the exercise on a desktop computer by following the alternative instructions provided.

 **BE SURE TO** open Control Panel before beginning this exercise.

1. In the **Control Panel** window, tap **Mobile PC**. Then in the **Mobile PC** window, tap **Tablet PC Settings**.

> **Troubleshooting** If your Control Panel does not include the Mobile PC category, click Hardware And Sound, and then click Tablet PC Settings.

The Tablet PC Settings dialog box opens. On the General tab, you can indicate whether you are right-handed or left-handed, and you can calibrate the screen for better pen tracking.

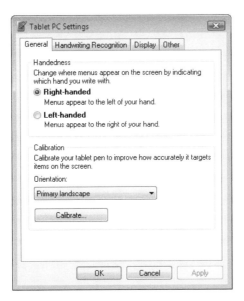

2. Tap the **Handwriting Recognition** tab.

   On this tab, you can set options that will allow the handwriting recognizer to progressively "learn" about your style of writing.

3. Tap the **Display** tab, and then tap the **Orientation** arrow. In the list, tap the **Primary** option that is not your current orientation, and then tap **Apply**.

   The screen orientation changes. If you do not want to keep this orientation, switch it back before continuing.

   > **Tip** If your Tablet PC has tablet buttons, you can tap the Change button and set up the orientation sequence for a button.

4. Tap the **Other** tab.

   This tab provides access to options for configuring your pen and the Input Panel.

5. Tap the **Go to Pen and Input Devices** link.

   The Pen And Input Devices dialog box opens. The Pen Options tab displays a list of the pen equivalents of various mouse actions. You can adjust the settings for each pen action other than single-tapping to conform to the way you use the pen. You can change the size of the gesture required to start Input Panel, the speed and duration of the pen equivalent of right-clicking, and the speed and location variance that constitute a double-tap. (You cannot change the single-click action.)

6. Tap the **Press and hold** action, and then click **Settings**.

   In the Press And Hold Settings dialog box, you can turn the press and hold for right-clicking action on or off, and you can set the speed and duration of the action.

7. Tap **Cancel**, and then in the **Pen and Input Devices** dialog box, tap the **Pointer Options** tab.

   The options on this tab control the feedback you receive in response to pen actions.

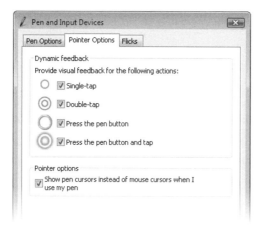

8. Tap the **Flicks** tab.

On this tab, you can set whether you can navigate and edit content with a flick of the pen.

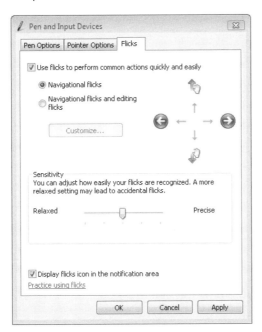

You cannot customize navigation flicks, but you can customize editing flicks.

9. Experiment with the options on this tab, and then tap **Cancel** to close the **Pen and Input Devices** dialog box.

10. On the **Other** tab of the Tablet PC Settings dialog box, tap the **Go to Input Panel Settings** link.

The Options dialog box opens, with the Settings tab active. On this tab, you can specify the location and functionality of the Insert button that appears when you are writing in the Input Panel. You can also turn the AutoComplete feature on or off and restore the default Input Panel settings.

> **Tip** You can also open this dialog box from the Input Panel, by tapping Tools and then Options.

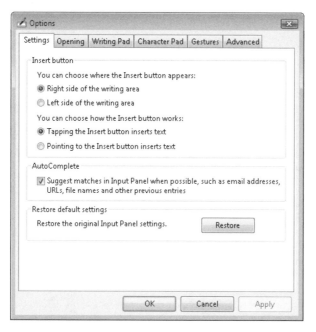

11. Tap the **Opening** tab.

On this tab, you can choose how to open the Input Panel and where its tab and icon appear on the screen.

12. Explore the other tabs of the **Options** dialog box. Then close the dialog box and the Mobile PC window.

13. Locate the **Input Panel** tab on your screen, point to it to open the tab, and then tap it to open the Input Panel.

    By default, the Input Panel floats on the screen and can be dragged to any convenient location.

14. On the **Input Panel**, tap **Tools**, and then in the list, tap **Dock at Top of Screen**.

    The Input Panel stretches to fill the full width of the screen and anchors itself at the top.

15. Restore the default **Float** setting, and then close the **Input Panel**.

Installing and Sharing a Local Printer

To print from a computer that is not part of a network, you must physically connect a printer to your computer, usually through either a USB port or a parallel port. A printer that is connected directly to your computer is called a *local printer*. The software to run the printer is installed on and run from your computer. When you connect a printer to your computer and then turn on the printer, Windows Vista recognizes that a device has been connected and identifies the type of device. It then searches through its database of drivers to locate the appropriate software to run the printer. If Windows Vista doesn't have the current driver for your particular printer, it asks you to provide the driver.

> **Troubleshooting** Many printers come with a CD containing installation files and drivers that were current at the time the printer was manufactured. If you don't have the current *printer drivers*, you can usually locate them on the printer manufacturer's Web site.

If your computer is connected to a network, you can share your local printer with the entire network or with a select group of people. When you share your printer, you assign it a name. This name might be based on the manufacturer or model of the printer (such as *HP LaserJet*), some special feature (such as *Color*), or perhaps the physical location of the printer (such as *Front Office*). Regardless, simple names work best because they are more likely to be easily identified by everyone who needs to use your printer.

> **Tip** Some printers suggest their own printer name during the sharing process. You can either accept the suggested name or replace it with one you choose.

In this exercise, you will install a local printer, test the installation by printing a test page, and then share the printer for use by other people. There are no practice files for this exercise, but if you are logged on to the computer with a standard user account, you need to have an administrator password available to share the printer.

> **Important** You do not need to be connected to a network to complete this exercise; you can share your printer even if no one but you will ever need to use it.

BE SURE TO have a printer and the appropriate connection cable available before beginning this exercise.

> **Tip** If you already have a working connection to your printer, skip to Step 14 to learn how to share it.

1. Connect the printer to the appropriate port on your computer.

2. Connect the printer to a power outlet, and then if necessary, turn it on.

   If your computer connects to the printer through a USB port, Windows Vista recognizes the device and displays an alert while it configures the necessary settings and drivers.

3. If Windows Vista does not recognize the printer, skip to Step 5. Otherwise, click the alert to display the progress of the printer installation.

4. After Windows declares the printer ready to use, close the **Driver Software Installation** window, and skip to Step 14. If the installation did not complete successfully, continue with Step 5.

5. Open **Control Panel**, and under **Hardware and Sound**, click **Printer**.

6. On the toolbar of the Printers window, click **Add a printer**.

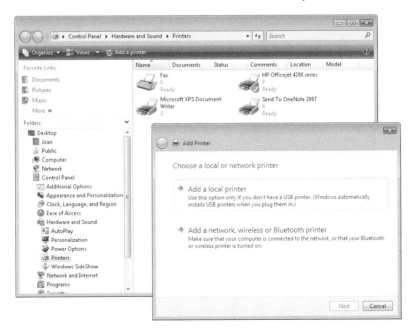

7. On the first page of the **Add Printer** wizard, click **Add a local printer**.

8. On the **Choose a printer port** page, select the port to which your printer is connected from the **Use an existing port** list, and then click **Next**.

> **Troubleshooting**   It is likely that the correct port will already be selected. If not, the installation instructions from your printer manufacturer will tell you which port you should use. Some manufacturers supply helpful drawings to guide you.

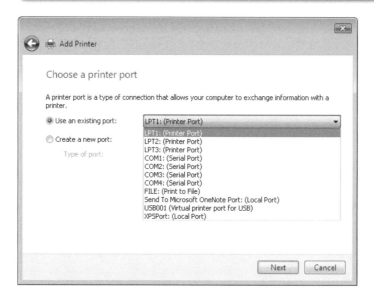

> **Tip**   While working through the wizard, you can return to a previous page by clicking the Back button in the upper-left corner.

9. If you have an installation CD for your printer, insert it in the appropriate drive, click **Have Disk**, and follow the instructions on the screen to install your printer. Otherwise, in the **Manufacturer** list, click the brand name of your printer.

> **Important**   Your installation CD must contain updated drivers that are compatible with Windows Vista. If your drivers are out of date, you might need to download current drivers from the printer manufacturer's Web site.

The Printers list changes to reflect a list of the printer drivers for that manufacturer that come with Windows Vista.

Tip Updated drivers are often available through Automatic Updates.

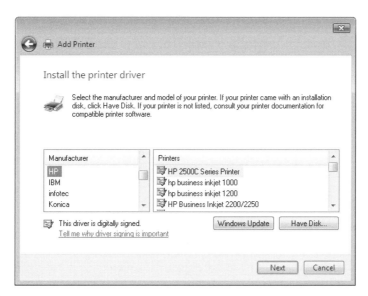

10. In the **Printers** list, click the model of your printer (which you can usually find printed on the top or front of the printer). Then click **Next**.

> **Troubleshooting** If the Printers list doesn't include your specific model, select a model with a similar name. Alternatively, download the necessary drivers from the manufacturer's Web site, return to the Install The Printer Driver page, and click Have Disk to install the printer manually.

11. On the **Type a printer name** page, change the printer name if you want to, or accept the default name. If you want Windows and any programs you install, such as Microsoft Office Word, to print to this printer when you click the Print button, select the **Set as the default printer** check box. Then click **Next**.

> **Tip** You can change your default printer at any time. To do so, display the Printers window, and double-click the printer you want to set as the default. Then on the Printer menu of the printer's management window, click Set As Default Printer.

12. On the wizard's confirmation page, click **Print a test page**.

After Windows Vista sends the test page to the printer, a confirmation message box appears.

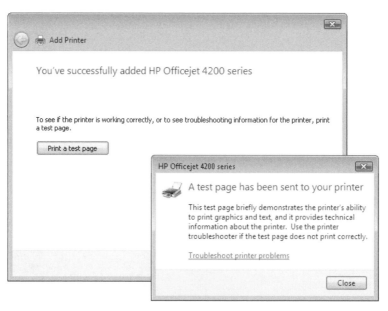

13. In the confirmation message box, click **Close**. Then in the **Add Printer** wizard, click **Finish**.

    Your local printer appears in the Printers window.

14. In the **Printers** window, right-click the icon representing your printer, and then click **Sharing**.

    The printer's Properties dialog box opens, displaying the Sharing tab.

15. Click **Change sharing options**. In the **User Account Control** dialog box, if you are logged on as an administrator, click **Continue**. Otherwise, enter an administrator password, and then click **OK**.

16. Select the **Share this printer** check box. Then in the **Share name** box, type a simple name for the printer (or leave the default).

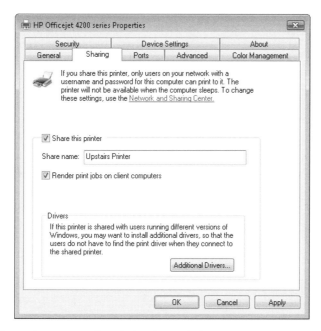

17. In the **Properties** dialog box, click **OK**.

In the Printers window, the printer's icon now indicates that it is shared.

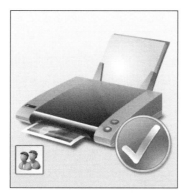

 CLOSE the Printers window and Control Panel.

Connecting to a Remote Printer

A *network printer* is a printer that is not connected directly to your computer but is available through a network. It might be a free-standing networked printer, or it might be accessible through someone else's computer, through a print server, or through a printer hub.

If the printer you are connecting to is available to everyone on the network, you will not need specific permission to connect to it. If the printer has been made available only to specific people or groups, you will have to ask the printer's "owner" or your network administrator to make the printer available to you.

In this exercise, you will connect to a network printer. There are no practice files for this exercise.

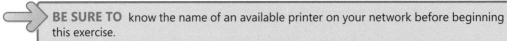

BE SURE TO know the name of an available printer on your network before beginning this exercise.

1. Open **Control Panel**, and under **Hardware and Sound**, click **Printer**.

2. On the toolbar of the Printers window, click **Add a printer**.

3. On the Add Printer wizard's first page, click **Add a network, wireless, or Bluetooth printer**.

   Windows Vista searches your network and then displays a list of available printers.

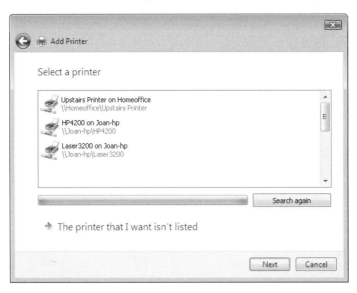

4. On the **Select a printer** page, click the printer you want to connect to, and then click **Next**.

> **Troubleshooting** If the printer you want to connect to isn't in the list, click The Printer That I Want Isn't Listed. Then on the Find A Printer By Name Or TCP/IP Address page, in the Select A Shared Printer By Name box, type \\ followed by the name of the computer to which the printer is attached, and the printer name, in the format shown, and then click Next. If not everyone on your network is allowed to use this printer, you might be prompted to enter your user account name and password to complete the connection.

Windows attempts to connect to the selected printer. If the drivers required by that printer aren't already installed on your computer, Windows Vista requests permission to install them.

5. In the **Printers** message box, click **Install driver**. In the **User Account Control** dialog box, if you are logged on as an administrator, click **Continue**. Otherwise, enter an administrator password, and then click **OK**.

After connecting to the printer, you can give it a name other than the one assigned by the printer's "owner."

6. On the **Type a printer name** page, change the printer name if you want to, or accept the default name. If you want Windows and any programs you install, such as Word, to print to this printer when you click the Print button, select the **Set as the default printer** check box. Then click **Next**.

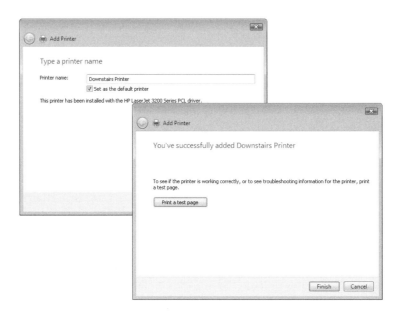

You can print a test page, and print to the network printer just as you normally would.

7. In the **Add Printer** wizard, click **Finish**.

The network printer appears in the Printers window. You can print to it as you would to a local printer.

 CLOSE the Printers window and Control Panel.

Updating Device Drivers

Device drivers are files containing information that Windows needs to communicate with your printer, fax machine, scanner, camera, or other device. Drivers can be specific to an individual device or to a family of devices (such as all HP LaserJet printers), and they are often specific to a certain version of Windows.

Device drivers can be found on the Web site of the device manufacturer or on certain Web sites that centralize driver information. (Be aware when you visit these unaffiliated sites that they might require a subscription, or they might be trying to sell tools that can detect your drivers and suggest updates.)

Setting Up Speakers

Computer systems that are equipped with *sound cards* usually come with a set of external speakers so that you can listen to music and other audio files. Some monitors come with built-in speakers that take the place of external speakers. If you're a real audiophile, you might want to purchase fancy surround-sound speakers for your computer. Or if you want to listen to audio output privately, you can connect headphones either directly to your computer or through the external speakers.

Most standard speaker systems consist of two speakers with one cord that connects them to each other, another that connects them to the computer, and a power cord that connects them to the power source. One speaker might have a volume control (independent of the computer's volume control) and a headset jack.

In this exercise, you will connect speakers to your Windows Vista computer and adjust the audio output levels. There are no practice files for this exercise.

> **BE SURE TO** have a set of computer speakers available before beginning this exercise.

1. Remove the speakers from their packaging, if you have not already done so.

   > **Tip** If you are using an alternate audio configuration, such as a headset microphone, connect the input and output cables appropriately and then skip to Step 6.

2. Link the two speakers using the connector cable.

3. Position the speakers to the left and right of your monitor to provide stereo sound quality.

4. Connect the speakers to a power outlet by using the AC adapter cord.

5. Plug the speakers into the speaker jack on the computer by using the connector cable.

   > **Tip** The speaker jack might be indicated by a small speaker icon or the words *Audio* or *Audio/Out*.

6. Open **Control Panel**, and then click **Hardware and Sound**.

   The Hardware And Sound window opens.

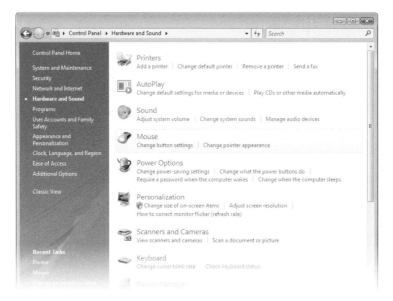

7. In the **Hardware and Sound** window, click **Sound**.

   The Sound dialog box opens.

8. Click each of the tabs, and explore the options available.

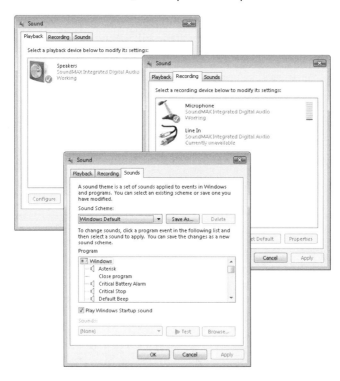

9. On the **Playback** tab, click your speakers, and then click **Configure**.

   The Speaker Setup wizard starts.

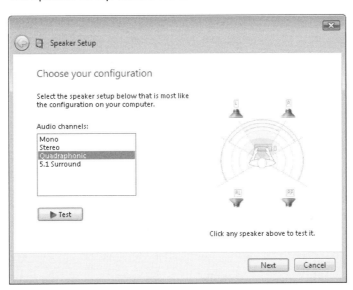

10. On the **Choose your configuration** page, select the appropriate audio channel, and then click **Test**. Test each of the channels to hear the different options, select the channel you want, and then click **Next**.

    If you choose any configuration other than Mono, the Select Full-Range Speakers page appears next. You can enable, disable, and test speakers from this page.

11. If the **Select full-range speakers** page appears, click **Next** to complete the configuration, and then on the **Configuration complete** page, click **Finish**.

 **CLOSE** the Sound dialog box and the Hardware And Sound window.

Setting Up a Microphone

With the rapid evolution of Internet-based communications, digital video, and speech-to-text technologies, microphones are being used more commonly with business and home computer systems. Microphones come in a variety of options, such as the following:

- Freestanding microphones
- Microphones that attach to your computer
- Headset microphones with built-in headphones that allow more private communication and consistent recording quality
- Boom microphones with a single headset speaker

If you will be recording a lot of speech or using the Speech Recognition feature, it is worth investing in a good-quality microphone. Buy anything less than the best you can afford, and you are likely to find yourself making a return trip to the store. To get the highest quality, it is critical that you choose the type of microphone that best fits your needs. Headset and boom microphones maintain a constant distance between the microphone and your mouth, which helps to maintain a more consistent sound level than a stationary microphone. The headphones built into headset and boom microphones provide the same privacy as a telephone, because the audio output is heard only by the wearer.

In this exercise, you will connect a microphone to your Windows Vista computer and adjust the audio input levels. There are no practice files for this exercise.

> **BE SURE TO** have a microphone available before beginning this exercise.

1. Remove the microphone from its packaging, if you have not already done so.

> **Troubleshooting** If you are using a USB microphone, ensure that you are logged in as an administrator before connecting the microphone to the USB port. If you connect the microphone while logged in as a standard user, the device installation might not succeed, but no obvious indicator of the problem appears.

2. Plug the microphone connector cable into the audio input jack on your computer, or into a USB port, depending on the connection type.

> **Tip** The audio input jack might be indicated by a microphone icon or the word *Mic* or *Microphone*.

3. Open **Control Panel**, and then click **Ease of Access**.

4. In the **Ease of Access** window, under **Speech Recognition Options**, click **Set up a microphone**.

   The Microphone Setup wizard starts.

5. Select the option for the type of microphone you are using, and then click **Next**.

6. On the **Set up your microphone page**, read the instructions, and then click **Next**.

   The Adjust The Microphone Volume page appears.

7. On the **Adjust the microphone volume** page, read the microphone test paragraph aloud in your normal speaking voice. Or just for fun, you might try singing a couple of lines from your favorite song!

   As you speak (or sing), the volume gauge moves in response to your voice, and the microphone settings (which you can't see here) adjust to your natural speaking volume.

   > **Troubleshooting** If the volume gauge does not move, your microphone might be incorrectly connected, or it might not be compatible with your computer. If this happens, hold the microphone close to your mouth and speak loudly—if the recording meter moves slightly, the connection is good, and the problem is between your microphone and your computer. You might be able to solve this problem by downloading new device drivers from the microphone manufacturer's Web site, or it might be simpler to replace the microphone.

8. When you finish reading the paragraph, click **Next**. Then click **Finish** to complete the wizard.

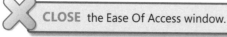 **CLOSE** the Ease Of Access window.

Key Points

- To fit more or less content on your screen, you can change the size at which your monitor displays information.

- You can output information from your computer to two (or more) screens, either displaying the same content on both screens or doubling the size of your desktop.

- Windows Vista automatically locates the drivers necessary to install USB devices, so you can connect a device and start using it without further effort.

- You can configure your computer to receive input from multiple language-specific keyboards and to send keystrokes from your keyboard as if it were a different-language keyboard.

- A variety of options allow you to tailor your mouse to suit the way your work.

- New Tablet PC functionality makes it easier to write and move around efficiently by using a pen or your finger.

- You can print to a printer that is connected directly to your computer, or to a printer that is connected to another computer on your network.

- You can increase the quality of audio output and input if you connect external speakers and a microphone to your computer.

Keyboard Shortcuts

Press this	To do this
Ctrl+Esc	Open the Start menu
Ctrl+Tab	Move forward through dialog box tabs
Ctrl+Shift+Tab	Move back through dialog box tabs
Esc	Cancel the current task
Enter	Replaces clicking the mouse for many commands
F1	Display Help

Chapter at a Glance

Display Web sites in Internet Explorer 7, **page 169**

Find, save, and return to Web sites, **page 182**

Discover and subscribe to RSS feeds, **page 190**

6 Safely and Efficiently Accessing the Internet

In this chapter, you will learn to:

✔ Connect to the Internet.

✔ Display Web sites in Internet Explorer 7.

✔ Block pop-up windows.

✔ Change your home page.

✔ Change the appearance of Web content.

✔ Find, save, and return to Web sites.

✔ Print Web pages.

✔ Send Web pages and links to other people.

✔ Discover and subscribe to RSS feeds.

✔ Restrict objectionable content.

The Internet is a worldwide network consisting of millions of smaller networks that exchange information. Originally constructed and used by governments and large organizations for the exchange of text-based data, the Internet evolved almost overnight with the implementation in 1990 of a prototype for the World Wide Web, known simply as the *Web*, by Tim Berners-Lee. While combining the existing concept of *hypertext* with the Internet, Berners-Lee developed the system of hyperlinks and Uniform Resource Identifiers, also known as Uniform Resource Locators (URLs) that paved the way for the global exchange of information we take for granted today.

Browsing the Internet (also known as *surfing the Web*) has become an entertainment medium in itself, as well as a simple and powerful research solution that puts a world of information at your fingertips, literally. Students, scholars, business people, shoppers, gamers, and others can now find almost any information or entertainment they want on the Web. Many television programs are now available for viewing on the Internet, because their producers recognize that people are looking for entertainment on their computers rather than turning on the television.

Moreover, the Web is no longer a one-way information highway for individual computer users. The advent of personal Web spaces called *Web logs*, or *blogs*, means that anyone can post anything on the Web for family, friends, and complete strangers to view and respond to. Blogs range from personal diaries and ways for communities to keep in touch to sources of information on a specific topic that are replacing traditional media in importance. They can provide on-the-spot news about current events, and because they are not constrained by printing and production processes, they can "scoop" other media with late-breaking news. They are also uncensored and largely unregulated, meaning that viewers need to bear in mind that their information is not necessarily unbiased or correct.

Windows Vista includes Windows Internet Explorer 7, a *Web browser* with which you can easily find, view, search, print, and save Web pages while shielding your computer and the people who use it from exposure to malicious or objectionable content. Internet Explorer provides a framework in which you can view Web pages, and an engine with which you can perform basic tasks.

In this chapter, you learn how to configure Internet Explorer 7 to best fit your needs and how to use some of the great features not available in previous versions of Internet Explorer. You will personalize the Internet Explorer browser window and content display, and specify the amount of objectionable language, nudity, sex, and violence users of your computer are able to see.

See Also Do you need only a quick refresher on the topics in this chapter? See the Quick Reference entries on pages xxxix–lxxiii.

> **Important** No practice files are required to complete the exercises in this chapter. For more information about practice files, see "Using the Book's CD" on page xxix.
>
> The exercises in this chapter assume that Internet Explorer 7 is your default Web browser. If it is not, you might have to vary the exercise steps slightly, but you will still be able to follow along with the exercises.

Connecting to the Internet

In the past, many employers were concerned that giving employees access to the Internet from their work computers would mean a loss of productivity, because people could receive and send personal e-mail messages, indulge in surreptitious Web surfing, or download objectionable content. These days, more and more employers are coming to the conclusion that Internet access can actually enhance the productivity of people in some jobs, and many provide organization-wide access.

In addition, Internet access is fast becoming one of the primary reasons for buying a home computer. Setting up a connection from your computer to the Internet is easier than ever with Windows Vista. The most difficult part of the process will likely be finding out what types of connections are available from Internet service providers (ISPs) in your area and deciding which one you want to use.

To use the Internet, you must connect to a computer or network of computers that acts as a go-between, by using one of the following types of connections:

- *Local area network (LAN).* If you connect to the Internet through a LAN, you are actually connecting to a computer on your network that has been set up to provide Internet access; connections to upstream providers are handled for you by that computer.

- *Cable*, *ISDN*, or *DSL*. If you are connecting through a dedicated cable, ISDN (integrated services digital network), or DSL (digital subscriber line) connection—one that doesn't require a user account name or password—you will connect your computer to a *router* (usually one leased or purchased from your service provider). After following the service provider's instructions to set up the router for the first time, Windows Vista will automatically handle the connection process.

- *Dial-up connection.* If you are connecting through a dial-up connection, you are making a connection from your computer to another computer using two *modems* and an ordinary telephone line. The remote computer usually belongs to the *Internet service provider (ISP)* with whom you have set up your user account.

Whichever type of connection you use, the Windows Vista Network And Sharing Center can help you with the necessary setup work.

To create an Internet connection through an ISP, you need to first set up a user account. The ISP will then provide the information you will need to provide to complete the connection process in the Network And Sharing Center, such as:

- The specific *IP address* or the address of the *DHCP server*
- *DNS* addresses and domain names
- *POP3* or IMAP settings for incoming e-mail
- *SMTP* settings for outgoing e-mail

In this exercise, you will use the Network And Sharing Center to connect to the Internet through a broadband or dial-up connection. There are no practice files for this exercise.

>
>
> **BE SURE TO** log on to Windows and have your Internet connection information available before beginning this exercise. If you are connecting through a dial-up connection, you must have the name and access number of your ISP and your dial-up user account name and password. If you are connecting through a password-protected broadband connection, you will not need the access number.

Start

1. Click the **Start** button, click **Control Panel**, and then in the **Control Panel** window, click **Network and Internet**.

2. Under **Network and Sharing Center**, click the **Connect to a network** task.

   The Connect To A Network wizard starts, displaying all available network connections. If you have several connections available, you can filter the list by clicking the Show arrow and then clicking Dial-up And VPN or Wireless.

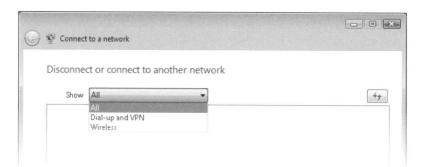

3. At the bottom of the page, click the **Set up a connection or network** link.

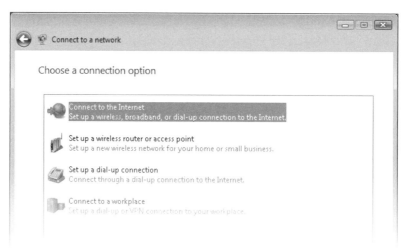

4. On the **Choose a connection option** page, click **Connect to the Internet**, and then click **Next**.

> **Tip** You can return to a previous page of the wizard at any time by clicking the Back button in the upper-left corner of the window

5. On the **How do you want to connect** page, click either **Broadband** or **Dial-up**, and then click **Next**.

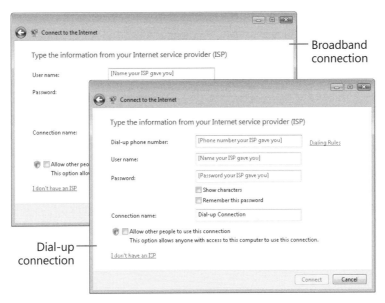

Broadband connection

Dial-up connection

6. Enter the requested connection information, and then click **Connect** to close the window and create the connection.

CLOSE the Network And Internet window.

> **Tip** To connect to an existing network connection, click Connect To on the Start menu. Then in the Connect To A Network wizard, click the connection you want to use, and click Connect.

Displaying Web Sites in Internet Explorer 7

Whether or not Internet Explorer 7 is your default browser, you can start it from the Windows Vista Start menu and use it to explore the Web. With all browsers, you navigate to a specific Web site by typing its address, or Uniform Resource Locator (URL), in an address box and then clicking *hyperlinks* to move to specific Web pages.

In the past, you needed to open your Web browser multiple times if you wanted to view multiple Web pages at the same time. Although you can still do that with Internet Explorer 7, you can also display multiple Web sites on separate *tabs* within one Internet Explorer program window. *Tabbed browsing* is convenient because it takes far less time to open a new tab than it does to start a new instance of Internet Explorer, and it's much easier to move between open sites by selecting from the tabs at the top of one window than by selecting from taskbar buttons that don't display as much information. When you have several pages open, you can display thumbnails or a list of all the open pages and then click the page you want to view. When the open tabs exceed the available space, navigation buttons appear to the right or left of the tabs.

Switch between Web sites — by clicking the page tabs   Click here to — display a new tab

For the duration of the session (until you close the tab), Internet Explorer keeps track of the pages you visit within each tab. You can move backward and forward between those pages.

While you are working in Internet Explorer, you might want or need to interact with other programs—for example, to edit an HTML file you are working with, or to send a Web page or link by e-mail. You can tell Internet Explorer which program to open for a specific task on the Programs tab of the Internet Options dialog box. Select an HTML editor from the list of those installed on your computer, and then if you want Internet Explorer to use different default programs for other tasks than those set in Windows, click Set Programs to open the Windows default program settings and make your changes.

See Also For more information about choosing a default Web browser, e-mail client, media player, contact management system, and other programs, see "Specifying the Default Program for a Type of File" in Chapter 7, "Working with Programs."

In this exercise, you will start Internet Explorer and use various methods to open new, bookmarked, and linked Web sites and pages. You will open pages in the same window, on a new tab in the same window, and in a new window. You will navigate between sites and pages, close some sites, and then close them all. There are no practice files for this exercise.

Start

> **BE SURE TO** have an active Internet connection before beginning this exercise.

1. In the upper-left corner of the **Start** menu, click **Internet**.

> **Troubleshooting** The name of your default Internet browser appears below the word *Internet*. If Internet Explorer is not your default browser, point to All Programs on the Start menu, and then click Internet Explorer.

Internet Explorer starts, displaying your current home page.

Navigation bar   Address box   Command bar

> **See Also** For information about changing the site that opens when you start Internet Explorer, see "Changing Your Home Page" later in this chapter.

Go

2. Click once in the **Address** box to select the URL of the currently displayed page. Type http://www.microsoft.com, and then click the **Go** button or press Enter.

The Microsoft Web site replaces your home page.

3. In the **Address** box, replace *microsoft* with msn. Then press Alt + Enter.

> **Tip** You don't have to type a full Web site URL to move to a different site or a different page within the same site. You can change as much or as little of the URL as necessary.

The MSN site opens on a new tab.

4. Click the **Start** button (or press the ⊞ key).

When the Start menu opens, the insertion point is already in the Start Search box in the lower-left corner of the menu.

5. In the **Start Search** box, type http://.

Windows filters all the indexed information on your computer and displays a list of items containing the characters you've typed; in this case, items from your Favorites and History lists, as well as the entry you're currently typing.

You can click any Web site or page in the list to open it in Internet Explorer.

> **Tip** Internet Explorer records the Web sites you visit in your History list, so you can easily locate a site you have previously been to. Favorites are sites or locations that you save so you can return to them later.

6. In the **Start Search** box, complete the URL by typing money.msn.com. Then press Enter .

As you type, Windows continues to filter the item list shown on the Start menu. When you press Enter, the home page of the MSN Money site opens in a new tab, in the existing Internet Explorer window.

7. On the page, below the MSN Money title, click one of the links to other pages of the MSN Money site.

The selected page replaces the home page you were viewing.

8. Right-click another of the page links to display a menu of options for working with that page.

Page links

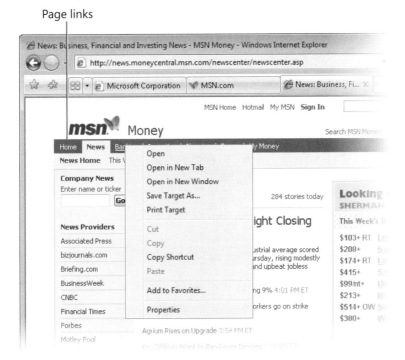

9. On the context menu, click **Open in New Tab**.

   The selected page opens in a *background tab*, so that the tab displaying the page you linked from is still on top of the others.

   > **Tip** Clicking Open In New Window starts an entirely new instance of Internet Explorer.

10. In the tab area, click the new tab to bring it to the front. (If you followed the instructions exactly so far, it is the fourth of four tabs.)

Back

11. Click the original MSN Money tab (the third tab), and then to the left of the **Address** box, click the **Back** button.

   You return to the MSN Money home page. Because you have visited only two pages on this tab, either the Back button or the Forward button is active at any one time.

Recent Pages

12. To the right of the Back and Forward buttons, click the **Recent Pages** button.

   A list of the pages visited on this tab appears, with a check mark indicating the current page.

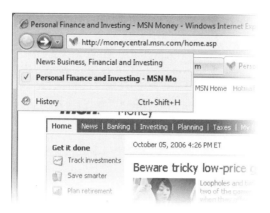

13. In the list, click the page that doesn't have a check mark next to it, to return to that page.

14. On the **Command** bar, click **Tools**. Then on the **Tools** menu, click **Internet Options**.

The Internet Options dialog box opens, displaying the General tab.

15. In the **Tabs** area, click **Settings**.

The Tabbed Browsing Settings dialog box opens.

16. Review the types of changes you can make, and change any settings that you want. Then click **OK** in the **Tabbed Browsing Settings** dialog box and again in the **Internet Options** dialog box.

Close Tab

17. In the browser window, click any one of the middle tabs, and then click the **Close Tab** button that appears.

    The tab closes, and the tabs to its right slide over to take its place.

Close

18. On the Internet Explorer window title bar, click the **Close** button.

    Because more than one tab is open, Internet Explorer prompts you to confirm that you want to close them all. (This is one of the settings you can change in the Tabbed Browsing Settings dialog box.)

19. In the message box, click **Show Options**.

You can have Internet Explorer reopen the current set of tabs the next time you start it (for example, if you have to shut down your computer but have a number of sites open that you want to return to) or you can disable the warning. This warning actually does come in handy sometimes while making the transition to tabbed browsing—it can be easy to forget that closing the window affects more than one site.

20. In the message box, click **Close tabs** to close all the tabs and quit Internet Explorer.

> **Tip** From time to time, Microsoft releases a new version of Internet Explorer. If you have configured Windows Vista for automatic updates, you will be informed of all the updates when they happen. You can always find the latest version of Internet Explorer at *www.microsoft.com/windows/ie/*.

Protecting Personal Information

Microsoft and MSN are licensees of the TRUSTe Privacy Program, which means that every Microsoft or MSN Web site contains a link to a privacy statement that must inform you of the following:

- The types of personal, identifying information that are collected from you through the Web site
- The name of the organization that is collecting the information
- How the information is used
- With whom the information might be shared
- Your choices regarding collection, use, and distribution of the information
- The kind of security procedures that are in place to protect against the loss, misuse, or alteration of your information
- How you can correct inaccuracies in the information

For more information about TRUSTe, you can visit *www.truste.org*. If you have concerns about the protection of your personal information while using MSN Explorer, you can send an e-mail message to *MSNPrivacy@msn.com*.

Blocking Pop-Up Windows

Pop-up windows (or just *pop-ups*) are the small Web browser windows that open on top of (or sometimes below) the Web browser window when you display a Web site or click an advertising link. Pop-ups frequently display annoying advertisements, adware (fake warning messages containing links to product sites), spyware (malicious software that can collect personal information from your computer), or other types of content you did not invite and probably don't want. Some types of pop-ups are valid; these might appear when you click a link for more information or when you log on to a secure site.

The Internet Explorer Pop-up Blocker is a feature through which you can prevent unwanted pop-ups from displaying. The Pop-up Blocker is turned on by default. When a pop-up tries to open, an audio alert sounds, and the *Information Bar* appears at the top of the Internet Explorer content pane, notifying you that a pop-up has been blocked. If you want to display the pop-up, you can click a link on the Information Bar to configure specific pop-up options for that site. You have the option of turning off the audio alert and/or Information Bar notifying you when a pop-up is blocked.

You can allow all pop-ups that appear when you are viewing a specific site by adding the site to either the Pop-up Blocker list of allowed Web sites or your Trusted Sites list. You can temporarily allow pop-ups from a site you are visiting, and configure the filter level to allow pop-ups from secure sites or to block most or all pop-ups.

To modify Pop-up Blocker settings:

→   On the Internet Explorer **Tools** menu, point to **Pop-up Blocker**, and then click **Pop-up Blocker Settings**.

To turn off Pop-up Blocker:

1. On the **Tools** menu, point to **Pop-up Blocker**, and then click **Turn off Pop-up Blocker**.

2. In the **Pop-up Blocker** message box requesting confirmation, click **Yes**.

Changing Your Home Page

Each time you open a new instance of Internet Explorer without specifying a target Web page, the browser window opens and displays your *home page*. This is generally the main page of a site to which you often refer, such as MSN for general information, your company's home page for internal news, or a financial Web site for tracking your investments. If you prefer, you can select a blank (Internet Explorer–generated) page as your home page and display a specific Web site only when you choose to visit one.

In this exercise, you will change your home page, add a second home page, and then set a blank home page. There are no practice files for this exercise.

> **BE SURE TO** have an active Internet connection before beginning this exercise.

1. On the **Start** menu, click **Internet**.

   > **Troubleshooting** If Internet Explorer is not your default browser, point to All Programs on the Start menu, and then click Internet Explorer.

   Internet Explorer starts, displaying your current home page on the default tab.

   When you purchase a new computer or upgrade your operating system, the computer or software manufacturer usually sets your home page as part of that process.

2. Replace the URL in the **Address** box with http://www.microsoft.com, and then press [Enter].

   The Microsoft home page replaces your default home page on the current tab.

Home

3. On the **Command** bar, click the **Home** arrow, and then in the list, click **Add or Change Home Page**.

   The Add Or Change Home Page dialog box opens, displaying the current URL.

4. In the dialog box, select the **Use this webpage as your only home page** option, and then click **Yes**.

Launch Internet Explorer Browser

5. Close the browser window. Then on the **Quick Launch** toolbar, click the **Launch Internet Explorer Browser** button.

Internet Explorer restarts, displaying the Microsoft Web site home page as your default home page.

6. In the **Address** box, replace *microsoft* with **msn**, and then press $\boxed{\text{Enter}}$.

The MSN home page opens on the current tab.

7. In the **Home** list, click **Add or Change Home Page**. Then in the dialog box, select the **Add this webpage to your home page tabs** option, and click **Yes**.

8. Click the **Home** button.

Internet Explorer displays the two home pages you have set, on separate tabs.

9. In the **Home** list, point to **Remove**, and then click **Remove All**. Then in the **Delete Home Page** dialog box, click **Yes**.

10. Click the **Home** button.

Internet Explorer displays your blank home page.

 BE SURE TO set your home page or pages as you want them before continuing.

Changing the Appearance of Web Content

Some Web sites set the formatting, such as fonts, font sizes, and text and background colors, used in their pages in order to control the way the site looks on your screen. Others don't. In the latter case, you can change the appearance of content displayed in the Internet Explorer browser window by changing the formatting. You might make these changes for personal preference or for readability if, for instance, you have trouble distinguishing certain colors or find it difficult to read small text on a computer monitor.

To change the size of the text on Web pages that don't specifically set the text size:

→ On the Internet Explorer **Page** menu, point to **Text Size**, and then click the size you want: **Smallest**, **Smaller**, **Medium** (the default), **Larger**, or **Largest**.

To change the text and background colors used on Web pages that don't specifically set the color:

1. On the Internet Explorer **Tools** menu, click **Internet Options**.

2. On the **General** tab of the **Internet Options** dialog box, in the **Appearance** section, click **Colors**.

3. In the **Colors** dialog box, clear the **Use Windows colors** check box.

4. Click the **Text, Background, Visited**, or **Unvisited** color button, select the color you want to use for that feature, and then click **OK** in each open dialog box.

To change the font size, text colors, and background color of all Web pages (even Web pages that specify those elements):

1. Complete the previous steps to change font sizes and set custom colors.

2. On the **General** tab of the **Internet Options** dialog box, in the **Appearance** section, click **Accessibility**.

3. In the **Formatting** area of the **Accessibility** dialog box, select the **Ignore colors specified on webpages** check box and the **Ignore font sizes specified on webpages** check box.

4. Click **OK** to effect your changes.

To change the fonts used on Web pages and in documents that don't specifically set a text font, follow the same procedures, but click Fonts to change the fonts, and then select the Ignore Font Styles check box in the Accessibility dialog box.

Finding, Saving, and Returning to Web Sites

To increase the efficiency with which you can move among sites you are currently viewing or have viewed in the past, and to make it easier to find sites that contain the information you need, Internet Explorer offers the following navigation tools, which put Web site information at your fingertips:

- **Live Search.** With this feature, you can perform plain-text searches on the Web, or search the files and folders on your computer.

- **Favorites Center.** This window contains links you have saved to Web sites, folders, and files; links to RSS feeds you have subscribed to; and a record of your Internet browsing history. You can display the Favorites Center as a multi-page window or pin it as a pane in the browser window.

- **Quick Tabs**. This feature displays screenshots of all Web pages currently open.

- **Tab List.** Clicking this button displays a submenu of the open Web pages.

Quick Tabs button ┐ ┌ Tab List button   Windows Live Search
                                                                                        input box

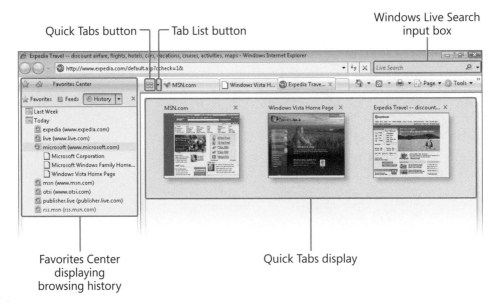

Favorites Center
displaying
browsing history

Quick Tabs display

In this exercise, you will conduct a simple search, expand the available search resources, save a page to your Favorites Center, and return to a page from your History list. There are no practice files for this exercise.

BE SURE TO start Internet Explorer before beginning this exercise.

Search

1. In the **Live Search** box at the right end of the Navigation bar, type a plain-text query, such as What types of plants grow on volcanoes?, and then click the **Search** button.

   Live Search searches the Web for pages containing content and keywords related to your question, and displays the results in the browser window. You can display any listed site by clicking its title, which is underlined to indicate that it is formatted as a hyperlink.

Search Options

2. At the right end of the **Live Search** box, click the **Search Options** arrow.

   Note that Live Search is the only search provider listed.

3. In the **Search Options** list, click **Find More Providers**.

   The Internet Explorer Web site appears, displaying links to two dozen search providers you can make available to the search utility. Adding a provider from this list makes it available in the Search Options list. To conduct a search through that provider, enter your search term, click the Search Options arrow, and then in the list, click the provider you want to use.

Add to Favorites

4. On the toolbar, click the **Add to Favorites** button, and then in the list, click **Add to Favorites**.

You can create additional folders within your Favorites Center by clicking New Folder.

5. In the **Add a Favorite** dialog box, click **Add** to make the current page available from your Favorites Center.

Favorites Center

6. On the toolbar, click the **Favorites Center** button.

The Favorites pane expands, displaying the page (Favorites, Feeds, or History) you most recently viewed.

7. If the Favorites page is not displayed, click **Favorites** to verify that the Add Search Providers page is there. Then click the **History** arrow, and in the list, click **By Site**.

The History page displays an alphabetical list of the sites you have visited in the last 20 days. You can click any site in the History list to open it in Internet Explorer.

> **Tip** On the General tab of the Internet Options dialog box, you can clear the History list or change the number of days (0 to 999) Internet Explorer retains your browsing history.

Pin the Favorites
Center

8. In the upper-right corner of the **Favorites Center**, click the **Pin the Favorites Center** button to convert the temporary window to a pane.

9. In the **History** list, click **By Date**, click **Today**, click **search.live (search.live.com)**, and then click **Live Search: What plants grow on volcanoes?** to return to your original search results.

Close

10. Experiment with other aspects of the Favorites Center. When you finish, click the **Close** button in its upper-right corner.

> **Tip** To clear your Internet Explorer history, click Delete Browsing History on the Tools menu.

  CLOSE the Internet Explorer window.

Printing Web Pages

While you're browsing the Web, Internet Explorer makes it easy to print the Web page you're viewing, either on paper, to a file, or if you have Microsoft Office OneNote 2007 installed on your computer, to your OneNote notebook. Before printing the page, you can preview it and adjust settings such as the paper size, the orientation, and the margins.

> **Tip** You can quickly send the contents of a Web page and a link to that page to your default OneNote notebook by clicking Send To OneNote on the Internet Explorer Tools menu. You must have previously started OneNote at least one time before you can send information to it from Internet Explorer.

In this exercise, you will preview and print a Web page. There are no practice files for this exercise.

  BE SURE TO install a printer before beginning this exercise.

1. On the **Start** menu, type http://www.otsi.com in the **Start Search** box, and then press Enter .

   The home page of our company Web site opens. The size and orientation of the page content is defined so that the content is in a horizontal format.

Print

2. On the **Command** bar, click the **Print** arrow, and then click **Print Preview**.

The OTSI home page appears in a Print Preview window, in the default portrait (vertical) orientation. Because the page content is restricted to a horizontal format, accepting these default settings will result in a small version of the Web page at the top of the printed page. Around the page, four Adjust Margin icons indicate the page margins; you can change the left, right, top, or bottom margin by dragging the appropriate Adjust Margin icon.

Adjust Margin icon

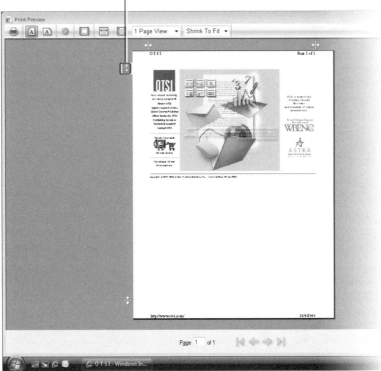

3. On the Print Preview window toolbar, click the **Landscape** button.

In landscape (horizontal) orientation, the content fits more appropriately on the page.

Landscape

4. On the toolbar, click the **View Full Width** button.

The page expands to fill the width of the window.

View Full Width

Print Document

5. Experiment with other adjustments. Then on the toolbar, click the **Print Document** button.

The Print dialog box that opens is similar to the Print dialog box that opens when you print a document from another program, such as Microsoft Office Word. Rather than having their own printing capabilities, programs that you run on your computer simply use the built-in Windows printing function.

6. Select the printer you want to use, and then click **Print** to print the page exactly as shown in the Print Preview window. (Or if you would prefer to not actually print the page, click **Cancel**.)

The Print dialog box and Print Preview window close, and your document is printed, with the Web page title and page number at the top of each page and the URL and date of printing at the bottom of each page.

 CLOSE the Internet Explorer window.

Sending Web Pages and Links to Other People

Sharing information from Web pages can be very useful—for example, when you're researching information (such as travel plans) on behalf of a group, or come across an article that you know would be of interest to a co-worker, friend, or family member. To share the information, or to simply keep a copy of it handy in an easily accessible electronic format, you can send a static copy of the page (to someone else or to yourself) embedded in an e-mail message. Alternatively, you can send the page URL in a message, and the recipient can click the URL to link to the "live" Web page.

In this exercise, you will first send a Web page in an e-mail message, and then send a link to a Web page. There are no practice files for this exercise.

BE SURE TO   configure a working e-mail account on your computer before beginning this exercise.

1. Start Internet Explorer to display your default home page.

2. On the **Command** bar, click the **Page** button to display a menu of actions you can perform with the current Web page.

3. On the **Page** menu, click **Send Page by E-mail**. Then in the **Internet Explorer Security** message box that appears, click **Allow**.

A new e-mail message opens in your default e-mail program. A copy of the currently displayed page is embedded in the message, not as a graphic, but as individual HTML and graphic elements. You can click any text or graphic in the embedded page and work with it as you would work with other e-mail message content.

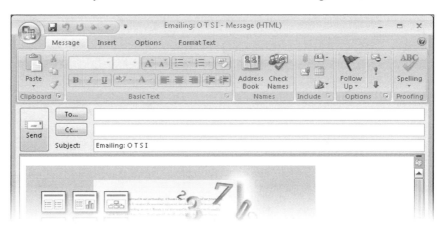

4. Change the size of the message window, and notice that (if the Web page is designed to fill a percentage of an Internet browser window rather than to be a fixed size) the content changes to fill the space.

5. Address the e-mail message to yourself, and then send it. (Or if you prefer, close the message window without sending the message.)

   You can work with the message you receive as you would with any other—you can view it, delete it, save it for later reference, or forward it to someone else.

6. On the **Page** menu, click **Send Link by E-mail**.

   The message created this time contains only the URL of the current Web page. Notice the variation in the message subject between the two methods of sending the Web page information.

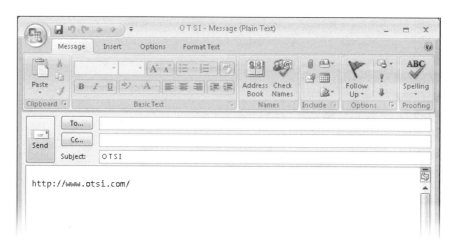

7. Address the e-mail message to yourself, and then send it. (Or if you prefer, close the message window without sending the message.)

CLOSE the Internet Explorer window.

Discovering and Subscribing to RSS Feeds

Really Simple Syndication (RSS) is a technology with which Web sites and blogs can send information to you, so that you don't have to visit the site. You can subscribe to an RSS feed from any site that offers one. Although RSS is a recent technology, RSS feeds are available for thousands of Web sites.

In the past, you had to install a newsreader program on your computer to subscribe to and view RSS feeds. Now you can subscribe to feeds directly from Internet Explorer 7. When you visit a site that has one or more RSS feeds, the RSS button on the Command bar becomes active (orange). You can click the button to view the default feed, or click the RSS arrow to display a list of feeds available from the site. You can also choose to have Internet Explorer play an audio alert when it finds an available feed on a Web page.

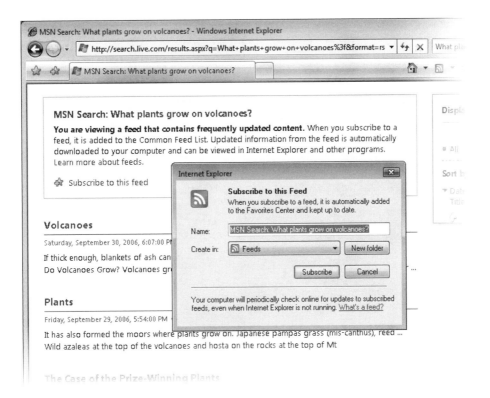

Web-based newsreaders and many other sites, such as the MSN Syndicated Content (RSS) Directory at *rss.msn.com* offer directories of RSS feeds. You simply click the link next to a site you like to subscribe to it.

Subscribing to an RSS feed adds it to the Feeds page of your Internet Explorer Favorites Center. You can return to it at any time to view up-to-date article synopses, and click any headline that interests you to display the article. RSS feeds can include the publisher's recommendation for how often subscribers will receive updates. You can stipulate the minimum update frequency for the feeds you subscribe to from Internet Explorer 7. To control the feed settings, display the Content tab of the Internet Options dialog box, and then in the Feeds area, click Settings.

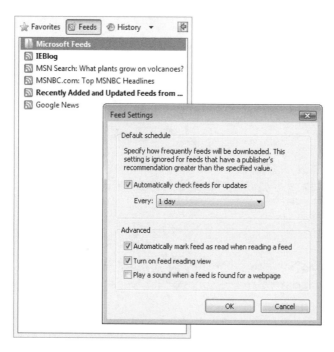

Your Favorites Center is available to you only on the computer it is stored on. If you want to access your newsfeeds from any computer, you can connect to a Web-based newsreader such as one of the following:

- My MSN, a home page you can personalize with the elements you want to see when you start your Web browser, accepts RSS feeds. To use this site, you need to register an e-mail address as a .NET Passport or Windows Live ID. (You might already have done this for another purpose.) For more information, visit

  my.msn.com

- Google Reader displays all your RSS feeds without all the extra information that might be on your My MSN page. To use this reader, you need a Google account. For more information, visit

  www.google.com/reader/

- My Yahoo! also supports RSS feeds. To use this reader, you need a Yahoo! account. For more information, visit

    my.yahoo.com

Web-based RSS readers do not require that you install any software on your computer. To locate other readers, search the Internet for *RSS reader.*

Restricting Objectionable Content

In addition to the basic ways you can tailor your Web-browsing experience, Internet Explorer includes settings that protect your privacy and offer peace of mind regarding the types of content that can be viewed on your computer. The Content Advisor feature controls the types of content that Internet Explorer may display by monitoring Web sites in accordance with the Internet Content Rating Association, an independent organization that catalogs Web sites within rating categories that cover:

- Content that creates feelings of fear or intimidation, sets a bad example for young children, or encourages children to perform or imitate dangerous or harmful behavior
- Depictions of gambling or of the use of weapons, alcohol, tobacco, or other drugs
- Depictions of discrimination or encouragement to engage in discriminatory behavior
- Offensive language including profanity, expletives, terms for bodily functions, anatomical references, obscene gestures, explicit sexual references, and otherwise vulgar, discriminatory, or crude language
- Partial, frontal, or full nudity, revealing attire, and provocative displays
- Mild or explicit sexual activity, passionate kissing, and clothed or non-explicit sexual touching
- Violence, including aggressive, natural, or accidental violence; fighting in which creatures are injured or killed or damage is inflicted on realistic objects; injuring or killing of humans or non-threatening creatures; injuring or killing of humans with blood and gore; or wanton and gratuitous violence
- User-generated content, such as chat rooms, that is not controlled by a site owner and might or might not be moderated

You can add other rating systems such as SafeSurf (*www.safesurf.com*) to Content Advisor, to increase your level of control. Web site authors and owners who are aware of Internet rating systems voluntarily submit their sites for rating. You can allow only sites with a certain rating, and you can block the display of unrated sites (although this might result in a lot of sites being blocked because their owners don't know about the program).

> **Tip** For information about the Internet Content Rating Association and tips for ensuring safe Web browsing for kids, or to apply for an ICRA label for a Web site you control, visit *www.icra.org*.

For each of the content categories, you can specify the level of that type of content Internet Explorer may display: None, Limited, Some, or Unrestricted.

In this exercise, you will configure the Content Advisor settings, and then see Content Advisor in action. There are no practice files for this exercise.

> **BE SURE TO** start Internet Explorer before beginning this exercise.

1. On the Internet Explorer **Tools** menu, click **Internet Options**, and then in the **Internet Options** dialog box, click the **Content** tab.

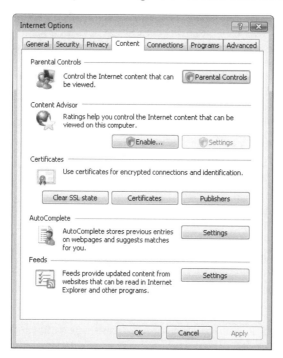

2. In the **Content Advisor** area, click **Enable**.

3. In the **User Account Control** dialog box, if you're logged on as an administrator, click **Continue**. Otherwise, enter an administrator password, and then click **OK**.

> **Troubleshooting** Repeat Step 3 each time the User Account Control message box appears while completing the remaining steps of this exercise.

The Content Advisor dialog box opens, displaying the Ratings tab.

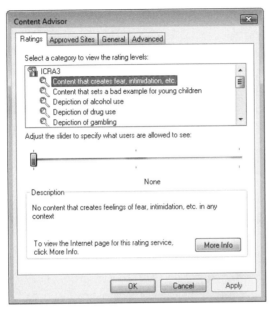

4. In the **Select a category** list, click each category in turn and move the slider located below the category list to display descriptions of each restriction level.

   Some categories have three levels of restriction and others have four.

5. Set the restriction level for each category as you want it, and then click the **Approved Sites** tab.

   You can allow or deny the display of specific sites regardless of their content, by entering the site URL in the Allow This Website box and then clicking the Always button or the Never button.

> **Troubleshooting** Don't be misled by the names of the tab and text box—you can block sites as well as allow them by entering their information here.

6. Add any sites you want to this list, and then click the **General** tab.

If you activate Content Advisor without selecting the Users Can See Websites That Have No Rating check box, Internet Explorer blocks the display of any site that hasn't been submitted for rating by ICRA or another rating organization you specify, or whose site administrator hasn't added the rating code to the Web site's pages.

7. For the purposes of this exercise, leave the **Users can see websites that have no rating** check box cleared, and the **Supervisor can type a password** check box selected. Then in the **Supervisor password** area, click **Create password**.

If you don't proactively create a password, Content Advisor prompts you to do so the first time you activate it.

8. In the **Create Supervisor Password** dialog box, type P@ssw0rd in the **Password** and **Confirm password** boxes, and click **OK**. Then click **OK** in the message box confirming that the password was successfully created.

You can display the Internet Explorer Web page that lists currently available rating systems by clicking Find Rating Systems in the Rating Systems area.

9. In the **Content Advisor** dialog box, click **OK**. Then click **OK** in the message box confirming that Content Advisor has been enabled.

In the Internet Options dialog box, the buttons in the Content Advisor area change to Disable and Settings.

10. Close the **Internet Options** dialog box, and then close the **Internet Explorer** window.

   The Content Advisor settings are applied to all windows opened after this point. If you try to open a site that does not meet your criteria, Internet Explorer displays a dialog box restricting access to the site.

   You must enter the supervisor password to access sites that don't meet the established criteria. You can browse the Web to see if you come across a site restricted by Content Advisor. Keep in mind that only sites that include their ratings within the page code are filtered by Content Advisor.

11. Click the **Start** button, type http://www.microsoft.com in the **Start Search** box, and then press [Enter].

   Internet Explorer starts and displays the Microsoft Corporation Web site home page. Content Advisor displays a warning that the page has been rated by a rating system that you don't have installed.

   Troubleshooting In fact, the RSACi rating system used by the Microsoft Web site has been merged into the ICRA rating system, but at the time we wrote this book, Content Advisor wasn't aware of that. Perhaps it will be by the time you work through this exercise.

12. Select the **Always allow this website to be viewed** option, type P@ssw0rd in the **Password** box, and then click **OK**.

13. Click any of the links in the **Product Families** list.

Content Advisor again restricts you from displaying the page. Obviously, this type of constant restriction can be quite irritating. After you view a few other Web sites with your criteria in place, you might want to make adjustments to the Content Advisor settings to fine-tune the way it works.

14. To disable Content Advisor, click **Internet Options** on the **Tools** menu, and on the **Content** tab of the **Internet Options** dialog box, click **Disable**.

To prevent other people from changing the restrictions you have set on your computer, after activating Content Advisor, you must enter the supervisor password to change its settings or disable it.

15. In the **Supervisor Password Required** message box, type P@ssw0rd in the **Password** box, and then click **OK**. If a message box notifies you that Content Advisor has been turned off, click **OK**. Then close the **Internet Options** dialog box.

 CLOSE the Internet Explorer window.

> **Tip** On the Advanced tab of the Internet Options dialog box are many settings that affect various aspects of Internet Explorer, such as accessibility, browsing, printing, and searching. For the most part, you are unlikely to need to change these options. However, if you find yourself wishing that some aspect of Internet Explorer worked a different way, you might want to display the Advanced tab to see if one of its options will do the trick.

Key Points

- The Windows Internet Explorer 7 tabbed browsing interface lets you open multiple Web sites in a single instance of Internet Explorer. You don't clutter up the taskbar, and it's faster and easier to open and switch between sites.

- If you want to quickly return to a site you've already visited, you can locate and open it from the Start menu.

- Not only can you change the home page that opens when you start Internet Explorer, but you can open multiple home pages.

- You can personalize the look of the browser window as well as the way content appears and performs within the window.

- Windows Vista incorporates safeguards that shield computer users from objectionable Internet content. What you see is up to you: You can specify the level of protection you want for yourself and for other users of your computer.

Keyboard Shortcuts

Press this	To do this
Ctrl+click	Open links in a new tab in the background
Ctrl+Shift+click	Open links in a new tab in the foreground
Ctrl+T or double-click an empty space on the tab row	Open a new tab in the foreground
Ctrl+Tab or Ctrl+Shift+Tab	Switch between tabs
CTRL+W or ALT+F4	Close current tab (or current window when there are no open tabs)
Alt+Enter	Open a new tab in the foreground from the Address bar
Ctrl+n (where *n* is a number between 1 and 8)	Switch to a specific tab number
Ctrl+9	Switch to the last tab
Ctrl+Alt+F4	Close other tabs
Ctrl+Q	Open Quick Tabs (thumbnail view)

Chapter at a Glance

Start programs automatically, **page 207**

Install and remove programs, **page 202**

Specify the default program for a type of file, **page 209**

Use and modify Sidebar, **page 223**

7 Working with Programs

In this chapter, you will learn to:

✔ Install and remove programs.

✔ Start programs automatically.

✔ Specify the default program for a type of file.

✔ Use the programs that come with Windows Vista.

✔ Use and modify Sidebar.

Nowadays you can purchase a computer, plug it in, and start working without installing any additional software. New name-brand computers usually come with the operating system (in this case, Windows Vista) already installed. They often also include software packages that provide the programs you need to carry out specific tasks, such as word processing. Sooner or later, however, you will want to install additional programs, from a CD, a network server, or a Web site.

Most programs place a link on the Start menu. You can start the program by clicking that link or by opening a file of a type that is associated with the program. For example, double-clicking an image file in Windows Explorer starts Windows Photo Gallery and then displays the graphic. You can change the program associated with a file type. For example, if you are more likely to want to work with photographs in an image-editing program, you can instruct Windows to open any file with a *.jpg* extension in that program when you double-click it. To save time, you can have Windows start programs for you, when you log on to the computer. You can easily change a few settings to make working with programs more efficient.

When you are ready, you will want to explore the programs that come with Windows Vista. Some of these programs are in the form of *gadgets* displayed on Windows Sidebar that keep tools such as a calculator or notepad immediately available. Others are stand-alone programs that provide tools to help you perform common tasks, such as scheduling appointments, keeping track of contact information, communicating via e-mail, or collaborating with co-workers. Previously you might have had to purchase a special software program to provide these functions that now come already installed. Although you still have that option, these built-in programs can provide invaluable time-saving support by putting specialized tools at your fingertips.

In this chapter, you will learn about installing new programs on your computer and re-moving programs you no longer need. You will set up a program to start automatically when you turn on your computer, and you will specify which program will open files of a particular type when you double-click them. Finally, you will take a tour of some of the programs that come with Windows Vista, and you will experiment with Sidebar.

See Also Do you need only a quick refresher on the topics in this chapter? See the Quick Reference entries on pages xxxix–lxxiii.

> **Important** Before you can use the practice files in this chapter, you need to install them from the book's companion CD to their default location. See "Using the Book's CD" on page xxix for more information.

Installing and Removing Programs

With so many programs available to help save you time, increase your productivity, broaden your knowledge base, or simply entertain you, one of your first tasks with a new computer system is usually installing programs. When you upgrade from a previous version of Windows, your installed programs remain available. If you regularly use several different programs, not having to reinstall them on your new system can save you a lot of time. When you purchase a new name-brand computer it might come with several programs pre-installed that you are not interested in using. If you no longer use a program—it didn't live up to your expectations, your interests changed, you replaced it with something better, and so on—and you don't intend to ever use it again, you should remove it to avoid taking up valuable disk space.

Installing Programs

You can install programs from a variety of sources, including physical media that you can hold in your hand—such as a CD, DVD, or floppy disk—and less tangible sources such as a file stored on your computer, on your network, or on a Web site. Regardless of the source of the installation files, you install almost all programs by running an executable file, which is often named *Setup.exe*. However, the precise installation process varies from program to program.

Here is what you might expect to encounter when installing from various sources:

- **CD or DVD installation.** Many software manufacturers use an *autorun file*, which is located in the *root* directory of the CD or DVD. When you insert a disc in a drive, Windows Vista looks for an autorun file and, if one is available, starts it automatically. The autorun file in turn starts an executable file that either leads you through a setup process or simply starts the program stored on the CD or DVD. Autorun files take the guesswork out of the setup process, because they don't require you to browse to a specific location, find a specific file, run a specific program, or make decisions about how to install the program.

- **Network installation.** If you work for a company that keeps the most current versions of its licensed software on one or more servers rather than distributing it on CD to its employees, you will likely install programs directly from a network server. Your network administrator will give you instructions for locating and installing these programs.

- **Internet installation.** Many companies supply free software or software upgrades that you can download or install from a Web site. To install a program over the Internet, click the link that is provided. If your Internet browser security settings allow file downloads and are set to prompt you for permission, you will have two options—to run the installation file from its current location on the Internet, or to download the installation file to your computer and run it from there. If you have a high-speed Internet connection through a DSL modem or a cable modem, and the installation file is small, it is simplest to run the installation file from the Internet. If you have a slower or less reliable connection, or the installation file is large, it is a good idea to download the file and run it locally.

Depending on the program you are installing, you might have to enter a unique registration code, called a *product key* or *CD key*, during the setup process. Product keys are issued by the software manufacturer, either physically or electronically:

- If you are installing the program from a CD or DVD, the product key is usually located on a sticker on the back of the jewel case.

- If you are installing the program from a network server, your network administrator will be able to supply the product key.

- If you are installing the program from the Internet, the software owner will supply you with a product key when you pay for it; free software might not require a product key, but the software supplier might request or require you to register with the company before installing the software. The information you provide might be used to register your interest in the product for support purposes, for statistical purposes, or so that the supplier can follow up with marketing materials and other information.

> **Tip** In the United States, the E-mail User Protection Act (HR 1910) requires that companies provide you with a means to remove yourself from mailing lists, and you can generally find a removal link or instructions at the bottom of the e-mail messages you receive from the company if you would prefer not to receive further messages.

Product keys are one of the methods software manufacturers use to try to prevent software piracy. A program that requires a product key for installation can't be installed without it. If you lose your product key, you won't be able to install the program in the future, unless you have registered your copy of the software and can successfully appeal to the software manufacturer for a replacement product key.

See Also   For information about software piracy, see the sidebar "The Perils of Piracy" in Chapter 1, "Getting Started with Windows Vista."

Most software companies require that you read and acknowledge a license agreement before you can install their software. You might be tempted to just click I Agree so that you can move on, but bear in mind that the license agreement is a legal contract. As with any contract, it is a good idea to read the agreement before consenting to it and installing the software.

> **Troubleshooting** With Windows Vista, only a user with *administrative privileges* can install some types of programs on your computer. If you do not have administrative privileges for the computer on which you want to install a new program, or if you are logged in with a Standard account (which we recommend for security), Windows prompts you to enter an administrative password to continue.

Many programs offer multiple installation options, such as *typical*, *complete*, or *custom*. Some programs that you install from a CD or DVD offer the option of copying large files to your computer or accessing them from the CD or DVD when needed. To save space on your hard disk for the features you will use most, you might have the option of waiting to install rarely used program features until the first time you need them. When choosing your installation type, consider the way in which you will use the program, the amount of space it requires, and how much space is available on your hard disk. Also think about whether the installation source will be available to you later, in case you need to reinstall the program or access features that weren't installed initially. In most cases, the default (typical) installation fits the needs of the average user and is the best choice.

When you start the installation process, most programs offer you the opportunity to accept or change the installation location, which is usually a product-specific sub-folder within the *Program Files* folder on your drive C. Unless you have a very specific reason for doing so, there is no need to change this default location; accepting it guarantees that the program and Windows know where to find program files. While actively installing files, the installation program might display a progress bar to keep you informed about what is going on during the installation process, and you might be informed of specific actions and file installations as they occur.

When the installation process is complete, you might be required to restart your computer. Restarting the computer allows the installation program to replace older versions of files that are in use and to clean up after itself.

> **Tip** If you would prefer not to restart your computer after installing a program, you can close the dialog box by clicking its Close button. The final setup tasks will then be completed the next time you start or restart the computer.

Removing Programs

Most commercial programs have many components—executable files, reference files, theme or graphic files, shortcuts, registry settings, and so on—and each component has to reside in a specific location for the program to work correctly. If you want to remove a program from your hard disk, it would be tedious—and with some large programs, virtually impossible—to track down and delete all its components. To ensure that a program is removed completely, instead of deleting the program's files and folders directly, you should always uninstall the program through Control Panel, as described in the following steps.

1. Display **Control Panel**, and under **Programs**, click the **Uninstall a program** task.

   The Programs And Features window opens.

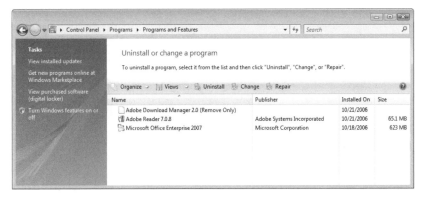

2. In the list of installed programs, select the one you want to remove.

   Uninstall and Change buttons appear on the toolbar.

> **Tip** If you want to change the setup of a program after you have installed it—for example, to install parts of the program that weren't included in the original installation—you can click the Change button on the toolbar to re-run the program setup from files installed on your computer.

3. On the toolbar, click **Uninstall**.

   Simple programs might be deleted immediately, and you can then simply close Control Panel. For programs with multiple components, the process is a little more complicated. A message box asks you to confirm that you want to proceed.

4. In the message box, click **Yes**. In the **User Account Control** dialog box, if you're running as an administrator, click **Continue**. Otherwise, enter an administrator password, and then click **OK**.

   The uninstall program gathers information from your computer, including information about any shared components (files that are commonly required by many programs) used by the program you are removing. Then it deletes the files, shortcuts, and registry entries associated with the program.

> **Tip** The uninstall program should not remove any documents or other personal files you created by using the program. Nevertheless, it is a good idea to back up any information you don't want to lose.

If the program you are removing makes use of shared components, it might be necessary to restart your computer to complete the process. If a restart is necessary, a message box appears, and you have the opportunity to save files and quit programs before continuing.

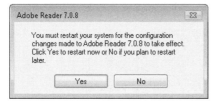

5. After saving and closing files, click **Yes** to restart your computer now, or click **No** to complete the uninstall process when you next restart or start your computer.

   If you click No, the program will remain in the list in the Programs And Features window until the next time you start or restart your computer.

Starting Programs Automatically

If you use certain programs every day, you can have Windows start them for you whenever you log on to your account. For example, many people start their e-mail programs first thing in the morning; other people might work all day in a particular accounting program. You might open your organization's intranet site each morning to look for announcements or open a news Web site to stay up to date on the headlines.

To specify that a particular program should start automatically, you place a shortcut to the program in your *Startup* folder. Each user has his or her own *Startup* folder, and there is also a *Startup* folder that applies to all users, so you can choose to make a program start automatically for everyone, or just for yourself.

> **Tip** If the program you're starting requires a user account name and password, you will be prompted to enter that information when Windows starts the program.

You can access your *Startup* folder or the *Startup* folder that belongs to all users of your computer through the Start menu or through Windows Explorer. You cannot access another user's *Startup* folder.

In this exercise, you will specify that a program start automatically when anyone logs on to your computer. This example uses Microsoft Paint, but you can substitute any other program. There are no practice files for this exercise.

> **BE SURE TO** log on to Windows before beginning this exercise.

1. On the **Start** menu, point to **All Programs**, right-click **Startup**, and then click **Explore All Users**.

    > **Tip** Clicking Explore opens your own *Startup* folder.
    >
    > If you only want to check the contents of the *Startup* folder and not change them, you can click Open All Users to open Windows Explorer with the Folders list closed.

    Windows Explorer opens with the *Startup* folder for all users displayed in the Content pane. (Whether or not the folder contains any files depends on your installation.) Even if you usually work in Windows Explorer with the Navigation pane or the Folders list closed, choosing Explore All Users opens Windows Explorer with them both open.

2. Under **Programs** in the **Folders** list, click **Accessories** to display the contents of that folder in the Content pane.

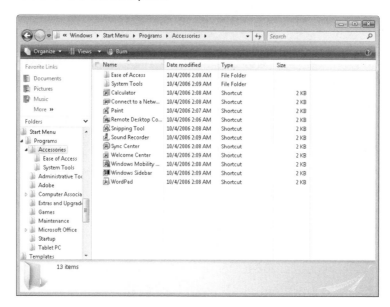

> **Troubleshooting**   If the Navigation pane and Folders list aren't open, open them now.

3. If necessary, scroll the **Navigation** pane until the *Startup* folder is visible.

4. In the **Content** pane, point to the shortcut to the **Paint** program, hold down the secondary mouse button, and drag the program to the **Startup** folder in the **Navigation** pane, releasing the mouse button when you see the *Move to Startup* ScreenTip.

   When you release the mouse button, a context menu (also called a shortcut menu) appears.

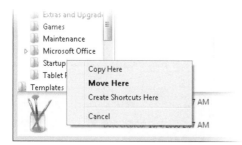

> **Troubleshooting** The context menu appears because you used the secondary mouse button to drag the file, rather than the primary mouse button. If you use the primary mouse button, the Paint shortcut simply moves to the folder, and you don't see the context menu. You would then need to copy it back into the *Accessories* folder.

5. On the context menu, click **Copy Here**. In the **User Account Control** dialog box, if you're running as an administrator, click **Continue**. Otherwise, enter an administrator password, and then click **OK**.

A copy of the shortcut is created in the *Startup* folder for all users of your computer. Paint will start automatically for each user as she or he logs on to Windows.

6. In the **Folders** list, click the **Startup** folder to display your new shortcut.

Shut Down
Options

7. On the **Start** menu, click the **Shut Down Options** button, and then click **Log Off**. Then log on again.

After Windows starts, a new Paint window opens.

> **CLOSE** the Paint window.
>
> **BE SURE TO** delete the Paint shortcut from the Startup folder if you don't want Paint to start every time you open Windows.

Specifying the Default Program for a Type of File

Usually you have just one program of a particular type installed on your computer—one word processor, one spreadsheet program, one database program, and so on. In each program, you create files of a specific type, identified by the file name extension. For example, the documents you create and save in Microsoft Office Word 2007 have the *.docx* extension appended to their file names. By default, these extensions are hidden from your view, and you never have to type them when you assign a name to a file. But they are there nevertheless.

One of the functions of the file name extension is to identify programs that can open the file. If you double-click the file in Windows Explorer and the default program associated with the file's extension is installed on your computer, Windows Vista starts the program, and that program then opens the file. This system is all well and good as long as each extension is "owned" by a single program.

> **Tip** When you double-click a file with an extension for which Windows has no program association, or if the associated program is not installed on your computer, Windows displays the Open With dialog box so that you can select the program you want to use. You might be able to open the file in a different program that creates similar files. For example, you can often use Microsoft Office Excel to open older spreadsheet files with the *.wks* extension, which were probably created in either Microsoft Works or Lotus 1-2-3.

However, the system breaks down if a file name extension represents a format that more than one installed program can work with. The classic example of file-type conflict arises with graphics files. The extensions of these files represent the format of the file rather than the program that created it. By design, most graphics programs can open and create files in several different graphics formats, because different formats are suited for different types of output. For example, one format might produce superior results in print, and another might be great for on-screen viewing. Of the files suited to viewing on a computer, some might produce high-quality images but also large file sizes; whereas others might produce acceptable quality with smaller sizes that are faster to download from the Web.

Until you install a graphics program on your computer, double-clicking a graphics file in Windows Explorer displays the graphic in Windows Photo Gallery. When you install a different graphics program, its installation program might lay claim to all graphics file formats. Then if you double-click a file with any of those extensions, Windows Vista calls upon that program to open the file. Or it might not. Double-clicking a file might continue to open it in Windows Photo Gallery, when you really want to work with the file in your new graphics program.

You can right-click a file and then click Open With to display the dialog box from which you can select the program you want to use. If you always want to open all files of a certain type with a different program than the one Windows Vista currently calls on for that task, you can change the default program for the type.

In this exercise, you will change the default program for a bitmap graphic from Windows Photo Gallery to Paint.

> **USE** the *03_MusicBox* graphic. This practice file is located in the *Chapter07* subfolder under *SBS_WindowsVista*.
>
> **OPEN** your Documents folder in Windows Explorer, and navigate to the *MSP\ SBS_WindowsVista\Chapter07* folder.

1. In the **Content** pane, double-click the *03_MusicBox* image.

Unless the default program for opening bitmap files has changed, the image opens in Windows Photo Gallery

See Also For information about Windows Photo Gallery, see "Viewing and Cataloging Pictures" in Chapter 9, "Working with Digital Media."

2. Close the **Windows Photo Gallery** window. Then in the **Content** pane, right-click the *03_MusicBox* image, point to **Open With**, and click **Choose Default Program**.

The Open With dialog box opens, displaying the different programs you have installed that will open this type of file.

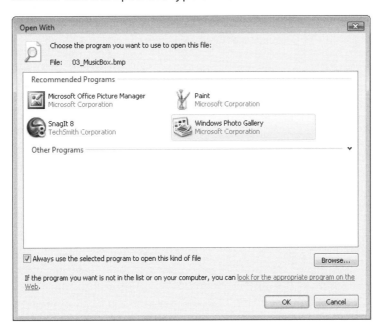

3. Under **Recommended Programs**, click **Paint**, and then click **OK**.

> **Tip** If you don't want to use any of the recommended programs, you can click Browse and navigate to the program you want to use.

Paint starts and opens the graphic file. Any files with the .bmp extension that you open after this will open in Paint, unless you change the default program to something else.

CLOSE the Paint window.

BE SURE TO reset the default program for bitmap graphics if you don't want them to continue opening in Paint.

Changing Your Default Middleware Programs

Middleware is software that connects two or more otherwise separate programs, which could be applications or system programs. Common types of middleware include transaction processing monitors and terminal emulation, messaging, and database access programs. Many middleware applications are Web-based. Because middleware is merely a connector and not part of the programs being connected, middleware programs are interchangeable. For example, you might choose to use Windows Internet Explorer or Firefox to browse the Internet, and you might choose to use Microsoft Office Outlook or Windows Mail to send e-mail messages from within those programs.

Windows Vista comes with a standard set of Microsoft middleware programs (Microsoft Windows Media Player, WIndows Internet Explorer, and Windows Mail). On a new computer, the original equipment manufacturer (OEM) might have in-stalled and selected other middleware programs as the defaults. However, the Microsoft middleware programs are available as part of the Windows Vista installa-tion, and you can select one or more of them as the default at any time.

To change the default settings:

1. On the **Start** menu, click **Default Programs.**

   The Default Programs window opens to the Choose The Program That Windows Uses By Default page.

2. Click the **Set program access and computer defaults** task. In the **User Account Control** dialog box, if you're running as an administrator, click **Continue**. Otherwise, enter an administrator password, and then click **OK**.

   In the Set Program Access And Computer Defaults dialog box, you have three choices:

   - *Microsoft Windows* sets all the standard Microsoft middleware programs as the defaults.

   - *Non-Microsoft* sets the current Web browser, e-mail program, media player, and instant messaging program as the defaults.

   - *Custom* sets the defaults for each of the five middleware options to your choice of either the Microsoft middleware program or the current program.

3. Make any necessary changes to your default middleware programs, and then click **OK**.

Using the Programs That Come with Windows Vista

A variety of useful programs are installed on your computer along with the Windows Vista operating system. The following brief introduction to some of these programs will help you decide whether you want to explore them on your own.

Windows Fax and Scan

With Windows Fax and Scan, you can send and receive faxes through an analog phone line and a modem, or through a fax server. After ensuring that the internal or external modem is correctly installed and turned on and that the phone line is plugged in, you need to set up a fax account to tell Windows how you will send and receive faxes. (If you want to send a fax via a fax modem but do not want to receive faxes, you don't have to set up an account.) Thereafter, you can start Windows Fax And Scan from the All Programs menu.

To send a fax from Windows Fax And Scan, click Fax in the Navigation pane, and then click the New Fax button on the toolbar to display a New Fax window. After entering the receiving phone number (or the contact to whom you are sending the fax) and a subject, you can compose the fax or a cover sheet, attach a file or insert a picture or scanned document, and then click Send.

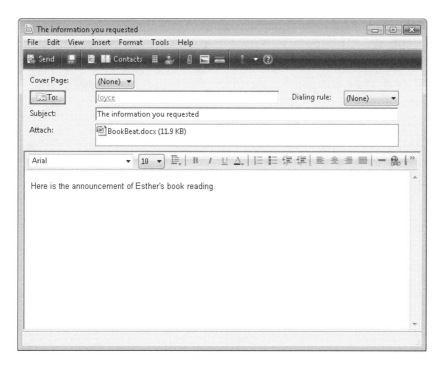

Received faxes appear in your Inbox in the Windows Fax And Scan window and can be viewed in much the same way as an e-mail message in an e-mail program.

If you have a scanner connected to your computer, you can also use Windows Fax And Scan to scan text documents and graphics to your computer as digital files that you can send as faxes or e-mail message attachments. Most modern scanners are Plug and Play devices that you can simply plug into an appropriate port on your computer.

To scan a printed document, turn on the scanner and insert the document you want to scan. Start Windows Fax And Scan, click Scan at the bottom of the Navigation pane, and then click the New Scan button on the toolbar. Adjust the settings in the New Scan window, and then click Preview to see how the scanned document will look.

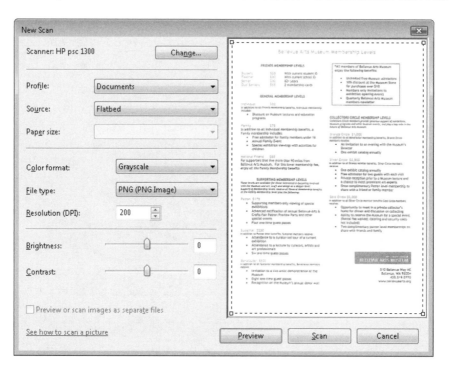

If you are satisfied with the preview, click Scan. Windows Fax And Scan scans the document and displays the scanned image. You can then send it directly by clicking the Forward As Fax or Forward As E-Mail button on the toolbar, or you can click the Save As button to save it as a file on your computer.

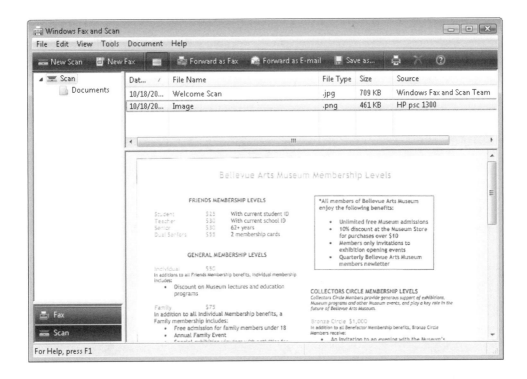

Windows Calendar

To simply check a date, you can click the clock in the notification area at the right end of the Windows taskbar to display a calendar for the current month. However, if you don't use Microsoft Office Outlook and want to track your schedule in an electronic calendar, you can use the new Windows Calendar program that comes with Windows Vista.

To open a personalized window where you can make appointments, point to All Programs on the Start menu, and then click Windows Calendar. When you select a time slot in the center pane and click the New Appointment button on the toolbar, a new appointment appears in the calendar. Type the name of the appointment, fill in information in the Details pane, and if you want, instruct Windows Vista to remind you about the appointment in advance.

In addition to keeping track of your schedule, you can also keep track of your tasks. Clicking the New Task button on the toolbar creates a new task in the Tasks pane in the lower-left corner of the window. Type the name of the task, and fill in information in the Details pane.

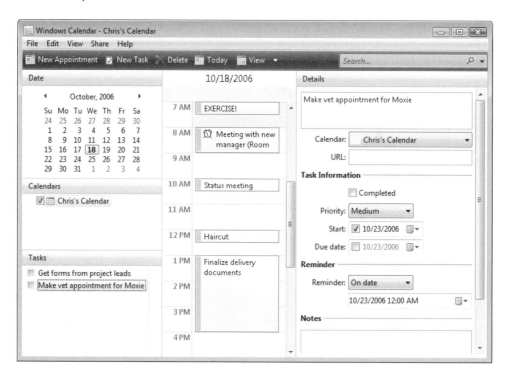

Windows Contacts

The contact program that comes with Windows Vista can be used as a stand-alone electronic address book or it can be used in conjunction with Windows Mail and Windows Fax And Scan to provide ready access to your contact information. With Windows Contacts, you can:

- Store e-mail addresses, street addresses, phone numbers, and personal information about a contact. You can associate each contact with a picture.

- Create contact groups so that you can send e-mail messages to the entire group. For example, you might create a group for each project you're working on, or you might want a group for family members.

- Import contact information from programs that export comma-separated text files, and export information from Windows Calendar in that format for use in other programs.

- Send and receive electronic business cards that contain contact information in a format that can easily be merged into other people's contact databases.

- Print your contact information in a variety of formats so that you can carry it with you when you don't have access to your computer or handheld electronic organizer.

You can easily add contact information by clicking Windows Contacts on the All Programs list to open the Contacts window. Clicking the New Contact button on the toolbar displays the Properties dialog box, where you can fill in all the information you have for a contact on multiple tabs.

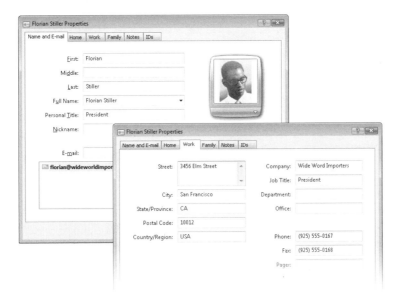

After you create your contacts, you can view and organize them in various ways, in much the same way that you view and organize files in any folder window.

Windows Mail

With computer communications, the world has become a much smaller place. It used to take months for a letter to travel from one side of the world to the other; it now takes seconds for an electronic message to make the same trip. Windows Vista comes with an e-mail program called Windows Mail that you can quickly and easily configure to send and receive e-mail messages.

The first time you start Windows Mail by clicking it on the All Programs menu, you are prompted to set up an account by entering information provided by your Internet service provider (ISP) or network administrator. Thereafter, starting Windows Mail displays your Inbox with any messages downloaded from your mail server.

Windows Mail is a rich e-mail program with many sophisticated features and customizable options. To read a message, you can click it in the header pane to display its contents in the reading pane, or you can double-click it to open it in its own window. Either way, you can click buttons on the toolbar to reply to the sender, reply to the sender and all the people who also received the message, or forward the message to someone else. To send a new message, you click the Create Mail button on the toolbar to open a New Message window, where you can enter the address of the recipient and any people to whom you are sending courtesy copies, and type a subject and the text of the message. You can format the message, check its spelling, and attach files to it before clicking the Send button to send it on its way.

Clicking Options on the Tools menu displays a multi-tabbed dialog box, where you can tailor the way the program operates to meet your needs.

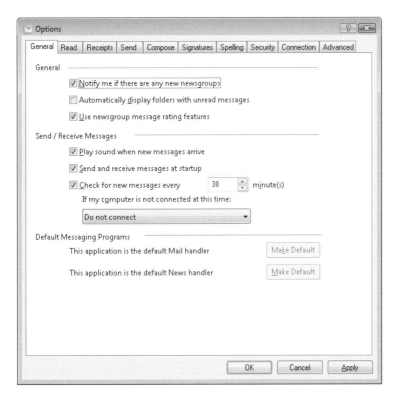

In addition to using Windows Mail to send and receive e-mail messages, you can configure it to connect to newsgroups. *Newsgroups* are moderated or unmoderated "message boards" on which people communicate about a specific subject. If people are talking about it, there is probably a newsgroup for it. Although this mode of communication has been somewhat eclipsed by blogs, which incorporate the graphics and pizzazz typical of a Web page, newsgroups are nevertheless an important resource. You can subscribe to a newsgroup by clicking Newsgroups on the Tools menu of the Windows Mail window.

Tip *Instant messaging (IM)* is a real-time electronic communication system that allows you to "chat" with contacts by typing in a window on your computer screen. Windows Vista does not come with its own instant messenger program. However, you can click Windows Live Messenger Download in the All Programs list to start your Web browser and display a Windows Live Services Web page from which Windows Live Messenger is available as a free download. This page also describes the features of the program and the things you can do with it in addition to chatting.

Playing Games

Windows Vista comes with these nine games, of varying difficulty, to entertain you when you have a few spare minutes.

- **Chess Titans.** A three-dimensional chess game with colored squares to guide you.

- **FreeCell.** A version of solitaire with all the cards visible. New look in Windows Vista.

- **Hearts.** A card game where having hearts and the queen of spades is bad and having the jack of diamonds is good. New look in Windows Vista.

- **InkBall.** Pinball for the Tablet PC, where bouncing balls are controlled by ink strokes.

- **Mahjong Titans.** A solitaire-like version of the classic Chinese game, played with tiles instead of cards.

- **Minesweeper.** A board game involving hidden mines and number clues. New look in Windows Vista.

- **Purble Place.** Three children's games in one: Comfy Cakes, Purble Shop, and Purble Pairs. New in Windows Vista.

- **Solitaire.** The classic card game, whose goal is to reorder randomly displayed cards by suit and rank. New look in Windows Vista.

- **Spider Solitaire.** A two-deck version of solitaire. New look in Windows Vista.

With the Business and Enterprise editions of Windows Vista, the Games folder and the games that come with Windows Vista are not installed by default. If a Games link does not appear on the right side of the Start menu, you can display it by following these steps:

1. Right-click the **Start** button, click **Properties**, and on the **Start Menu** tab of the Properties dialog box, click **Customize**.

2. Scroll the list in the **Customize Menu** dialog box, and under **Games**, select the **Display as a link** option. Then click **OK** in each of the open dialog boxes.

   A link to the Games folder now appears on the right side of the Start menu.

If the folder that opens when you click the Games link is empty, you need to turn on the display of Games from the Windows Features dialog box.

See Also For information about making games available, see "Turning Windows Features On and Off" in Chapter 11, "Optimizing Your Computer System."

To play a game, you double-click it in the Games folder. Clicking a game icon displays information about the game's publisher, developer, and genre (type) in the Details pane at the bottom of the folder window and information about how well it will perform on your computer in the Preview pane on the right side.

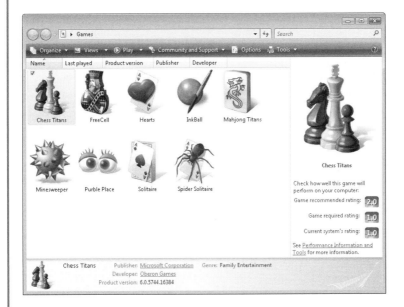

You might also want to while away some time playing games other than those that come with Windows Vista. You can find thousands of games in stores and online for purchase, and many are available for free download.

Installing a game adds a link to the game to your Games folder so that you can easily start all games from one central location.

Windows Meeting Space

No matter what type of job you have, you probably attend your fair share of meetings. In the past, meetings almost always involved sitting down in an office or conference room for a face-to-face discussion. Although advances in telephony have created the possibility of teleconferencing, this type of meeting is unsatisfactory if documents or supporting information need to be exchanged and discussed. That's where Web conferencing comes in. This latest evolution of the traditional meeting allows people in dispersed locations to meet, share content and ideas, collaborate on documents, and communicate using their computers.

With Windows Meeting Space, which comes with Windows Vista, you can set up an on-screen meeting for up to ten people. (You might want to supplement the meeting with a conference call or instant messaging.) The first time you start the program by clicking Windows Meeting Space in the All Programs list, you need to do a little setup work so that Windows Vista can identify the people near you who are using computers. Then to initiate a meeting, in the Windows Meeting Space window, click Start A New Meeting, assign the meeting a name, enter a password, and click the Create A Meeting button.

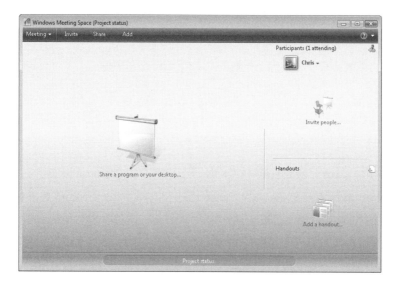

You can invite people to a Windows Meeting session by sending an electronic invitation. If you want to make the meeting available to an entire group of people, you can make it visible through a local network to people near you so that they can join the meeting.

As participants join the meeting, their names appear in the Windows Meeting window. You can share a file such as a schedule or budget with participants by clicking Share A Program Or Your Desktop and then browsing to and double-clicking the file. It opens on your computer for editing, but all participants can see it. You can give control of the file to another participant so that she or he can edit the file on his or her computer. You can also share your entire desktop in a way that is similar to Remote Assistance. You can distribute a file such as an agenda to participants by clicking Add A Handout and then browsing to and double-clicking the file to make it available from the Windows Meeting Space window. Each participant then double-clicks the handout in the window to open a copy on his or her computer. One at a time, participants can make changes that are re-flected in all the open copies of the handout file.

If you have been invited to a meeting, in the Windows Meeting Space window, you can either click Join A Meeting Near Me and supply a password, or click Open An Invitation File (if that is the way you were invited).

Privacy and security are maintained in a meeting because of the precautions taken when inviting people and because all communications are encrypted.

Using and Modifying Sidebar

Windows Sidebar is a cool new feature introduced with Windows Vista. Sidebar displays a number of small programs called gadgets that provide dynamic content (up-to-date information or entertainment) on a transparent vertical bar. Initially, Sidebar displays a large analog clock, a newsreader, and a slideshow display of the contents of your Pictures folder. (If you purchased a new computer with Windows Vista already installed, the OEM might have added other gadgets to Sidebar.) You can move, change, resize, or delete any of the default gadgets, and you can add other gadgets that come with Windows or new gadgets that you download from the Internet.

Sidebar opens by default in certain editions of Windows Vista and must be manually started in others.

In this exercise, you will change the appearance of the analog clock, display news head-lines and open an article, and then add a gadget to Sidebar. There are no practice files for this exercise.

> **BE SURE TO** display the Windows Vista desktop before beginning this exercise.

1. If Sidebar is not open on your desktop, point to **All Programs** on the **Start** menu, click **Accessories**, and then click **Windows Sidebar**.

   Sidebar opens on the right side of your screen, displaying the default gadgets.

Gadget controls

2. Point to the **Clock** gadget to display the gadget controls, and then click the **Options** button, labeled with a wrench icon.

The Clock dialog box opens, displaying an example of the current clock.

3. In the preview area, click the **Next** button to display an alternative clock face.

A different clock face style appears in the preview area.

Next

4. View the six other clock face options, and then return to the one you like best.

5. In the **Clock name** box, type My Clock. Select the **Show the second hand** check box if you want the analog clock to display the passing of seconds, and then click **OK**.

Your personalized clock appears on Sidebar.

6. If headlines aren't already shown in the **Feed Headlines** gadget, click **View Headlines** to load current news headlines.

News headlines cycle through the Feed Headlines gadget four at a time. You can move back or forward through the headlines by clicking the arrows at the bottom of the gadget.

7. Click any headline that interests you.

A window displays a synopsis of the associated article. You can view the entire article by clicking the headline at the top of the synopsis window.

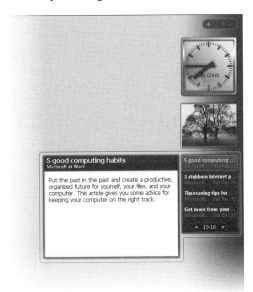

Sidebar control

8. On the **Sidebar control** at the top of Sidebar, click the **Add** button (labeled with a plus sign).

The Gadgets window opens, displaying the available gadgets. (Your Gadgets window might include more than those shown here.)

9. Drag a couple of gadgets you think might be useful from the **Gadgets** window to Sidebar. Then close the **Gadgets** window.

> **Tip** You can download other gadgets supplied by Microsoft and other companies by clicking Get More Gadgets Online.

For the purposes of this exercise, we've chosen the Stocks gadget, which you can use to quickly check stock prices, and the Weather gadget, which displays the current temperature and a photographic representation of the current weather conditions for any area you choose. Feel free to choose any other gadget that interests you; if you're feeling adventurous, you can click Get More Gadgets Online, in the lower-right corner of the window, to browse and download other gadgets from the Microsoft Web site.

> **Troubleshooting** Hundreds of gadgets are available from the Windows Vista gadget gallery. Very few of these were officially created by Microsoft, and therefore Microsoft does not offer guarantees or provide product support for any of these gadgets you choose to download.

10. Right-click the **Slide Show** gadget, and then click **Detach from Sidebar**.

    The Slide Show moves to the upper-left corner of your screen, and appears in a larger window.

11. Point to the **Slide Show** gadget to display controls to its right and on the gadget itself. On the gadget, click the **View** button (the right-most button, which has a magnifying glass icon).

    The currently displayed picture opens in Windows Photo Gallery. The slide show continues behind the photo gallery.

12. Close the **Windows Photo Gallery** window.

13. Right-click the **Slide Show** gadget, and click **Attach to Sidebar**. Then drag the reattached gadget to the bottom of Sidebar.

    The other gadgets move up to make room for the Slide Show.

14. Right-click an empty area of **Sidebar**, and then click **Properties**.

    The Windows Sidebar Properties dialog box opens.

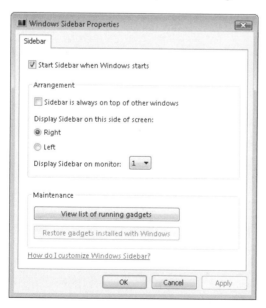

15. Experiment with the Sidebar properties, clicking **Apply** to see the effects of different settings. When Sidebar is configured the way you want it, click **OK**.

> **Tip** You can make Sidebar available at all times by selecting the Sidebar Is Always On Top Of Other Windows check box in the Windows Sidebar Properties dialog box. Then when you maximize other windows, they won't overlap Sidebar. To remove Sidebar from the Windows desktop, right-click Sidebar, and then click Close Sidebar.

Key Points

- When installing new programs, you can usually answer a few setup questions and then leave most of the details to Windows Vista. Similarly, Windows Vista provides a safe way of completely removing programs you no longer use.

- You can instruct Windows Vista to automatically start a program when you log on to your computer.

- You can choose the program Windows Vista starts when you double-click a file of a particular type.

- The programs that come with Windows Vista can help you be more efficient and productive by taking care of a variety of common business tasks.

- Windows Sidebar is an innovative tool that puts information that is constantly updated on your desktop, where you can glance at it throughout the day.

Keyboard Shortcuts

Press this	To do this
Windows logo key	Open or close the Start menu
Ctrl+Esc	Open the Start menu
Shift+F10	Display the shortcut menu for the selected item
Windows logo key+Spacebar	Bring all gadgets to the front and select Windows Sidebar
Windows logo key+G	Cycle through Sidebar gadgets
Tab	Cycle through Sidebar controls

Chapter at a Glance

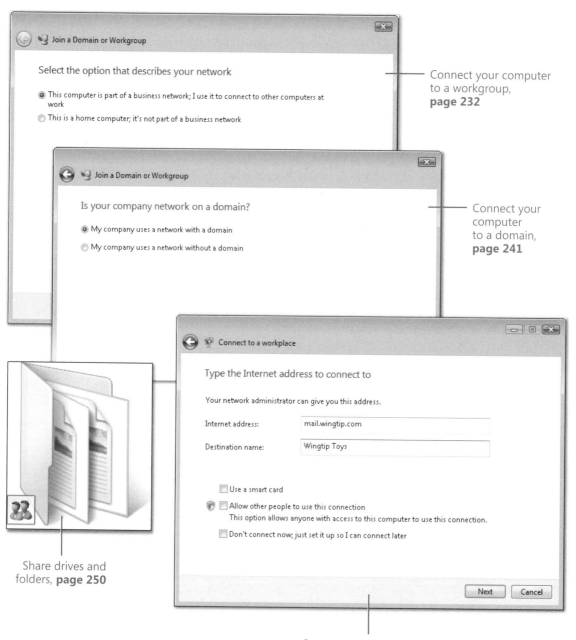

Connect your computer to a workgroup, **page 232**

Connect your computer to a domain, **page 241**

Share drives and folders, **page 250**

Connect to a domain from another location, **page 235**

8 Making Connections

In this chapter, you will learn to:

- ✔ Connect your computer to a workgroup.
- ✔ Connect to a domain from another location.
- ✔ Connect your computer to a domain.
- ✔ Access your domain computer remotely.
- ✔ Share drives and folders.

Every Windows Vista computer is set up to connect to a network through either a domain or a workgroup. If your computer is part of a domain, you are probably well aware of it—most networked computers within commercial office environments are on a domain. If your computer is part of a workgroup, you might not be aware of it—if your computer is the only one in your office or home, for example, you might not realize that your computer is the basis of its own network.

See Also For information about domains and workgroups, see the sidebar "Networks, Domains, and Workgroups" in Chapter 1, "Getting Started with Windows Vista."

There are various ways to connect to a network. When you are in the office or at home, you connect by means of a network cable or wireless network adapter. If you have a user account on a domain, and your network administrator has configured the system to allow *virtual private network (VPN)* connections, you can access domain resources when you are away from the office by setting up a VPN connection from a remote computer to the domain, over the Internet. If you set up your domain computer to allow Remote Desktop connections, you can not only access the information stored on it, but also log on to it remotely, and work on it as though you were working directly on it at the office.

In this chapter, you will learn how to join your computer to a new or existing work group, and how to set up your computer to log on to a domain. You will set up a VPN connection to a domain from an off-network location, and explore how to access domain resources. You will configure your computer to allow Remote Desktop connections, and then connect to a computer by using Remote Desktop. Finally, you will explore ways of sharing drives and folders on your computer with other network users.

See Also Do you need only a quick refresher on the topics in this chapter? See the Quick Reference entries on pages xxxix–lxxiii.

Important Before you can use the practice files in this chapter, you need to install them from the book's companion CD to their default location. See "Using the Book's CD" on page XXX for more information.

Connecting Your Computer to a Workgroup

If you have several computers in your household and have set up a home network so that you can share resources such as printers, the computers are probably part of a workgroup. If there are fewer than 20 networked computers in your office, they might be part of a workgroup or they might be part of a domain. (If you have more than 20 networked computers, they are almost certainly part of a domain.) The main difference between the two is in how the network resources are managed. In a workgroup:

- No computer has control over any other.
- User accounts for each computer are administered individually; you need a user account on a specific computer to log on to that computer.
- All computers must be on the same local network (wired or wireless).

All the computers in a workgroup must be on the same network, but a network can include multiple workgroups. Windows Vista automatically joins your computer to a workgroup during installation. During a new installation, Windows Vista uses the default workgroup; during an upgrade, it retains the existing workgroup setting. You can change the workgroup you're joined to at any time, and you can create a new workgroup for specific resource-sharing purposes.

Tip You can reconfigure a workgroup-joined computer to connect to a domain; for example, if you take your personal laptop to the office, or want your home computer to be visible to other domain users.

In this exercise, you will join your computer to a new workgroup that you will create for the purpose of sharing resources. There are no practice files for this exercise.

 BE SURE TO start Windows Vista and display Control Panel before beginning this exercise.

1. In **Control Panel**, click **System and Maintenance**, and then click **System**.

   The System window opens, displaying information about your computer.

2. Under **Computer name, domain, and workgroup settings**, click **Change settings**. In the **User Account Control** dialog box, if you're logged on as an administrator, click **Continue**. Otherwise, enter an administrator password, and click **OK**.

   The System Properties dialog box opens, displaying the Computer Name tab.

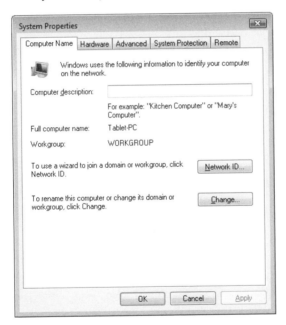

3. To the right of **To use a wizard to join a domain or workgroup**, click **Network ID**.

   The Join A Domain Or Workgroup wizard starts.

4. With the **This computer is part of a business network** option selected, click **Next**.

   > **Troubleshooting** It might seem logical to select the This Is A Home Computer option, but that option does not allow you to create a new workgroup.

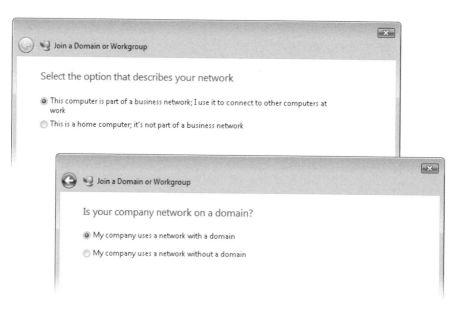

5. Select the **My company uses a network without a domain** option, and then click **Next**.

6. In the **Workgroup** box, type a descriptive name for the new workgroup. (No matter how you type it, the name appears in all capital letters.) Then click **Next**.

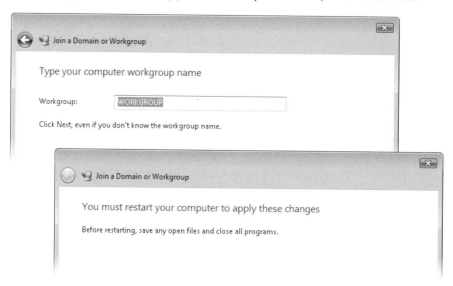

7. On the wizard's final page, click **Finish**.

8. In the **System Properties** dialog box, click **OK**.

You must restart your computer for the change to take effect.

9. Close any open files, and quit any running programs. Then in the message box, click **Restart Now**.

10. After restarting, display the **System** window, and verify that your computer is now joined to the new workgroup.

 CLOSE the System window.

Connecting to a Domain from Another Location

Virtual private network (VPN) connections are becoming increasingly common in the corporate world. With a VPN connection, a domain user can access a private (corporate or institutional) network via the Internet, thus extending the private network so that she or he is virtually, if not physically, part of it.

If your organization has set up a *remote access server*, you can create a VPN connection to your domain over the Internet. Using this connection, you have full access to network resources while you are away from the office, which is extremely useful when you are traveling or working from home.

The speed of your VPN connection is limited by the speed of your Internet connection. If you are connecting to a VPN through a dial-up connection, you might run out of patience while waiting for your computer to access common network resources. However, if you are connecting through a broadband connection, access speeds can be nearly as good as being physically there.

In this exercise, you will create a VPN connection over the Internet. There are no practice files for this exercise.

Troubleshooting If your organization does not have a remote access server, you cannot complete this exercise.

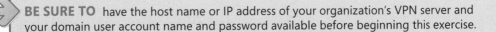 **BE SURE TO** have the host name or IP address of your organization's VPN server and your domain user account name and password available before beginning this exercise.

1. Display **Control Panel**, and then click **Network and Internet**.

The Network And Internet window opens.

2. Under **Network and Sharing Center**, click the **Connect to a network** task, and then at the bottom of the **Connect to a network** window, click the **Set up a connection or network** task.

The Connect To A Network wizard starts.

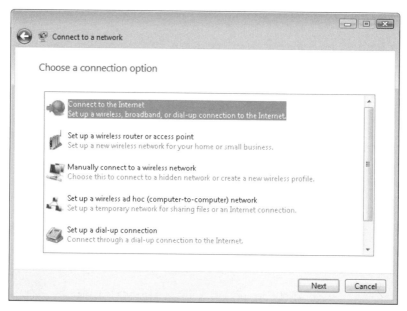

3. Scroll to the end of the **Choose a connection option** list, click **Connect to a workplace**, and then click **Next**.

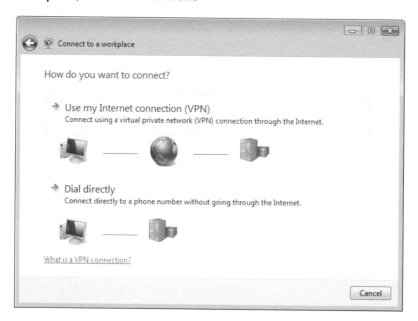

4. On the **How do you want to connect** page, click **Use my Internet connection (VPN)**. The Type The Internet Address To Connect To page opens.

5. In the **Internet address** box, type the remote access server's host name or IP address, and in the **Destination name** box, type a name for the connection (for example, the company name).

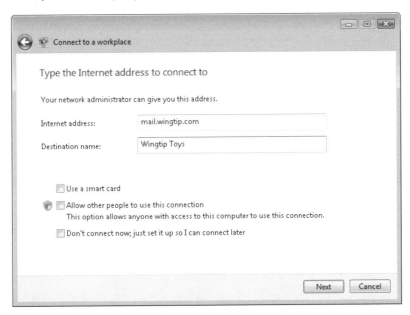

6. Specify whether you want to make the connection available to other users of your computer or keep it to yourself, and then click **Next**.

7. On the **Type your user name and password** page, enter your network credentials.

Notice that you can display the characters of your password to confirm it before proceeding. If you select this option, your password will be visible only on this page, not during the actual logon process.

8. Click **Connect**.

You connect to the network. The network verifies your user account name and password, and then logs you on.

While your computer is connected to the network, a network icon appears in the notification area, and you can connect to the same network resources as you could if you were sitting at your desk at work.

Network icon

9. In the **Connect to a workplace** wizard, click **Close**.

The first time you connect to the network, Windows Vista might prompt you to specify whether it is a private or public network.

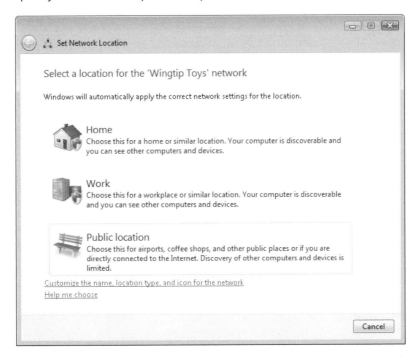

10. If the **Set Network Location** window appears, click **Work**. Then in the **User Account Control** dialog box, if you're logged on as an administrator, click **Continue**. Otherwise, enter an administrator password, and click **OK**.

CLOSE the Network And Internet window.

> **Tip** To disconnect from a VPN connection, right-click the network icon, point to Disconnect From, and then click the VPN connection.

Creating an Ad Hoc Wireless Network

If you want to share information stored on your computer with other people nearby and everyone's computer has a wireless network adapter, a simple method of sharing is to set up an ad hoc wireless network. In spite of the fact that members must be within 30 feet of each other, this type of network presents a lot of possibilities. For example, you might consider establishing an ad hoc network at a meeting of mobile computer users so that you can share information with other attendees on their own screens rather than an overhead projector. (After establishing the network, you can do this is by using Windows Meeting, a really cool new feature of Windows Vista.)

See Also For information about Windows Meeting, see "Using the Programs That Come with Windows Vista" in Chapter 7, "Working with Programs."

Ad hoc networks are by definition temporary; they cease to exist when members disconnect from them, or when the computer from which the network was established moves beyond the 30-foot effective range of the others.

You can share an Internet connection through an ad hoc network, but keep in mind that the Internet connection is then available to anyone logging on to a computer that is connected to the network, and thus is likely not very secure.

To set up an ad hoc network:

1. On the **Start** menu, click **Connect To**.

2. In the **Connect to a network** window, click the **Set up a connection or network** task.

3. On the **Choose a connection option** page, click **Set up a wireless ad hoc (computer-to-computer) network**, and then click **Next**.

> **Troubleshooting** The Set Up An Ad Hoc Network option appears only on computers that have wireless adapters.

4. Read the ad hoc network information, and then click **Next**.

5. Provide a network name, select whether the network is open or requires authentication, provide a security phrase if necessary, and then click **Next**.

After Windows Vista sets up the ad hoc network, you have the option of sharing your Internet connection.

To disconnect from an ad hoc network, display the Connect To A Network window, click the ad hoc network, and then click Disconnect.

Connecting Your Computer to a Domain

If you work in an organization that has a domain, you probably have a desk with a computer on it that you identify as your own. But as far as the domain is concerned, there is no connection between that computer and you as a domain user.

Logging on to a domain requires a password-protected domain user account. Domain user accounts (not to be confused with Windows user accounts) are administered centrally and are not associated with any particular computer. As a result, any domain user can log on to any computer on the domain.

For a computer to be visible to other domain computers, a network administrator must create a machine account for the computer. The machine account is linked to the computer name; no two computers on any one domain can have the same name. Changing the name of a domain-connected computer may require an update to the machine account information. However, you can replace a computer with another that has the same name and connect that computer to the domain using the original machine account.

> **Tip** You can connect to a domain from a computer that doesn't have a machine account on that domain. Other domain users will not see the computer when browsing the domain, but they can connect to shared folders on it if they know the computer name.

In this exercise, you will connect a computer for which a machine account has already been created to a domain. There are no practice files for this exercise.

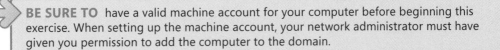

BE SURE TO have a valid machine account for your computer before beginning this exercise. When setting up the machine account, your network administrator must have given you permission to add the computer to the domain.

1. Connect your computer to your corporate network, either physically or through a VPN connection.

2. Display **Control Panel**, click **System and Maintenance**, and then click **System**.

3. In the **System** window, under **Computer name, domain, and workgroup settings**, click **Change settings**. Then in the **User Account Control** dialog box, if you're logged on as an administrator, click **Continue**. Otherwise, enter an administrator password, and click **OK**.

4. In the **System Properties** dialog box, click **Network ID**.

5. In the **Join a Domain or Workgroup** wizard, with the **This computer is part of a business network** option selected, click **Next**.

6. With the **My company uses a network with a domain** option selected, click **Next**.

The wizard displays a list of the information you need to have before proceeding.

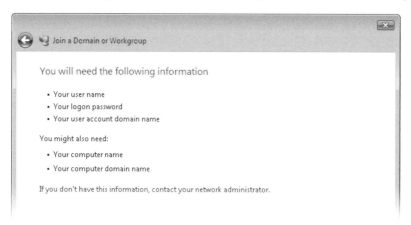

7. Make sure you have all the necessary information, click **Next**, and then enter your user name, password, and domain name.

No matter how you type it, the domain name is displayed in all capital letters.

8. Click **Next**.

Windows Vista searches the specified domain for a machine account with the same name as your computer and displays a message if it finds one.

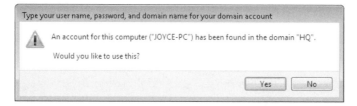

9. Click **Yes**.

Windows Vista asks whether you want to enable your user account on the computer.

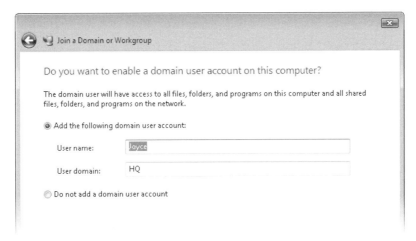

10. If you want to enable your user account, click **Next**. Otherwise, select the **Do not add a domain user account** option, and then click **Next**.

Windows Vista asks whether you want to have administrator privileges on this computer. Unless you are the domain's network administrator, it is safest to accept the default Standard Account option.

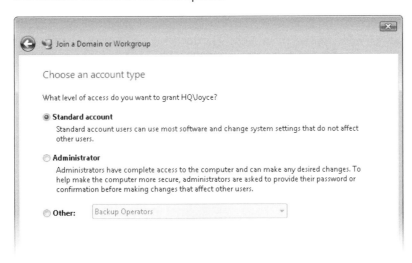

Troubleshooting Removing a computer from a domain requires Administrator privileges. Any administrator can enter his or her credentials to allow Windows Vista to complete that task. But if you plan to frequently switch between domains or between a domain and a workgroup, it might be more convenient to select the Administrator option.

11. Click **Next**, and then click **Finish**.

12. In the **System Properties** dialog box, click **OK**.

    A message box tells you that you must restart your computer for the change to take effect.

13. Close any open files, and quit any running programs. Then in the message box, click **Restart Now**.

14. When your computer restarts, press `Ctrl`+`Alt`+`Del` to display the Welcome screen. Then enter your domain credentials, and press `Enter` to log on to the domain.

Accessing Your Domain Computer Remotely

If you frequently travel with a mobile computer, or if you work from locations such as a central office, branch office, and home office, you don't need to have all your programs and data files on all the computers you work with. You can use the computer you have at hand to work virtually on your own computer by using *Remote Desktop*. If the computer is not on the same network as your own computer, you can use this handy feature only if you first establish a VPN connection to the domain.

Before you can connect to your own computer, you need to configure it to allow remote access. You can allow access via Remote Desktop from computers running a previous version of Windows or only from computers running Windows Vista. Restricting access to computers running Windows Vista provides a greater level of security because of its method of authentication (user verification).

> **Important** This level of security goes both ways. You can use Remote Desktop from your Windows Vista computer to connect to a computer running a previous version of Windows, but you will be asked to acknowledge that the Windows Vista security features will not be in effect for that connection.

After connecting to the remote computer, you see its desktop on your local computer's monitor. You use your computer's keyboard and mouse to start programs, move around, and work just as if you were sitting at the remote computer. Even the sound from the remote computer plays on your local system. You can select other local resources that you want to have available, such as printers, from the tab in the Remote Desktop Connection window.

During a remote session, the Connection bar (a yellow tab) appears at the top of the remote desktop. With the Connection bar buttons, similar to the window-management buttons found in the upper-right corner of a window, you can minimize or shrink the remote desktop to work on your local computer, while maintaining the connection to the remote computer. You can hide the Connection bar by clicking the thumbtack icon on its left edge, and display it again by pointing to the top of the remote desktop.

When you are ready to disconnect from a remote session, do not close the remote desktop or shut down the remote computer. Instead, you must log off from the remote computer by clicking the Shut Down Options button on that computer's Start menu, and then clicking Log Off (or if connected remotely to a computer running Microsoft Windows XP, clicking Log Off on that computer's Start menu). If you shut down the remote computer, it will actually turn off, and you won't be able to access it again until you or someone else physically restarts it.

> **Important** Logging off from a remote desktop connection does not close files or quit programs in the way that logging off from a local computer session does. Unless you want them to remain open while you are disconnected from the remote computer, you should always close files and quit programs manually before logging off.

See Also For more information, search for *Remote Desktop* in the Help And Support Center.

In this exercise, you will set up your computer so that it can be accessed via Remote Desktop. Then you will connect to a computer configured for Remote Desktop from another computer. There are no practice files for this exercise.

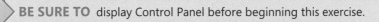

BE SURE TO display Control Panel before beginning this exercise.

1. In **Control Panel**, click **System and Maintenance**, and then under **System**, click the **Allow remote access** task. Then in the **User Account Control** dialog box, if you're logged on as an administrator, click **Continue**. Otherwise, enter an administrator password, and click **OK**.

The System Properties dialog box opens, displaying the Remote tab.

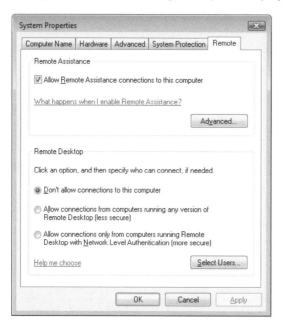

2. Under **Remote Desktop**, to allow Remote Desktop connections from any other Windows computer, select the **Allow connections from computers running any version of Remote Desktop** option. To restrict connections to computers running Windows Vista, select the **Allow connections only from computers running Remote Desktop with Network Level Authentication** option.

3. If your computer is set up to go to sleep after a specific period of non-use, a **Remote Desktop** message box advises you that you won't be able to connect through Remote Desktop while the computer is in sleep mode. Click **OK** to close the message box.

See Also For information about managing your computer's power plan, see "Improving Your Computer's Performance" in Chapter 11, "Optimizing Your Computer System."

Tip Any administrator of your computer is by default authorized as a remote user. If you want to authorize additional remote users, click Select Users, and then in the Remote Desktop Users dialog box, click Add. You can add individual users or groups of users.

---

4. In the **System Properties** dialog box, click **OK**.

5. From another computer on the domain, on the **Start** menu, point to **All Programs**, click **Accessories**, and then click **Remote Desktop Connection**.

The Remote Desktop Connection opens.

6. If the Remote Desktop Connection dialog box does not display the multi-tabbed area, click **Options**.

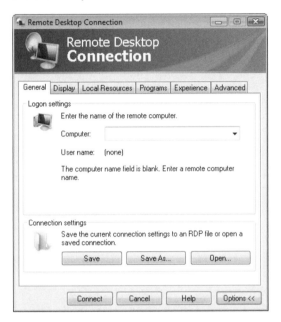

> **Tip** You can control the availability of your computer's resources during a remote session by selecting options on the Local Resources tab.

7. In the **Computer** box, type the name of the remote computer you want to access, and then click **Connect**.

> **Tip** If you don't know the computer name, you can click the Computer arrow, click Browse For More in the list, locate the computer you want to connect to in the Browse For Computers dialog box, and then click OK.

The Windows Security dialog box opens.

8. Enter your computer or domain credentials and, if you will be connecting to the remote computer from this computer on a regular basis, select the **Remember my credentials** check box. Then click **OK**.

> **Tip** To connect to a computer on a domain, enter your domain user name in the User Name box, in the format *DOMAIN\user name*. The domain shown below the Password box updates to reflect whether you are using computer or domain credentials.

A new window opens on your screen, displaying the desktop of the remote computer.

9. Explore the remote computer, and then when you are ready, log off from it.

 BE SURE TO repeat Steps 1 through 4 to turn off remote access, if you do not want to allow access from now on.

Storing and Managing Network Passwords

When you connect to a domain remotely, Windows Vista automatically stores your user name and password (collectively, your *credentials*) on the computer. You can change a password even if your computer is not connected to the domain. You can also remove passwords that you no longer use. If you change the credentials stored on your computer, Windows Vista passes the new credentials to the domain the next time you connect.

To store a network password:

1. In **Control Panel**, click **User Accounts and Family Safety**, and then click **User Accounts**.

2. In the Tasks list, click **Manage your network passwords**.

3. In the **Stored User Names and Passwords** dialog box, click **Add**.

   The Stored Credential Properties dialog box opens.

4. In the **Log on to** box, enter the server, Web site, or program for which you want to store credentials.

5. In the **User name** and **Password** boxes, enter your credentials for the server or Web site.

6. Under **Credential type**, select the type of entity for which you are storing credentials. Then click **OK**.

Sharing Drives and Folders

Whether you work on your computer in an office environment or a home environment, you might need to share files with other people on your domain or in your workgroup. Rather than sending copies of files to everyone who might need them, you can place the files on a *shared drive* or in a *shared folder* from which other people can access them.

> **Tip** A shared drive might be the entire contents of a hard disk or of another internal or external storage device, such as a CD drive or USB flash drive.

You control which drives and folders on your computer are shared. By default, when you share a drive or a folder, any other user on the network can access the files stored there whenever your computer is turned on. They can see the contents of the drive or folder, open files, save changes, create new files on the drive or in the folder, and delete files from the drive or folder. You can limit access so that only selected people or groups of people can work with the contents, and you can limit the types of access granted to each person or group.

> **Tip** A shared drive or folder is indicated by an icon that includes the head-and-shoulders images of two people.

The Windows Vista user profile structure includes a Public user profile folder that contains the Public Documents, Public Downloads, Public Music, Public Pictures, and Public Videos folders. The contents of these shared folders are available to anyone using the computer, meaning that multiple users of the same computer can share files with each other by placing the files in these folders.

> **Tip** If you collaborate with a team of people on a document and you want to avoid the risk of one person overwriting another person's changes, you need to use a system with version control. If your organization has a collaboration site built with Microsoft SharePoint products and technologies, such as Microsoft Office SharePoint Server 2007, you can store the document in a document library so that only one person at a time can check out and work on the document.

In this exercise, you will share a folder on your computer with everyone else on your domain or in your workgroup.

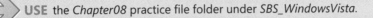

USE the *Chapter08* practice file folder under *SBS_WindowsVista*.

1. Display your **Documents** folder. Then browse to the *MSP\SBS_WindowsVista* subfolder.

2. In the **Content** pane, click the *Chapter08* folder, and on the toolbar, click **Share**.

   The File Sharing wizard starts.

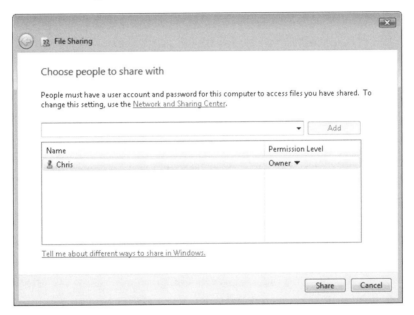

3. Click the arrow to the right of the empty box, click **Everyone**, and then click **Add**.

   Any person with a user account and password for this computer will now have read-only access to the *Chapter08* folder. You can change the access level from Reader to Contributor or Co-owner by clicking the Permission Level arrow and then clicking the type of access you want to allow.

4. Click **Share**. Then in the **User Account Control** dialog box, if you're logged on as an administrator, click **Continue**. Otherwise, enter an administrator password, and click **OK**.

Restricting Permission to a Shared Folder

By default, a shared drive or folder is available to everyone on your network. You can limit access to specific people or groups by removing Everyone from the permitted user list and adding only the people or groups you want.

To customize permissions for a shared folder:

1. Open the shared folder's **Properties** dialog box.

2. On the **Sharing** tab, click **Advanced Sharing**. Then in the **User Account Control** dialog box, if you're logged on as an administrator, click **Continue**. Otherwise, enter an administrator password, and click **OK**.

3. In the **Advanced Sharing** dialog box, select the **Share this folder** check box, and then click **Permissions**.

4. In the **Permissions** dialog box, with **Everyone** selected, click **Remove**. Then click **Add**.

5. In the **Select Users or Groups** dialog box, enter the Windows user account names or domain user account names of the people you want to have access to the shared folder, and then close the four open dialog boxes.

5. After the folder is shared, click **Done**.

In the Folders list and Content pane, the folder icon changes to reflect that the folder is shared.

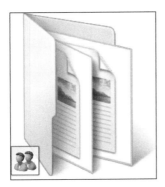

 CLOSE the Chapter08 window.

Key Points

- Every Windows Vista computer is part of either a workgroup or a domain. You can share resources with other computers through either of these networks. You can change your network configuration and switch between workgroup and domain connections.

- If your domain supports VPN connections, you can connect your computer to a domain over the Internet, from any location.

- You can connect to a domain computer from another computer and work on it as though you were sitting in front of it, by using Remote Desktop.

- You can connect over the Internet to a remote computer and interact with it directly as though it were your own desktop.

Keyboard Shortcuts

Press this	To do this
Ctrl+Esc	Open the Start menu
Alt+Up Arrow	View the folder one level up in Windows Explorer
F1	Display Help
Windows logo key+Break	Display the System Properties dialog box

Chapter at a Glance

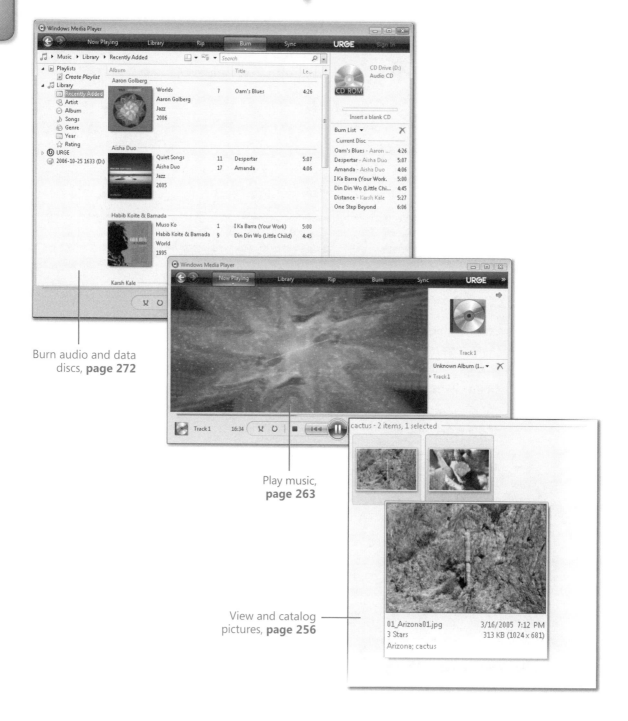

Burn audio and data
discs, **page 272**

Play music,
page 263

View and catalog
pictures, **page 256**

9 Working with Digital Media

In this chapter, you will learn to:

✔ View and catalog pictures.

✔ Play music.

✔ Configure Windows Media Center options.

✔ Burn audio and data discs.

✔ Share pictures and other digital media files.

These days, most people use their computers for more than simply creating documents, performing calculations, sending messages, and browsing the Internet. You might want to manage, manipulate, and print photographs; download, catalog, and listen to music; watch and create movies; and share digital pictures and media files with colleagues, friends, and family.

Windows Vista comes with built-in tools to help you make the most of your increasingly available digital media options. Whether you're working with media for personal or business purposes, you can use these tools to achieve professional results.

In this chapter, you will view and catalog pictures, play music, burn an audio CD or photo disc, and share pictures with other people on your network.

See Also Do you need only a quick refresher on the topics in this chapter? See the Quick Reference entries on pages xxxix–lxxiii.

Important Before you can use the practice files in this chapter, you need to install them from the book's companion CD to their default location. See "Using the Book's CD" on page xxix for more information.

Viewing and Cataloging Pictures

Windows Vista includes a powerful new tool for viewing, cataloging, and editing pictures, called Windows Photo Gallery. Photo Gallery is a substantial upgrade of the Windows Picture And Fax viewer available in Microsoft Windows XP. In addition to viewing, rotating, saving, and opening image files, you can do the following from the Photo Gallery window, without opening the file:

- Create and manage image collections
- Delete, rename, or copy a file
- View and edit file properties, including keywords
- Adjust photo exposure and color settings
- Fix red eye effects
- Precisely crop images to a standard or custom proportion

When opening a file from Photo Gallery you can select the image-editing program you want to use from those installed on your computer. After you finish manipulating image content, you can print pictures, order prints from a professional printing vendor, send pictures in e-mail, or burn them to a disc—all from the simple Windows Photo Gallery interface. If your computer system supports Windows Movie Maker, which also comes with Windows Vista, you can assemble pictures into a movie and view and catalog videos through Photo Gallery.

Designed for use with digital pictures from cameras and scanners, Photo Gallery supports the following file formats:

Image formats
Bitmap (.bmp)
Joint Photographic Experts Group (.jpeg)
JPEG File Interchange Format (.jfif)
Portable Network Graphics (.png)
Tagged Image File Format (.tiff)
Windows Portable Devices (.wpd)

Video formats
Advanced Systems Format (.asf)
Audio Video Interleave (.avi)
Microsoft Digital Video Recordinger-MS (.dvr-ms)
Moving Picture Experts Group (.mpeg)
Microsoft Windows Media Video (.wmv)

> **Troubleshooting** Pictures saved in other formats, such as Graphics Interchange Format (.gif) and Raw Image Data (.raw), will not show up in Photo Gallery even if they are stored in a cataloged folder. You will need to convert the picture to a supported format to be able to see and work with it in Photo Gallery.
>
> To run Movie Maker, your video card must support DirectX 9, and you must have video drivers designed for Windows Vista installed.

Double-clicking any file type associated with Windows Photo Gallery opens Photo Gallery and displays that file. The toolbar at the top of the window displays buttons and menus of commands for working with the displayed picture.

You can use the controls at the bottom of the Photo Gallery window to move forward or backward in the folder containing the selected file, display a slideshow of the images, reduce or magnify the image view, and rotate or delete selected images. The Info pane on the right displays properties of the selected image; you can add and edit information within the pane.

> **Tip** Click Info on the Windows Photo Gallery toolbar to display the Info pane.

When you click the Add Folder To Gallery or Go To Gallery button while viewing a picture in Photo Gallery, or when you click Windows Photo Gallery in the All Programs list on the Start menu, a Photo Gallery window opens in which you can view and work with all the supported-format pictures in all the folders you have added to the gallery. From this window, you can do the following:

- Select and work with one or more pictures.
- Sort all the pictures that have been added to the gallery, regardless of which folder they are stored in, by keyword (tag), date, or rating.
- View the pictures in a particular folder.

In this exercise, you will display a photo in Photo Gallery and then add the folder in which the photo is stored to the gallery. Then in the Photo Gallery window, you will sort and filter the files in various ways to find the ones you want. You will also add tags and adjust the properties of some photos so that they are easier to find.

> **USE** the practice files in the *Chapter09* folder under *SBS_WindowsVista*.
> **BE SURE TO** log on to Windows Vista and display your *Documents* folder before beginning this exercise.

1. In Windows Explorer, browse to the *MSP\SBS_WindowsVista\Chapter09* subfolder of your **Documents** folder.

2. In the **Content** pane, double-click the *01_Arizona10* image.

Windows Photo Gallery opens and displays the picture file.

Toolbar

Info pane

View controls

3. Without clicking the Add Folder To Gallery button, click each of the other toolbar buttons in turn to see what you can do with the displayed picture.

4. When you've finished exploring, click **Add Folder To Gallery**.

> **Troubleshooting** If the displayed picture is already part of a gallery, the Go To Gallery button appears in place of the Add Folder To Gallery button.

The Windows Photo Gallery window displays thumbnails of all the pictures in the *Chapter09* folder, where the *01_Arizona10* image is stored.

At the bottom of the Navigation pane, the *Chapter09* folder appears in the list of folders that are part of the gallery, along with your personal *Pictures* and *Videos* folders and the *Public Pictures* and *Public Videos* folders.

You can filter pictures in the gallery by tag, date taken, and rating.

5. At the top of the **Navigation** pane, under **Tags**, click **cactus**.

   The Content pane displays two pictures from the *Chapter09* folder.

6. If the Info pane isn't open, click **Info** on the toolbar.

7. With the *01_Arizona10* image selected, look at the file properties displayed in the Info pane.

   The *cactus* tag is one of the four tags associated with this image.

8. Point to the other image.

Photo Gallery displays a larger thumbnail that includes the file name, rating, tags, date and time taken, size on disk, and dimensions in pixels.

9. In the **Navigation** pane, under **Tags**, click **Flowers**.

The Content pane displays 13 items—12 pictures and a video—stored in several folders on your computer.

10. In the **Navigation** pane, under **Tags**, click **Wildlife**.

The Content pane displays four pictures and three videos. The videos are indicated by filmstrip markings on the left and right edges of the opening image of the video.

Obviously, tagging files with keywords provides a powerful way to locate pictures and videos about a particular subject. But it works best only when you tag all your images.

11. At the bottom of the **Navigation** pane, under **Folders**, click the *Chapter09* folder. Then in the **Content** pane, click the picture of the frog (*01_Frog*).

12. In the **Info** pane, click **Add Tags**. Then in the box that appears, type wi.

After a short pause, Windows Photo Gallery displays a list of existing tags that begin with these letters.

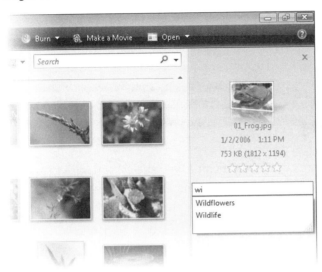

13. In the list, click **Wildlife**, and press the [Enter] key to apply the selected tag to the *01_Frog* image. Then close the **Info** pane.

14. In the left pane, click the **Wildlife** tag.

    The frog picture appears among the other Wildlife-tagged pictures.

Play Slide Show

15. At the center of the **View** controls at the bottom of the window, click the **Play Slide Show** button.

    Photo Gallery displays a full-screen slide show of the five pictures in the Wildlife category, shown in the order they appear in the Content pane (ascending file name order).

16. After viewing the slides once through, right-click the displayed image, and then click **Shuffle**.

    The slide display changes to a random order.

17. Press the [Esc] key to end the slide show.

CLOSE Windows Photo Gallery.

Retrieving Images from a Digital Camera or Scanner

If you have a digital camera or a scanner, you can easily download photographs to a computer that is running Windows Vista. If your camera or scanner is a USB device, Windows Vista recognizes the device and installs the drivers for it the first time you connect it. If your camera or scanner is not a USB device or a Plug And Play device, after connecting the device to your computer, open Control Panel, click Hardware And Sound, and then click Scanners And Cameras to start the Scanner And Camera Installation wizard, which will lead you through the connection process.

Your camera or scanner might come with special software to enable enhanced features. Some manufacturers recommend that you install this software before connecting the device to your computer, so it's a good idea to read the camera or scanner's manual first.

After Windows installs the drivers for your camera, the AutoPlay dialog box guides you through the process of importing or viewing photographs whenever you connect the camera to your computer. If you choose to import the photos, they are copied to your Pictures folder or another location you choose. Many digital cameras not only take photos but can also record video clips. You can download these clips in the same way you do photos.

> **Tip** If your digital camera stores images on some kind of removable memory media such as a compact flash card, you can transfer the images to your computer by using an appropriate adapter. Some computers come equipped with built-in cardreader drives for this purpose.

After Windows installs the drivers for your scanner, you can use Windows Fax And Scan, a program that comes with Windows Vista, to scan your photographs and store them on your computer.

See Also For information about Windows Fax And Scan, see "Using the Programs That Come with Windows Vista" in Chapter 7, "Working with Programs."

Playing Music

Windows Media Player is an easy-to-use program for managing catalogs of music, pictures, and videos, including recorded television programs. You can play or display any of these types of media by simply inserting a CD or DVD into your computer's CD or DVD drive, or by selecting the media you want to play from the Windows Media Player catalog or from a file on your computer. No special instructions are necessary for this simplest use of Windows Media Player. In this topic, we will discuss ways in which you can refine the Player's performance.

The first time you start Windows Media Player—for example, by inserting an audio CD into your CD drive and selecting the Play option in the AutoPlay dialog box—you have the option of manually setting up Windows Media Player. You can change the initial settings at any time, so it is simplest to select the Express Settings option and then click Finish, to get started with the most commonly used settings.

You can display the Player on your computer screen in any of these five modes:

- **Full mode.** The default mode. The CD plays in a window that includes a toolbar with navigation buttons and tabs that provide access to tasks you might want to perform with the media, a video display, a List pane displaying information about the media, and controls for playing the media and changing the window size.

Toolbar

List pane

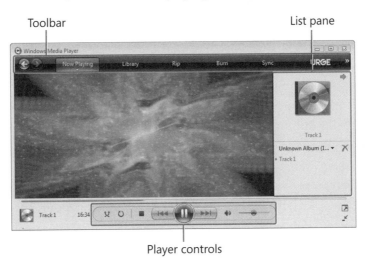

Player controls

The video pane can display the album cover art or a visualization of the music, or remain blank. To change the display, click the Now Playing arrow, point to Visualizations, and then click the option you want.

● **Compact mode.** Displays only the Player controls. You switch between full mode and compact mode by clicking the Switch Mode button in the lower-right corner of the Windows Media Player.

— View Full Screen
— Switch Mode

● **Mini Player mode.** Minimizes the Player to the Windows taskbar with access to the Player controls and other information. To display the Mini Player, right-click the Windows taskbar, point to Toolbars, and then click Windows Media Player. To switch back to the previous mode, click the Restore button.

Restore button

● **Full-screen mode.** Makes a video or picture fill the entire screen. Moving the mouse displays the Player controls. To switch to full-screen mode, click the View Full Screen button in either full or compact mode. Click the button again to switch back to the previous mode.

● **Skin mode.** Displays a small Player window with full controls. Can be customized with "skins" by means of which the Player takes on the shape and look of radios or other gadgets, mythical creatures, movie characters, or other animated graphic themes.

To switch to skin mode from full mode, right-click a blank area of the tab area or Player controls, point to View, and then click Skin Mode. The Player appears in the current skin in the upper-left corner of the desktop. To change the skin, click Skin Chooser on the View menu, select the skin you want, and then click Apply Skin. To return to full mode, right-click the skin mode Player, click Switch To Full Mode, and then click the Now Playing tab.

> **Tip** You can download skins from the Web by clicking More Skins in Skin Chooser.

Display ScreenTips to find the Player control you need

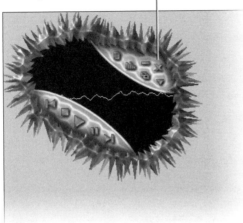

In full mode, the Windows Media Player toolbar includes tabs for the following tasks:

- **Now Playing.** Clicking this tab displays a menu from which you can play the current CD, show and hide the List pane, enhance the audio quality, display visual accompaniment to music, and download and install plug-in (helper) programs.

- **Library.** Clicking this tab lists the audio files stored on your computer that you have added to the library. They are cataloged by album, artist, and genre. Your *play lists* (compilations of tracks from various CDs and other sources) are also listed. You use commands on the tab's menu to create play lists, view the various types of media stored on your computer, add media files to the library, share media files, and download updated information about your media files from the Internet.

- **Rip.** Clicking this tab displays the tracks on the CD currently installed in your CD drive. You can select the tracks you want and rip (copy) them to your computer so that you can play them without the CD being inserted in the drive. Commands on this tab set the format and bit rate of the copy (which affects the size of the file and quality of the sound), and determine whether CDs are automatically ripped and whether the CD is ejected after ripping.

- **Burn.** Clicking this tab lists the audio files in the library so that you can select tracks to create a burn list. Commands on the tab enable you to specify whether the disc is ejected after burning and whether the sound should be adjusted so that it is consistent across tracks.

- **Sync.** Clicking this tab lists the audio files in the library so that you can select tracks to copy to a portable music device. You can also copy files from the device to your computer. In this way, any changes you make to one are synchronized with the other.

- **URGE.** Clicking this tab displays the URGE Web site, which is hosted on the Windows Media Web site. It includes links to various entertainment options on the Internet, including music download sites.

All the tabs except URGE include a More Options command that displays the Options dialog box where you can change Windows Media Player settings. If you have worked with a previous version of Windows Media Player, you can display the classic menu bar above the taskbar in the window.

> **Tip** You must be in full mode to display the classic menu bar.

In this exercise, you will view the Windows Media Player 11 Series settings, display the menu bar, and personalize the look and feel of the Player by changing the skin.

> **BE SURE TO** have an active Internet connection before beginning this exercise.

1. On the **Start** menu, point to **All Programs**, and then click **Windows Media Player**.

> **Troubleshooting** If this is the first time you have started Windows Media Player, select the default Express Settings installation option, and then click Finish.

2. On the toolbar, click each tab except URGE to see its display in the window, and then click each tab's arrow to see its commands.

3. Click the **Rip** tab's arrow, and then click **More Options**.

   The Options dialog box opens with the Rip Music tab active.

4. Explore the tabs of the **Options** dialog box, noticing how you can customize many different types of Player settings.

5. Make any changes you want, and then click **OK**, or simply click **Cancel** to close the dialog box without making any changes.

6. Right-click a blank area of the toolbar or the **Player controls** area, and then click **Show Classic Menus**.

    The available commands are arranged on the menu bar in five menus: File, View, Play, Tools, and Help.

7. Click the **File** menu, and then point to each menu in turn to see its commands. Then on the **View** menu, click **Skin Chooser**.

    The window changes so that you can choose a skin. The available skins are listed on the left and a preview of the selected skin appears on the right.

8. Click **More Skins**.

   The Skins For Windows Media Player page opens in your Web browser.

9. Scroll the list of skins, and follow the directions to download a few that you like.

   For the purposes of this exercise, download only skins created by Microsoft. You can come back and explore other skins later.

10. When you have finished downloading skins, close your browser window.

11. In the Skin Chooser window, click your favorite skin, and then click **Apply Skin**.

   Windows Media Player changes to reflect your selection and switches to skin mode. For example, the *gadget* skin looks like a space-age burled wood jukebox.

> **Tip** Move the mouse pointer over the buttons on the skin you select to learn what features are available for that skin.

Return to Full Mode

12. On the skin, click the **Return to Full Mode** button to redisplay the Skin Chooser window.

> **Troubleshooting** The appearance of the Return To Full Mode button changes to match the skin, but the icon is the same for all skins.

BE SURE TO apply the skin you want to use and, if you want to, repeat Step 6 to hide the menu bar before continuing.

CLOSE the Windows Media Player window.

Configuring Windows Media Center Options

You no longer need to purchase a separate edition of the operating system to enable the powerful Windows Media Center functionality on your computer or designated media server—it is built right into Windows Vista. Although it provides capabilities for viewing and cataloging photographs that are superior to those of Windows Photo Gallery and capabilities for collecting and playing music and videos that are superior to those of Windows Media Player, the main appeal of Windows Media Center is its ability to expand your television into a total entertainment center that accesses content on or through your computer. With a built-in or external analog or digital TV tuner, you can use Windows Media Center to pause, rewind, and record television programs (more than one at a time), including high-definition television (HDTV). And you can do it all from across the room with a remote control.

As with Windows Media Player, you can choose an Express or Custom setup the first time you start Windows Media Center. The Express setup takes less than one minute, and you can immediately get started. For example, you can display a dramatic slide show of photos, with Media Center automatically panning, zooming, and transitioning in a highly professional fashion. By default, Windows Media Center scans your Music, Pictures, and Videos folders for media files. You add or remove any folders you like.

At any time after you complete the initial setup process, you can change settings for all of your media-related tasks through the Windows Media Center. To configure the options, open Windows Media Center from the Start menu, go to Tasks, and then click Settings.

General settings include:

- **Startup and Window Behavior.** Automatically start Media Center when you log on and control window and taskbar interactions.

- **Visual and Sound Effects.** Control transitions between screens and images, sounds, color scheme, and the background color displayed behind images or videos.

- **Program Library Options.** Control which of the programs installed on your computer are available from within Media Center and whether those programs can control content and access media information through Media Center.

- **Windows Media Center Setup.** Manually set up the Internet connection, TV signal, speakers, and display used by Media Center.

- **Parental Controls.** Block the display of content you deem inappropriate for your children. You can temporarily unblock content by entering a four-digit access code of your choosing.

- **Automatic Download Options.** Retrieve media display information from the Internet manually or automatically.

- **Optimization.** Schedule regular maintenance of Windows Media Center at a time that is convenient to you.

- **Privacy.** Control the sending of anonymous usage and reliability information from your computer system to Microsoft, and prevent Media Center from keeping track of the shows you view the most.

If your computer system has a built-in or external TV tuner, you can watch and record television programs on your computer. Windows Media Center downloads television program listings from the Internet. TV settings include:

- **Set Up TV Signal.** Configure Media Center as a television receiver.

- **Configure Your TV or Monitor.** Control the way Media Center displays content on your monitor or another display you connect to the computer.

- **TV Audio.** Choose the audio output you want; available options depend on your system.

- **TV Closed Captioning.** When watching television programs through Media Center, you control the display of closed captioning (when available).

When displaying a slide show of images from your Pictures folder or another folder you select, you can control the following settings:

- **Show pictures in random order.** Display a slide show of pictures in the order they appear in the folder or in random order.

- **Show pictures in subfolders.** Include or exclude images stored in subfolders of your Pictures or other selected folder.

- **Show caption.** If caption information is saved with an image, you can display it as part of a slide show.

- **Show song information during slide show.** If a slide show is accompanied by music, you can display the song title and artist during each song or only at the beginning and end.

When playing music through Windows Media Center, you can display graphic visualizations of the melody, and show the song title, artist, and other available information during the song or at its beginning and end.

DVD settings include:

- **DVD Language.** You can select language preferences for subtitles, audio tracks, and menus. Your preferences will be automatically selected when viewing a DVD with alternative language selections.

- **Closed Captioning.** Control the display of closed captioning when available on a DVD.

- **Remote Control Options.** Program the actions of remote control buttons.

If you are a serious collector of digital photos, music, and movies, or a television aficionado, you will likely find the Windows Media Center experience a delight.

Burning Audio and Data Discs

With CD and DVD burners becoming increasingly standard with new computer systems and increasingly affordable additions to older ones, *burning* audio and data CDs and DVDs is becoming more common as a means of backing up documents, pictures, and music. You don't need to buy a special program to burn your own discs—all the necessary software is part of Windows Vista.

You can create CDs and DVDs in one of two formats:

- **Live File System.** This new disc format is the Windows Vista default format for saving data to a disc. Files are copied, rather than burned, to the disc, without being "staged" in an area of your computer's memory first. You can copy additional files to the disc at a later time and erase files you no longer need from the disc. When you eject the disc from the drive, Windows Vista finalizes the session before opening the drive. Live File System discs are compatible only with Windows XP and later computers.

- **Mastered.** This disc format was the standard when burning discs with Windows XP. A Mastered disc creates a closed session, meaning that no additional data can be added to the disc after you burn it. Files are first gathered into a Temporary Burn Folder and then burned to the disc in one session. After burning the files, the disc is closed and you cannot add or delete data. Mastered discs are compatible with earlier versions of Windows.

To burn a folder of picture files from Windows Explorer:

1. In Windows Explorer, navigate to the folder containing the files you want to burn to CD or DVD. Select either the entire folder or individual files, and then on the toolbar, click Burn.

Windows Vista copies the selected files to a Temporary Burn Folder, then opens your disc burner drive and prompts you to insert a writable disc. If you view the disc burner drive in Windows Explorer, you can see the files that will be burned to the disc.

2. Insert a blank CD or DVD in the drive.

   After scanning the inserted disc, the Burn A Disc dialog box opens.

   > **Troubleshooting** If the disc you insert is write-protected due to a previous mastered burn attempt, Windows Vista rejects the disc and asks you to insert another.

3. In the **Burn a Disc** dialog box, enter a name in the **Disc title** box. This is the name that will appear next to the drive letter in Windows Explorer when the disc is in a drive.

4. If you don't intend to burn more data to the disc or want to ensure that the disc is compatible with older operating systems and with CD or DVD players, click the **Show formatting options** button, and in the expanded **Burn a Disc** dialog box, select the **Mastered** option.

5. Click **Next**.

   If you are creating a Live File System disc, Windows Vista formats the disc and copies the selected files to it, and then displays the files in Windows Explorer under the heading Files Currently On The Disc. You can leave the disc in the drive and continue to update its contents, or remove the disc from the drive. When you eject the disc from the drive, Windows Vista first prepares the disc by closing the session.

To copy additional data to a Live File System format disc, insert the disc in the drive, and then either select the files you want to copy in Windows Explorer and click the Burn button, or display the disc contents in Windows Explorer and drag additional files to it.

If you are creating a Mastered disc, Windows Explorer displays the drive, with the selected files listed under the heading Files Ready To Be Written To The Disc, and you then need to click Burn To Disc on the toolbar to initiate the burn.

> **Tip** You can delete files from the Files Ready To Be Written To The Disc list, and add others, before burning the disc.

To burn music tracks to disc from Windows Media Player:

1. In full mode, click the **Burn** tab.

2. Drag the album, play list, or tracks you want to burn into the **Burn List** area of the **List** pane.

3. At the bottom of the **List** pane, click **Start Burn**.

4. When prompted, insert a writeable CD or DVD into your computer's disc burner.

   Windows Media Player burns the music files to the disc, and after burning the last track, it finalizes (closes) the disc and then ejects it.

Sharing Pictures and Other Digital Media Files

If several people work on your computer, you can make your pictures, music, and video files available to them by storing them in your computer's Public folders. If your computer is connected to a network, you can share the folders in which you store your media files so that other people on your network can access them.

See Also For information about sharing folders, see "Sharing Drives and Folders" in Chapter 8, "Making Connections."

You can also use Windows Photo Gallery or Windows Media Player to share a collection of media files with other computers running Windows Vista. Usually this type of sharing happens on a home network.

In Windows Photo Gallery, you turn on media sharing by clicking the File button on the toolbar and then clicking Share With Devices. In Windows Media Player, you click the Library arrow and then click Media Sharing. In either case, the Media Sharing dialog box opens. However, in the case of Windows Media Player, you can look for media files that have been shared by other people in addition to sharing your own media files.

In this exercise, you will use Windows Photo Gallery to share your media files with other people on your network.

USE the practice files in the *Chapter09* folder under *SBS_WindowsVista*.

 1. On the **Start** menu, point to **All Programs**, and then click **Windows Photo Gallery**.
 2. On the toolbar, click the **File** button, and then click **Share With Devices**.

    The Media Sharing dialog box opens.

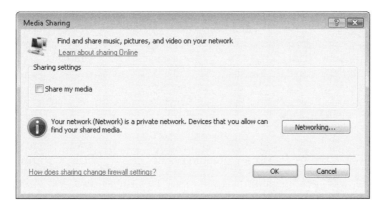

3. Under **Sharing settings**, select the **Share my media** check box, and click **OK**. Then in the **User Account Control** dialog box, if you're logged on as an administrator, click **Continue**. Otherwise, enter an administrator password, and click **OK**.

   The Media Sharing dialog box expands so that you can allow or deny specific users.

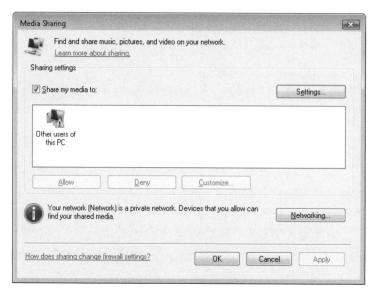

4. In the expanded dialog box, click **Settings**.

   The Media Sharing - Default Settings dialog box opens.

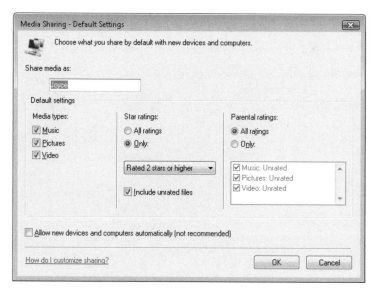

In the **Share media as** box, you can change the name of the collection of media files you are sharing.

5. Select or clear the check boxes under **Media types**, **Star ratings**, and **Parental ratings** to include only the specific media files you want to share.

6. Click **OK** to close the Media Sharing – Default Settings dialog box, and then click **OK** to close the Media Sharing dialog box.

   Nothing appears to have happened, but the specified media files are now available to other people on your network.

7. Display **Control Panel**, click **Network and Internet**, and then click **Network and Sharing Center**.

   Under Sharing And Discovery, Media Sharing is now turned on.

 CLOSE the Control Panel and Windows Photo Gallery windows.

Key Points

- With Windows Photo Gallery, you can view, catalog, search, and sort all the pictures stored on your computer.

- With Windows Media Player, you can create play lists of music tracks from various sources and play music in various modes on your computer.

- Windows Vista makes it easy to burn CDs and DVDs without third-party software. You can burn additional files to a disc at a later time.

- You can share digital media that meets specific criteria with other people on your network without having to share drives or folders.

Keyboard Shortcuts

Press this	To do this in Windows Media Player
Ctrl+M	Show or hide the menu bar
Ctrl+2	Switch to skin mode
Shift when you insert a CD	Stop a CD from playing automatically

Press this	To do this in Windows Photo Gallery
Ctrl+F	Open the Fix pane
Ctrl+P	Print the selected picture
Enter	View the selected picture at a larger size
Ctrl+I	Open or close the Details pane
Ctrl+period (.)	Rotate the picture clockwise
Ctrl+comma (,)	Rotate the picture counter-clockwise
F2	Rename the selected item
Ctrl+E	Search for an item
Alt+Left Arrow	Go back
Alt+Right Arrow	Go forward
Plus sign (+)	Zoom in or resize the picture thumbnail
Minus sign (-)	Zoom out or resize the picture thumbnail
Ctrl+B	Best fit
Left Arrow	Select the previous item
Down Arrow	Select the next item or row
Up Arrow	Previous item (Easel) or previous row (Thumbnail)

Page Up	Previous screen
Page Down	Next screen
Home	Select the first item
End	Select the last item
Delete	Move the selected item to the Recycle Bin
Shift+Delete	Permanently delete the selected item
Left Arrow	Collapse node
Right Arrow	Expand node
J	Move back one video frame
K	Pause the video playback
L	Move forward one video frame
I	Set the start trim point
O	Set the end trim point
M	Split a video clip
Home	Stop and rewind all the way back to the start trim point
Alt+Right Arrow	Advance to the next video frame
Alt+Left Arrow	Go back to the previous video frame
Ctrl+K	Stop and rewind video playback
Ctrl+P	Play video from the current location
Home	Move the start trim point
End	Move to the end trim point
Page Up	Seek to nearest split point before the current location
Page Down	Seek to nearest split point after the current location

Chapter at a Glance

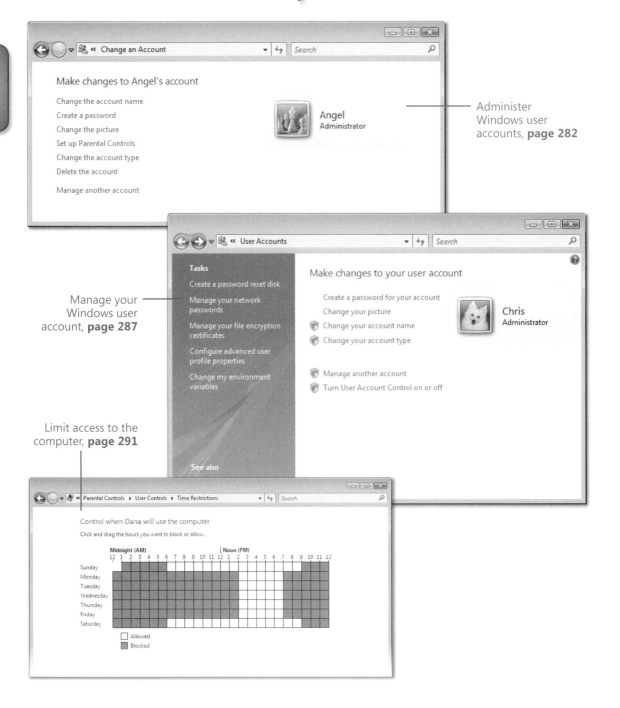

Administer Windows user accounts, **page 282**

Manage your Windows user account, **page 287**

Limit access to the computer, **page 291**

10 Managing Computer Security

In this chapter, you will learn to:

✔ Administer Windows user accounts.

✔ Manage your Windows user account.

✔ Limit access to the computer, to programs, and to the Internet.

✔ Analyze your computer's security.

✔ Configure Internet security zones.

In the old days, computers were isolated from each other, and the only way to transfer information among them was on a floppy disk (now referred to as "sneaker net"). With the advent of networks, information transfer became easier, but so did the possibility that the information stored on a computer would be accessed inappropriately or even illegally from another computer. As networks have grown from small to large, and worldwide access to local area networks has become simple and commonplace, concerns about information security have also increased.

Computer security is a hot topic these days. The proliferation of Internet access and e-mail in homes and workplaces around the world has provided a new (and relatively simple) avenue for malicious intrusion into our lives. It is important to be aware of the possible security vulnerabilities of each computer you work on, whether at home, at school, at work, or in a public place such as an Internet café. It is also important to protect yourself on all these computers through correct network setups, appropriate virus scanning software, and informed computing habits.

In this chapter, you will create user accounts, change user account information, restrict user account access, and manage some of your computer's security settings.

See Also Do you need only a quick refresher on the topics in this chapter? See the Quick Reference entries on pages xxxix–lxxiii.

> **Important** Before you can use the practice files in this chapter, you need to install them from the book's companion CD to their default location. See "Using the Book's CD" on page xxix for more information.

Administering Windows User Accounts

Windows Vista protects the information on your computer through a system of *user accounts* and *passwords*, which at one time were available only for computers that were part of a domain. Windows Vista extends this account and password system to workgroup computers so that more than one person can use the same computer. For example, if you manage your family's financial records on a home computer that is also used by your children to do their homework, you can set up separate accounts for your children so that they can't view confidential information or change your files.

The great thing about user accounts and passwords is that they help keep your information private. You can prevent other users from reading or altering your documents, pictures, music, and other files by storing them in the subfolders automatically set up under your user folder. You can share files by placing them in a Public folder or any folder outside of your user folder. (You can also specifically share the subfolders under your user folder, but you don't have to.) With Windows Vista, each user can personalize his or her own working environment and have easy access to frequently used files and applications without worrying about other people making changes to personal settings.

The user account and password system also means that Windows Vista can help you protect your computer from unauthorized changes. Windows Vista supports two levels of computer-specific privileges: Administrator and Standard. The first user account created on your computer is designated as an administrator account. This type of account has higher-level permissions than a standard account, which means that an administrator account owner can perform tasks on your computer that a standard account owner cannot.

Administrator account permissions are necessary to do things such as:

- Create, change, and delete accounts.
- Make system-wide changes.
- Install and remove programs.
- Access all files.

Tasks that require administrator permissions are indicated by a Windows security icon.

Standard account permissions allow a user to do things that affect only his or her own account, including:

- Change or remove the password.
- Change the user account picture.
- Change the theme and desktop settings.
- View files he or she created and files in the Public folders.

> **Tip** Windows creates a special account called *Guest*, which is inactive by default and disabled on computers that are part of a domain. You can activate the Guest account to give people limited access to your computer without having to create individual user accounts.

If you have an administrator account, it is a good idea to also create a standard account for your day-to-day computing. Logging on with a standard account will not prevent you from installing software or taking other administrator-level actions, because when Windows Vista requires administrator permissions to complete a task, it displays the User Account Control dialog box, requiring that you enter an administrator password to continue, or if you are logged on as an administrator, confirm that you want to continue the restricted task. (Any administrator can enter his or her password.) After receiving the password, Windows continues with the task.

The advantage of logging on with a standard account is that if malicious software (malware) or spyware sneaks onto your computer or if another person gains access to your computer (either in person or over the Internet) while you are logged on as a standard user, they are blocked from performing administrative tasks because they can't supply the administrator password. If you are logged on as an administrator, you have already supplied the password, leaving you vulnerable to these types of intrusions.

A computer running Windows Vista supports multiple user accounts. Every account has an associated *user account name* and a *user account picture*. Any user can change his or her own account name and picture and can create or change his or her own password; users with administrator permissions can change any user's account name and picture.

> **Important** If your computer is part of a domain, network permissions are administered through your domain account. You might be able to create a new account on your local computer, but you cannot create or modify a domain user account.

In this exercise, you will create a new user account with administrative privileges on your computer, change its privileges, and create a password. You will then delete the account. There are no practice files for this exercise.

> **BE SURE TO** log on to Windows Vista and display Control Panel before beginning this exercise.

1. In **Control Panel**, under **User Accounts and Family Safety**, click the **Add or remove user accounts** task. Then in the **User Account Control** dialog box, if you're logged on as an administrator, click **Continue**. Otherwise, enter an administrator password, and click **OK**.

> **Troubleshooting** If you are running Windows Vista Business Edition, you have a User Accounts category rather than User Accounts And Family Safety. The steps to complete the tasks in this chapter vary slightly from those given.

The Manage Accounts window opens.

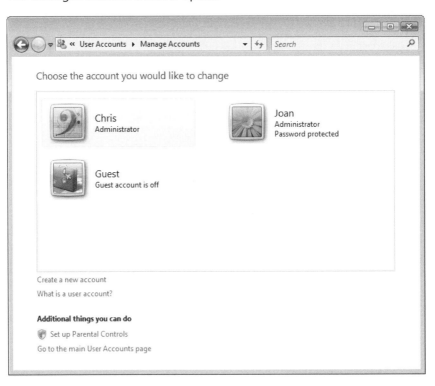

2. Click the **Create a new account** task.

The Create New Account page opens.

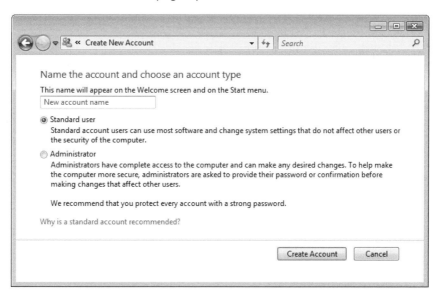

3. In the **New account name** box, type Angel. Select the **Administrator** option, and then click **Create Account**.

Windows Vista creates a new account called *Angel*, and assigns a user account picture to the account, which now appears in the Manage Accounts window.

4. In the **Manage Accounts** window, click **Angel**.

The Make Changes To Angel's Account page displays the options for changing the selected account.

5. Click the **Change the account type** task.

6. On the **Choose a new account type for Angel** page, select the **Standard user** option, and then click **Change Account Type**.

   On the Make Changes To Angel's Account page, *Standard user* appears under Angel's user account name.

7. Click the **Create a password** task.

   The Create A Password For Angel's Account page opens.

8. In the **New password** box, type Meow! and then press the ⌨Tab key to move to the next field.

   To ensure the secrecy of the password, the characters are displayed as dots as you type.

9. In the **Confirm new password** box, retype Meow!

10. In the **Type a password hint** box, type What does Angel say?

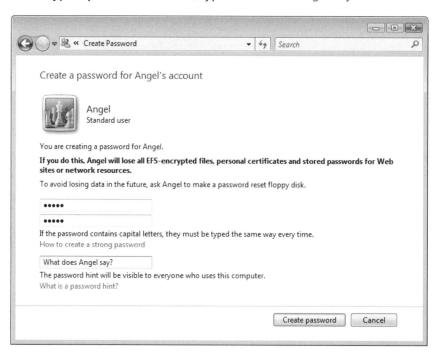

11. Click **Create password** to save the password as part of Angel's user account profile.

   On the Make Changes To Angel's Account page, *Password protected* appears under Angel's user account type.

12. Click the **Delete the account** task.

> **Troubleshooting** You cannot delete a user account while it is logged on to the computer; you must switch to that user account and log it off before you can delete it.

When you delete a user account, you can choose to keep the content of selected personal folders, to ensure that you don't delete files that person might want to keep.

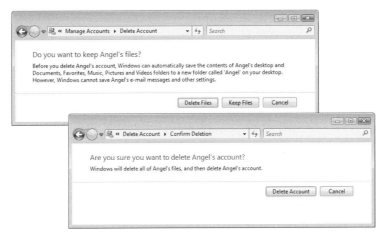

13. Angel has not created any files that you care about, so click **Delete Files**. Then on the **Confirm Deletion** page, click **Delete Account**.

Angel's account no longer appears among the active accounts.

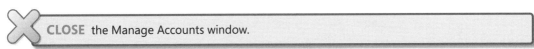

CLOSE the Manage Accounts window.

Managing Your Windows User Account

On the logon screen, each user account is represented by the user account name and also by a user account picture. Windows Vista comes with 12 user account pictures, representing a variety of animals, sports, and interests. You can select the picture that most closely matches your personality or interests. If none of the default pictures is to your liking, you can use a picture of your own.

You can use *bitmap (BMP)* files, *Graphic Interchange Format (GIF)* files, *Joint Photographic Expert Group (JPEG)* files, or *Portable Network Graphics (PNG)* files as user account pictures. The original graphic can be any size, but the user account picture is always displayed at 48 pixels high by 48 pixels wide. If you select a graphic whose height and width are not the same, the graphic will be stretched or cropped to a square shape when displayed.

In this exercise, you will first change your user account picture to one provided by Windows Vista, and then you will switch to a custom graphic.

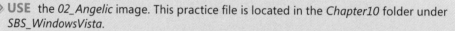

USE the *02_Angelic* image. This practice file is located in the *Chapter10* folder under *SBS_WindowsVista*.

OPEN Control Panel before beginning this exercise.

1. In **Control Panel**, click **User Accounts and Family Safety**, and then under **User Accounts**, click the **Change your account picture** task.

   The Change Your Picture window displays the built-in user account picture options.

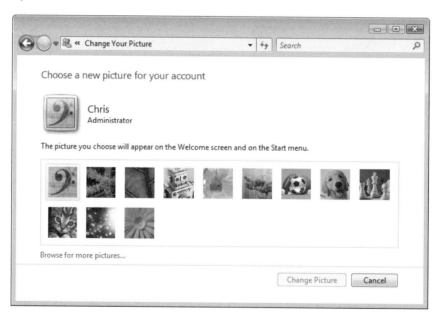

2. Click any picture that you like, and then click **Change Picture**.

Your new user account picture is shown in the User Accounts window. You can also see it at the top of the Start menu.

3. In the **User Accounts** window, click the **Change your picture** task. Then in the **Change Your Picture** window, click **Browse for more pictures**.

The Open dialog box displays the contents of your Pictures folder.

4. In the **Favorite Links** list, click **Documents**, and then navigate to the *MSP\SBS_WindowsVista\Chapter10* subfolder.

5. Click the *02_Angelic* image, and then click **Open**.

The User Accounts window displays your custom picture.

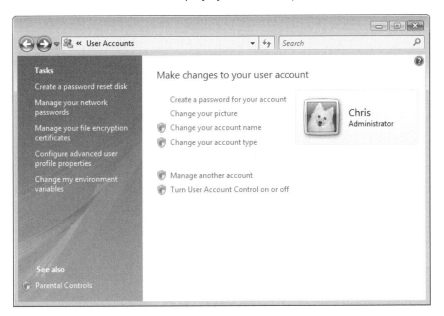

The custom picture is also now available in the Change Your Picture window.

CLOSE the User Accounts window.

Backing Up Your Windows Password

When you protect your Windows Vista user account by assigning a password, you have the option of creating a password hint. Windows Vista displays the password hint if you enter an incorrect password. If you didn't save a password hint, you can reset your password—but in order to do so you must first have created a password reset disk.

> **Tip** You can create a password reset disk only for a local user account, not for a domain user account.

If you password-protect your account, you might want to create a password reset disk in the event that you lose or forget your password. (It might sound unlikely, but it can happen, especially in an environment that requires you to change your password on a regular basis.) You can save the password reset file on either a USB flash drive or a floppy disk (but not on a CD).

To create a password reset disk:

1. Insert a USB flash drive or floppy disk in your computer.

2. In **Control Panel**, click **User Accounts and Family Safety**, and then click **User Accounts**.

3. In the **Tasks** list, click the **Create a password reset disk** task.

   The Forgotten Password wizard starts.

4. On the **Welcome** page, click **Next**.

5. On the **Create a Password Reset Disk** page, select the USB flash drive or floppy disk drive you want to use, and then click **Next**.

6. On the **Current User Account Password** page, enter the password you use to log on to Windows Vista, and then click **Next**.

7. When the **Progress** bar displays *100% complete*, click **Next**. Then click **Finish**.

Be sure to store the password reset disk in a safe place, because anyone can use it to reset your password and gain access to your computer.

Limiting Access to the Computer, to Programs, and to the Internet

If you want to allow or encourage your children to use the computer but are concerned about the amount of time or hours of the day they might spend "surfing" the Web or playing games, you can set time limits on their computer use and restrict access to games, to specific programs, and to Web sites displaying objectionable content. After setting up parental controls, you can generate activity reports to follow up on actual computer usage. And although this level of policing might not be necessary, perhaps just knowing that you can do it will provide some reassurance to you or reinforcement for your children.

> **Tip** Windows Vista parental controls are available only on computers that are part of a workgroup, not on computers that are part of a domain. Domain computers are administered centrally.

> **Important** Anyone with an administrator account on your computer can remove the parental controls you set. For the controls to be fully effective, you need to protect each administrator account with a password and disable the Guest account if it is not password-protected.

In this exercise, you will set parental controls for another user account on your computer to limit the amount of time that user is allowed on the computer. You will then view the activity report that will be generated. There are no practice files for this exercise.

> ▷ **BE SURE TO** set up a second user account on your computer before beginning this exercise.

1. Display **Control Panel**, and under **User Accounts and Family Safety**, click the **Set up parental controls for any user** task. Then in the **User Account Control** dialog box, if you're logged on as an administrator, click **Continue**. Otherwise, enter an administrator password, and click **OK**.

    The Parental Controls window opens.

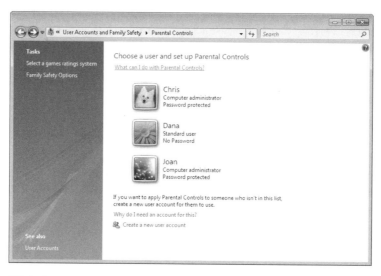

2. Click the user you want to set a time limit for.

   The User Controls window opens.

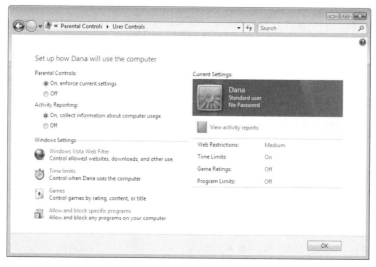

3. Under **Parental Controls**, select the **On, enforce current settings** option, and then under **Windows Settings**, click **Time limits**.

   The Time Restrictions window opens.

4. Click each hour in the grid that you want to block.

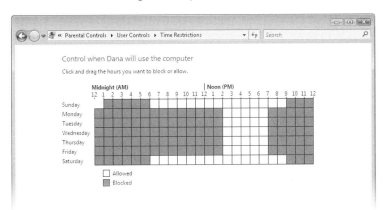

During the blocked time periods, if the selected user tries to log on to his or her account, Windows Vista denies access to the account and displays a message that the user account is blocked at that time.

5. In the **Time Restrictions** window, click **OK**.

6. In the **User Controls** window, with the **On, collect information about computer usage** option selected under **Activity Reporting**, click **View activity reports**.

The Activity Viewer displays the current (blank) report.

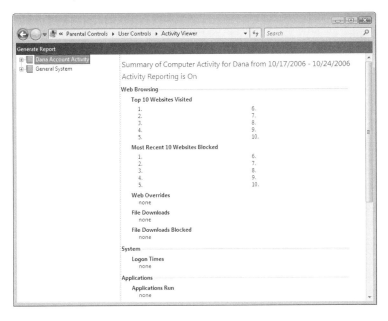

Back

7. Scroll the report to see the kinds of activities it tracks. Then in the upper-left corner of the Activity Viewer window, click the **Back** button.

8. Under **Windows Settings**, investigate the **Windows Vista Web Filter**, **Games**, and **Allow and block specific programs** controls. Adjust the parental controls as you want, and then click **OK**.

BE SURE TO turn off the parental controls if you don't want to use them.

CLOSE the Parental Controls window.

See Also For information about limiting access to objectionable Internet content on a broader scale, see "Restricting Objectionable Content" in Chapter 6, "Safely and Efficiently Accessing the Internet."

Analyzing Your Computer's Security

Most people think of security in terms of protecting a computer and the information stored on it against attacks by malicious programs such as *viruses* and malicious people known as *hackers*. Windows Vista is the most secure Microsoft operating system to date. It helps you protect your computer from these and other external threats with a number of built-in security features, including:

- *Windows Firewall*, which helps you prevent unauthorized transmissions to and from your computer.

- *Windows Defender*, which helps you detect software that might pose a potential threat to your privacy or your computer.

- *Windows Security Center*, which monitors the types of protection on your system.

- *User Account Control*, which requires specific acknowledgment and an administrator password when accessing settings that could disrupt your computer or affect its users.

- *Windows Update*, which makes it easy for you to ensure that your computer has the latest security tools.

Important Windows Vista does not include a virus scanning program, so you will need to purchase and install one yourself. Many commercial software packages that detect and treat computer viruses are available.

Any computer that is connected to the Internet, whether full-time or intermittently, is exposed to the risk of attack. This risk should always be taken seriously. You can protect your system in the following ways:

- **Work behind a firewall.** If you have a direct Internet connection, the firewall that is built into Windows Vista forms a secure bridge between the external Internet and your computer. If you are working on a home network, your firewall might be installed on the computer that controls communications between your home network and the Internet. If you're working on a domain, the firewall is a secure bridge between the Internet and your organization's intranet, to which your computer is connected. In all cases, the firewall protects your computer from intrusion.

  Windows Vista includes Windows Firewall, a program that protects your computer from initiating or receiving unauthorized external connections, such as those attempted by certain kinds of computer viruses. With Windows Firewall, the only connections that can be made to your computer are those either initiated or approved by you.

  Windows Firewall is turned on by default for all users and all connections to your computer, including local area network (LAN), Virtual Private Network (VPN), and dial-up connections. Windows Firewall settings are controlled from the Windows Security Center. You can make changes to the configuration of Windows Firewall for your own user profile without affecting other users' configurations.

- **Protect your computer with Windows Defender.** While you are connected to the Internet, malicious software (malware) and spyware might try to install themselves on your computer. They can also be attached to CDs and DVDs. Once installed, they can harm your computer or steal information, either immediately or at a future time. Windows Defender, which comes with Windows Vista, helps you protect your computer by alerting you when an installation program starts, or when a program tries to run itself or change your settings.

  As with a virus-protection program, you can use Windows Defender to scan your computer for suspicious software, either manually or on a regular schedule. It can quarantine or remove any malware or spyware it finds. It is important to keep the Windows Defender database of the software you don't want on your computer up to date, because Windows Defender uses this database (which consists of files called *definitions*) to identify the software. Fortunately, you can rely on Windows Update to automatically update the Windows Defender definitions.

- **Install all available security upgrades.** Use Windows Update to automatically keep your Windows Vista computer up to date with official Microsoft-issued product updates and Windows Defender definitions.

  See Also For more information about Windows Update, see "Updating Windows System Files" in Chapter 1, "Getting Started with Windows Vista."

- **Use third-party antivirus software.** Select a program that monitors your hard disk drive and external drives, as well as all incoming and outgoing files.

- **Never open unidentified e-mail attachments.** In particular, don't open any files that have an *.exe* extension.

  See Also For more information about e-mail security, refer to *Microsoft Office Outlook 2007 Step by Step* or *Windows Vista Step by Step, Deluxe Edition* by Joan Preppernau and Joyce Cox (Microsoft Press, 2007).

- **Regularly check Windows Security Center.** You can make sure all your computer systems are set for optimal protection in this one handy location.

In this exercise, you will examine your Windows Firewall setting options. Then you will explore and modify the Windows Defender options. Finally, you will view the status of your computer's protection against unauthorized external connections, viruses, spyware, and other threats. There are no practice files for this exercise.

> **BE SURE TO** display Control Panel before beginning this exercise.

1. In **Control Panel**, click **Security**, and then click **Security Center**.

   Windows Security Center opens.

2. In the left pane of the **Windows Security Center** window, click **Windows Firewall**.

   Windows Firewall opens.

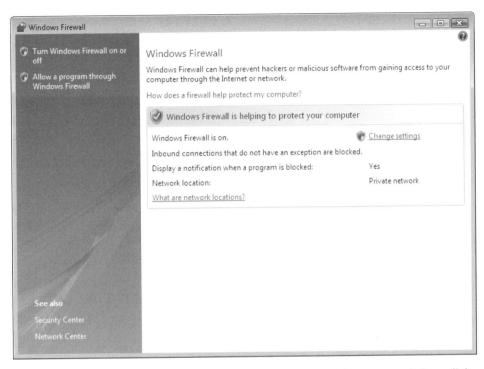

3. Read the information about your current Windows Firewall status, and then click **Change settings**. In the **User Account Control** dialog box, if you're logged on as an administrator, click **Continue**. Otherwise, enter an administrator password, and click **OK**.

The Windows Firewall Settings dialog box opens, displaying the General tab. If your computer is connected to a domain, the settings might be unavailable (gray), indicating that firewall policies are controlled by the domain administrator.

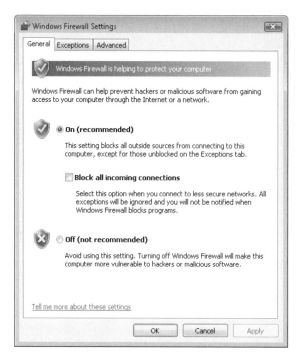

4. Read the descriptions of the three basic options: **On (recommended)**, **Block all incoming connections**, and **Off (not recommended)**.

Unless you have another firewall protecting your computer, the On option should always be selected. Before you use an unsecured or otherwise risky connection (such as a free Internet connection in a public location), return to this dialog box and select the Block All Incoming Connections check box.

> **Tip** Clicking the Tell Me More About These Settings link at the bottom of the tab displays the Understanding Windows Firewall Settings topic in Windows Help And Support. You can find further information about Windows Firewall here.

5. In the **Windows Firewall Settings** dialog box, click the **Exceptions** tab. Then scroll the **Program or port** list to see the basic exception types, noting which items are selected.

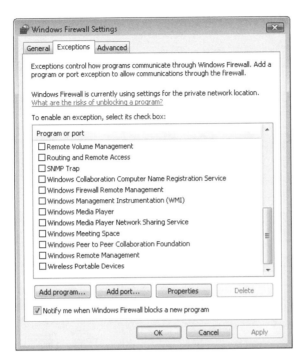

You can specifically allow external communications by certain types of programs by selecting the corresponding check boxes on this tab. When Windows Firewall prompts you to allow or deny a connection from a program you are using, connections that you allow are selected here. (And you can reverse your selection from here.) You can add a specific program or the port it uses to the list, and you can specify whether the program or port is unblocked for external communications with any computer, only the computers on your network, or only specific computers. (If you play interactive Internet games, you might find it necessary to unblock a specific port.)

6. Click the **Advanced** tab to display a list of the network connections currently protected by Windows Firewall.

You can select each individual network connection to be protected by Windows Firewall. If you are concerned that your firewall protection might be compromised by settings you've changed, you can restore the default Windows Firewall settings at any time.

7. In the **Windows Firewall Settings** dialog box, click **Cancel**. Then close the **Windows Firewall** window.

8. On the **Start** menu, point to **All Programs**, and then click **Windows Defender**.

Windows Defender opens.

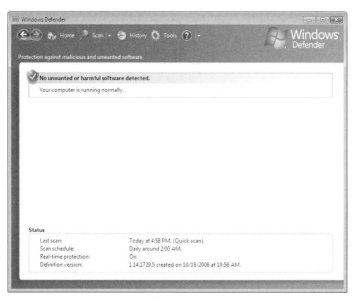

9. On the toolbar at the top of the window, click **Tools**.

The Tools And Settings page opens.

From this page, you can control the way Windows Defender works and monitor the software running on your computer.

10. In the **Settings** area, click **Options**.

The Options page opens.

From this page, you can control the frequency and type of automatic scanning, the actions taken by Windows Defender when encountering a suspicious item, the real-time protection in effect, and other options.

11. Scroll the page and notice the available options. Then in the **Automatic scanning** area, set the frequency and time for automatic scans to occur, select whether to perform a quick scan or full-system scan at that time, and click **Save**. In the **User Account Control** dialog box, if you're logged on as an administrator, click **Continue**. Otherwise, enter an administrator password, and click **OK**.

It is a good idea to keep the default setting to automatically scan your computer, but you can change the frequency and approximate time when you want the scans to take place to match a time your computer will be available.

12. In the **Security** window, click the **Check this computer's security status** task.

Windows Security Center opens, displaying the status of the four security essentials.

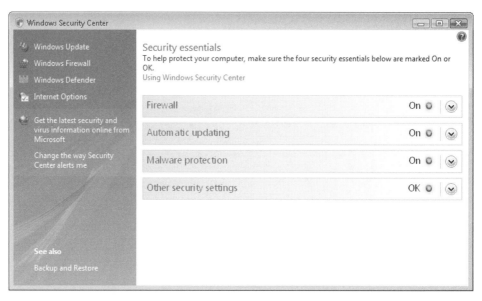

13. Make sure that all four settings are set to **On**. If any are not, click the corresponding **Find a program** button to locate and install the missing security application.

 CLOSE the Windows Security Center, Windows Defender, and the Security window.

Configuring Internet Security Zones

With Windows Internet Explorer, you can set different levels of security for different types of Web sites. For example, you might feel perfectly comfortable running programs that originate from your organization's intranet site or from specific Web sites that you trust (such as your own), but not want to allow certain types of programs to run on your computer from the Internet.

Internet Explorer divides the types of Web sites you visit into these four security zones:

- **Internet.** All external Web sites that are not in the trusted or restricted site lists.
- **Local intranet.** All Web sites that are part of your organization's local network.
- **Trusted.** Specific Web sites that you have designated as trustworthy; you believe that content from these sites will not damage your computer or data.
- **Restricted.** Specific Web sites that you have designated as untrustworthy; you believe that content from these sites might damage your computer or data.

You must specifically designate Web sites as part of the Trusted Sites and Restricted Sites zones; otherwise these zones are empty.

You can set the security level for each zone at one of five predefined levels, or you can customize the security level for your own or your organization's needs. The predefined security levels are:

- **High.** This level is appropriate for any Web sites you don't trust, or if you want to have full control over the content that is downloaded to and run on your computer. This is the default security level for the Restricted Sites zone. Internet Explorer prevents potentially harmful content from running on your computer, which might mean that the functionality or display of some Web sites is impaired.

- **Medium-high.** This level is appropriate for most Internet sites, and it is the default security level for the Internet zone. Internet Explorer prompts you before downloading any potentially unsafe content, and it does not download unsigned *ActiveX controls*.

- **Medium.** This is the default security level for the Trusted Sites zone. Internet Explorer does not download unsigned ActiveX controls, and prompts you for permission before downloading potentially unsafe content. Specific settings vary from the Medium-high security level.

- **Medium-low.** This is the default security level for the Local Intranet zone. Internet Explorer does not download unsigned ActiveX controls, but most other content runs without prompts.

- **Low.** This level is appropriate only for sites that you absolutely trust. Internet Explorer provides only minimal safeguards and warnings, and it downloads and runs most content without prompting you for permission.

Most people will find that the default settings are adequate for their needs, but from time to time you might want or need to customize a setting. Even if you never do, it's good to know what your options are so that you are confident that your Web browsing is done in a secure and sensible manner.

In this exercise, you will examine your current Internet Explorer security zone settings, experiment with changing your security options, and add and remove a Web site from the restricted sites list. There are no practice files for this exercise.

> **Important** If you have personalized your Internet security settings for a specific purpose and do not want them to be reset to the default settings, do not complete this exercise.

BE SURE TO display Control Panel before beginning this exercise.

1. In **Control Panel**, click **Security**, and then under **Internet Options**, click the **Change security settings** task.

   The Internet Properties dialog box opens, displaying the Security tab.

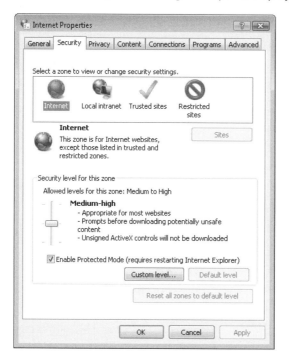

> **Tip** You can also display this tab by starting Internet Explorer and then double-clicking the zone name on the status bar.

Depending on your current security settings, the Security level for this zone area displays either a slide control like the one shown here or a custom setting.

2. If your screen shows a custom setting, click **Default level** to return the Internet zone to the default Medium-high security level.

Next you'll try customizing the security options.

3. Click **Custom level** to display the **Security Settings** dialog box for the currently selected Internet zone.

The default security level is shown in the Reset Custom Settings area.

4. Scroll through the options and change a few to see how changing security levels works. (Don't worry; you can undo the changes.) When you're finished making changes, click **OK**.

5. In the **Warning** message box prompting you to confirm your changes, click **Yes**.

   In the Internet Options dialog box, the security level for the Internet zone is now set to Custom.

6. In the **Select a zone** area, click **Restricted sites**.

   The security level for the Restricted Sites zone is set to High, and cannot be changed.

7. Click **Sites**.

The Restricted Sites dialog box opens.

Depending on your previous Internet Explorer use, the Websites list might already contain one or more site addresses.

8. In the **Add this website to the zone** box, type www.microsoft.com, and then click **Add**.

> **Important** If you do not want to temporarily implement any changes to your Internet zone security settings, skip to Step 12.

9. In the **Restricted Sites** dialog box, click **Close**. Then in the **Internet Properties** dialog box, click **OK**.

10. Click the **Start** button, and with the insertion point in the **Start Search** box, type http://www.microsoft.com. Then press [Enter].

Internet Explorer starts, and displays the Microsoft Corporation Web site.

The status bar at the bottom of the Internet Explorer window indicates that this is a restricted site.

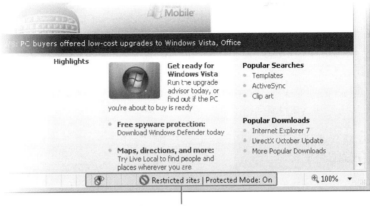

Site security status

Any scripts (small programs) or active content on this site will not run on your computer.

11. In the **Recent Tasks** list at the bottom of the left pane of the **Security** window, click **Change security settings**. In the **Internet Properties** dialog box, click **Restricted sites**, and then click **Sites**.

12. In the **Websites** list, click **www.microsoft.com**. Click **Remove**, and then click **Close**.

13. In the **Select a zone** area, click **Internet**, and then click **Default level** to return the Internet zone to the default security settings.

14. To implement this security level, click **OK**; otherwise, click **Cancel** to close the **Internet Properties** dialog box without implementing any of the changes.

CLOSE the Security window.

Protecting Yourself from Phishing Sites

Some Web sites are set up to collect information about users who visit them and use that data for fraudulent purposes. These "phishing sites" (so named because they "fish" for information) aren't Web sites that you would visit on purpose; links to them are distributed in e-mail messages, usually purporting to be from a bank or other financial institution. The phishing site link in the message is usually disguised as a valid link, but has code behind it that sends you to a site that is not the one you think you are visiting.

CHASE ○

Dear customer of JPChase Bank,

Technical services of the JPchase Bank are carrying out a planned software upgrade. We earnestly ask you to visit the following link to start the procedure of confirmation on customers data.

To get started, please click the link below:

https://chaseonline.chase.com/confirm.php?account42649 .

This instruction has been sent to all bank customers and is obligatory to fallow.

Thank you,
Customers Support Service.

Many phishing messages are immediately obvious due to the poor spelling and grammar they contain. Others claim to come from companies you don't actually have a financial relationship with. Even if you do business with the company, don't click the link! Instead, call the company to verify the validity of the request. Most reputable companies would never communicate with you about your personal or financial information in this way.

Internet Explorer 7 comes with a Phishing Filter that helps protect you by blocking known phishing sites. The filter is updated several times per hour using the latest security information from Microsoft and several industry partners. You can also use the filter to report suspicious sites or scams.

In addition to turning off automatic checking of visited sites against the list of known phishing sites, you can disable the Phishing Filter entirely. We would advise you to do this only if you feel confident that you will not be fooled by any phishing messages you receive.

Key Points

- User accounts can have associated passwords to protect the privacy of each person's data. You can back up your password information so that you can reset your password if you forget it.

- If you are concerned about how other people might use your computer, you can set limits on when it can be used, for how long it can be used, and what it can be used to do.

- You can easily analyze and optimize your computer's security settings.

- Internet Explorer has settings specifically designed to help you browse the Web without inadvertently exposing your computer and its information to risk of damage or theft.

Keyboard Shortcuts

Press this	To do this
Ctrl+Esc	Open the Start menu
Ctrl+Tab	Move through dialog box tabs
Ctrl+Shift+Tab	Move backwards through dialog box tabs
F1	Display Help
Windows logo key	Open or close the Start menu

Chapter at a Glance

Improve your
computer's
performance,
page 312

Turn Windows features
on and off, **page 318**

Remove unnecessary
files, **page 322**

11 Optimizing Your Computer System

In this chapter, you will learn to:

✔ Improve your computer's performance.

✔ Turn Windows features on and off.

✔ Manage cached files.

✔ Remove unnecessary files.

✔ Consolidate files on your hard disk.

You don't have to be a power user to be concerned about your computer's performance. Whether you use your computer for work, for gaming, or for occasionally browsing the Internet and sending e-mail messages to friends, you might find that your computer isn't as fast as you would like it to be. There are several ways to improve the performance of your computer and make the most of its resources. Some of them, such as increasing your computer's RAM, involve hardware. But you might get appreciable increases in speed and reliability just by giving your computer a system tune-up.

In this chapter, you will fine-tune some performance settings, turn off Windows features you never use, remove obsolete files, and rearrange files on your hard drive so that they can be accessed faster.

See Also Do you need only a quick refresher on the topics in this chapter? See the Quick Reference entries on pages xxxix–lxxiii

> **Important** No practice files are required to complete the exercises in this chapter. For more information about practice files, see "Using the Book's CD" on page xxix.

Improving Your Computer's Performance

If your productivity isn't what you think it should be and you suspect your computer is part of the problem, Windows Vista can give you information about your computer's performance and ways in which you might be able to improve it. Windows Vista indicates your computer's performance potential in various areas through the *Windows Experience Index*, which measures your processor, memory, graphics card, and hard disk. The lowest of these subscores is your computer's base score. The higher the base score, the better your computer's overall performance.

However, the base score you need depends a lot on what you intend to do with the computer. For example, you might receive a base score of 1 because you don't have a high-powered graphics card, even though you receive subscores of 3 or 4 in the processor, memory, and hard disk categories. Your computer would be more than adequate to run office applications such as word processing and spreadsheet programs; it just wouldn't be powerful enough to adequately display Windows Aero or sophisticated games. To optimize your computer for those purposes, you would need to upgrade your graphics card.

> **Tip** You can use the base score as an indicator of programs that will run well on your computer. Avoiding programs that require a higher base score than your computer's Windows Experience Index will help you avoid disappointing performance. In conjunction with the rating program, Windows Vista provides a link to software that will perform well on your computer.

If the Windows Experience Index memory subscore indicates that you would do well to upgrade your computer's memory, you don't necessarily have to crack open your computer's case to install new sticks of RAM or pay someone to do it for you. With a Windows Vista feature called *Windows ReadyBoost*, some types of *USB flash drives* can double as memory-expansion devices. If you insert a flash drive in a USB port, the AutoPlay dialog box that appears includes a Speed Up My System option. Clicking this option displays the ReadyBoost tab of the Properties dialog box for your flash drive, which tells you whether your flash drive has the type of "fast" flash memory that can be used for this purpose. If it does, you can select how much of your flash drive's capacity you want to use as auxiliary memory.

Tip When considering your desktop computer's performance, don't forget the most basic principle: keep it clean. The fans that keep your computer from overheating pull in air from outside the computer. With that air comes dust, dirt, pet hair, and other bits and pieces. This sediment clogs the fans and settles on the internal components, contributing to increased heat and decreased performance. Every three months or so, open the computer case. (Most cases now have a slide-off panel on the side, but if it's not obvious, consult the computer's manual.) With a vacuum hose or crevice tool, carefully vacuum the inside and outside of the case. Pay particular attention to both sides of the fan or fans. If you have had your computer for more than six months and haven't yet done this, you might be quite surprised at what you find inside!

Short of upgrading your computer system's hardware, some of the things you can do to improve performance are:

- Use Windows Defender to minimize the number of programs and services that start automatically when you start Windows.

- Speed up screen refresh rates by simplifying the visual effects Windows Vista has to create.

- Adjust your computer's power settings—for example, so that it wakes from a powered-down or sleeping state more readily.

> **Tip** If you use a mobile computer such as a laptop or Tablet PC, you can adjust the battery usage to prolong the period of time you can go without recharging.

- Streamline the indexing of files to focus on the ones you are most likely to want to find.

    See Also For information about searching for files, see "Finding Specific Information" in Chapter 3, "Working with Folders and Files."

- Increase file access speed by consolidating files and removing files you don't need.

    See Also For information about increasing file access, see "Removing Unnecessary Files" and "Consolidating Files on Your Hard Disk" later in this chapter.

In this exercise, you will examine the programs that Windows Vista starts when you turn on your computer, how Windows handles visual effects, and your computer's power settings. There are no practice files for this exercise.

BE SURE TO log on to Windows and display Control Panel before beginning this exercise.

1. In **Control Panel**, click **System and Maintenance**, and then click **Performance Information and Tools**.

    The Performance Information And Tools window displays your computer's Windows Experience Index.

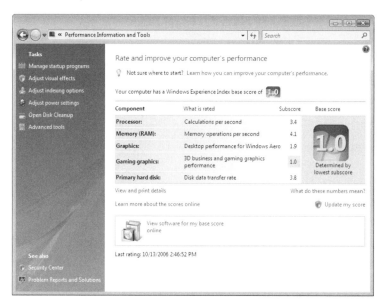

2. In the **Tasks** list in the left pane, click the **Manage startup programs** task.

    Windows Defender opens, displaying the Software Explorer page filtered to show only those programs that automatically start each time you log on to your computer.

    Details for the program selected in the left pane are shown in the right pane. If you can remove or disable a program, those buttons become active below the right pane when you select the program.

3. Close **Windows Defender**.

4. In the **Tasks** list in the left pane of the **Performance Information and Tools** window, click the **Adjust visual effects** task. In the **User Account Control** dialog box, if you're logged on as an administrator, click **Continue**. Otherwise, enter an administrator password, and then click **OK**.

   The Performance Options dialog box opens, displaying the Visual Effects tab. You can allow Windows Vista to select the optimum settings for your computer, or you can control the settings yourself. You can choose standard packages of settings configured to produce the best visual appearance (at the expense of speed) or the best performance (at the expense of looks). Or you can set each performance option individually.

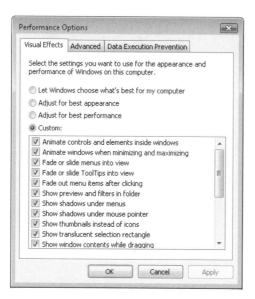

5. If you want to adjust the settings to improve your computer's performance, on the **Visual Effects** tab, select the **Adjust for best performance** option, and then click **OK**. Otherwise, click **Cancel**.

6. In the **Tasks** list in the left pane of the **Performance and Information Tools** window, click the **Adjust power settings** task.

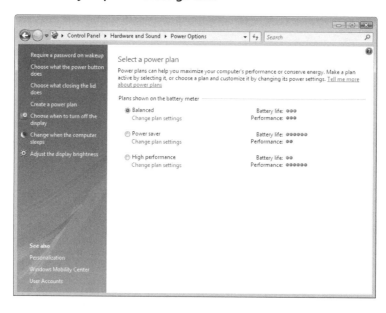

The Power Options window displays three default power plans offering energy savings, performance, or a balance between the two.

> **Tip** The available power options vary based on your computer. The window shown is that of a laptop computer.

7. Select the **High Performance** option, and then under the option, click **Change plan settings**.

In the Edit Plan Settings window, you can adjust the period of time you want Windows Vista to wait while the computer is idle before turning off the display and before putting the computer into Sleep mode, as well as the display brightness.

8. Click **Change advanced power settings**.

The Power Options dialog box opens, with the High Performance options listed. You can change any option to suit the way you work.

> **Troubleshooting** Don't be concerned if your list of options is different from the one shown. Windows Vista identifies the power settings that you can adjust for your computer and lists only those options.

9. Click **Cancel** to close the **Power Options** dialog box. Then click the **Back** button in the upper-left corner of the **Edit Plan Settings** window to return to the Power Options window.

10. If you want to change the power plan settings for your computer, select the option that represents the closest fit, and then to fine-tune the settings, click **Change plan settings**.

CLOSE the Power Options window when you finish making changes.

Turning Windows Features On and Off

Some of the features that come with Windows Vista are installed on your computer but are not immediately available for use because they are not turned on by default. Some features are turned on only in specific editions of Windows Vista, and some features aren't turned on in any edition. You can turn on a missing feature, such as Removable Storage Management, at any time. Or if your computer's performance seems unsatisfactory, you can try turning off Windows features you don't use to conserve system resources. You can always turn them back on if you find you need them.

In this exercise, you will explore the Windows Features dialog box so that you know how to turn Windows features on and off. There are no practice files for this exercise.

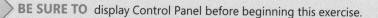

BE SURE TO display Control Panel before beginning this exercise.

1. In **Control Panel**, click **Programs**, and then under **Programs and Features**, click the **Turn Windows features on or off** task. Then in the **User Account Control** dialog box, if you're logged on as an administrator, click **Continue**. Otherwise, enter an administrator password, and click **OK**.

The Windows Features dialog box opens, and after a few seconds, a list of all the features appears. If all components of a feature are installed, its check box is selected. If some components of a multi-component feature are installed, its check box is shaded.

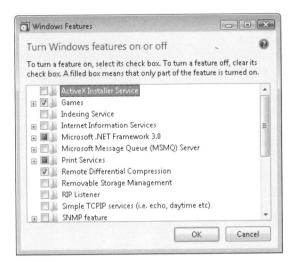

2. Scroll the features list, noticing which ones are installed and which aren't.

3. If you are not using an installed feature that you know it is safe to remove (such as Games), clear its check box, and then click **OK**.

   A message box tells you that configuring the change might take several minutes. When the process is complete, the message box and the Windows Features dialog box close.

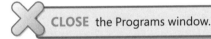 **CLOSE** the Programs window.

Managing Cached Files

When you visit a Web page, the page and its graphics are stored, or *cached*, in the Temporary Internet Files folder on your hard disk. The folder size is limited by default to 50 MB; you can increase (up to 1 GB) or decrease (down to 8 MB) the folder size to control how often the folder is purged. If you do a lot of Web surfing, particularly of graphic-intensive sites, the folder can fill up relatively quickly; after it is full, older files are deleted when newer files are cached.

> **Tip** If you would prefer that Internet Explorer not cache any temporary files, select the Empty Temporary Internet Files Folder When Browser Is Closed check box on the Advanced tab of the Internet Properties dialog box.

In this exercise, you will view your temporary Internet files and associated settings. There are no practice files for this exercise.

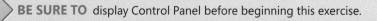

BE SURE TO display Control Panel before beginning this exercise.

1. In **Control Panel**, click **Security**, and then under **Internet Options**, click the **Delete browsing history and cookies** task.

   The Internet Properties dialog box opens, displaying the General tab.

2. In the **Browsing history** area, click **Settings**.

   The Temporary Internet Files And History Settings dialog box opens.

In this dialog box, you can specify how often Internet Explorer looks for updated versions of cached pages, and how much storage space is available for your temporary Internet files.

3. Click **View files**.

Your Temporary Internet Files folder opens, probably displaying a wide variety of cached files.

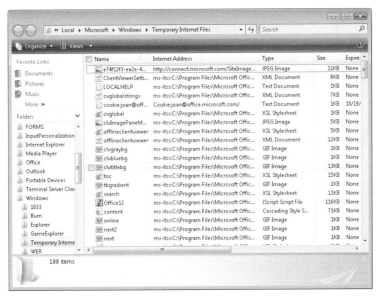

4. Close the **Temporary Internet Files** window, and then click **View objects**.

    Your Downloaded Program Files folder opens. This folder might contain very few (or no) files, depending on your Internet browsing habits.

5. Close the **Downloaded Program Files** window, and then click **Cancel** in the **Temporary Internet Files and History Settings** dialog box.

 CLOSE the Internet Properties dialog box and the Security window.

Tip You can clear the file cache by clicking Delete in the Browsing History area. Internet Explorer will recache any previously visited pages and cookies the next time you visit those sites. To delete only selected items—for example, to delete temporary files but retain cookies—display the Temporary Internet Files folder, select the desired files, and then press Delete. You can sort files by file type to quickly locate specific groups of files.

Removing Unnecessary Files

Every time you open a file, access a Web page, install a program, or download a file, Windows Vista creates a temporary file on your computer. In the case of program files such as documents, the temporary files contain autorecover information. Most of these temporary files are deleted automatically when they are no longer needed. However, poorly behaved programs sometimes don't clean up after themselves, resulting in megabytes of unnecessary files on your hard disk.

Other types of unused files can also clutter up your hard disk. A common culprit is the Recycle Bin—by default, deleted files are stored in the Recycle Bin until you empty it.

> **Tip** To delete a file without temporarily storing it in the Recycle Bin, press Shift+Delete instead of Delete. To always bypass the Recycle Bin, right-click the Recycle Bin, click Properties, select the Do Not Move Files To The Recycle Bin check box, and then click OK.

See Also For more information about the Recycle Bin, see "Rearranging and Deleting Items on the Desktop" in Chapter 2, "Working Efficiently in Windows Vista."

You can use *Disk Cleanup* to free up space on your hard disk by removing downloaded program files, temporary files, and offline files; compressing old files; and emptying the Recycle Bin. It is a good idea to use the *Task Scheduler* to schedule Disk Cleanup to run regularly. Then you don't have to remember the last time you ran it or when it's time to run it again.

> **Tip** Depending on the number of files to be compressed and deleted, Disk Cleanup can take from one to ten minutes to run.

In this exercise, you will run the Disk Cleanup utility on your computer and then schedule the utility to run once a month. There are no practice files for this exercise.

BE SURE TO display Control Panel before beginning this exercise.

1. In **Control Panel**, click **System and Maintenance**, scroll the window if necessary, and then under **Administrative Tools**, click the **Free up disk space** task.

The Disk Cleanup Options dialog box opens, prompting you to choose whether you want to clean up only your files or the files used by all users of your computer.

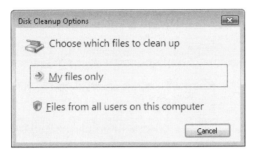

2. Click the option you want.

   After calculating the amount of disk space you can recover, the Disk Cleanup dialog box opens.

3. Click the name of each category of files in turn (not the category check box) to display its description.

   These descriptions will help you identify the categories that you can safely tell Disk Cleanup to delete. If a list of the files to be deleted is available, a View Files button is also displayed.

4. Click **Recycle Bin**, and then click **View Files**.

   The Recycle Bin window opens, giving you the opportunity to restore files before Disk Cleanup deletes them.

5. Close the **Recycle Bin** window.

6. Select the check boxes of all the categories you want to delete.

   The total amount of disk space you will gain is recalculated to reflect your selections.

7. Click **OK**. Then click **Delete Files** to confirm that you want to delete the selected categories of files.

   As Disk Cleanup completes the selected operations, a progress bar indicates how the cleanup is proceeding. You can cancel the cleanup at any point during the operation. The Disk Cleanup dialog box closes when the operation is complete.

8. Scroll the **System and Maintenance** window, and then under **Administrative Tools**, click **Schedule tasks**. In the **User Account Control** dialog box, if you're logged on as an administrator, click **Continue**. Otherwise, enter an administrator password, and then click **OK**.

   Task Scheduler starts.

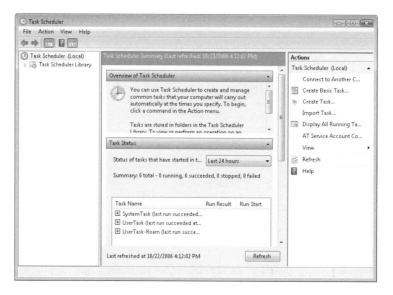

9. In the **Actions** pane on the right side of the window, click **Create Basic Task**. The Create Basic Task wizard starts.

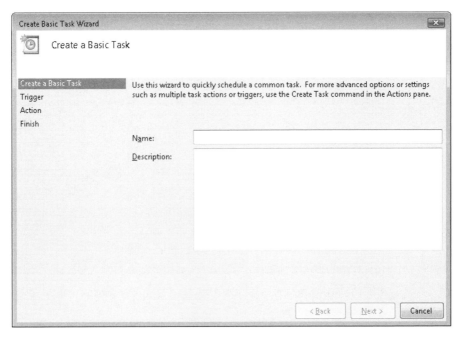

10. In the **Name** box, type Regular disk cleaning, and in the **Description** box, type Run Disk Cleanup once a month. Then click **Next**.

11. On the **Task Trigger** page, select the **Monthly** option, and then click **Next**.

12. On the **Monthly** page, click the **Months** arrow, and select the **<Select all months>** check box. Then click the **Days** arrow, select the **Last** check box to run the task on the last day of each month, and click **Next**.

13. On the **Action** page, with the **Start a program** option selected, click **Next**.

14. On the **Start a Program** page, click **Browse**. In the **Open** dialog box, type clean in the **File name** box, click **cleanmgr.exe** in the **File name** list that appears, and click **Open**. Then click **Next**.

The wizard displays a summary of the task instructions.

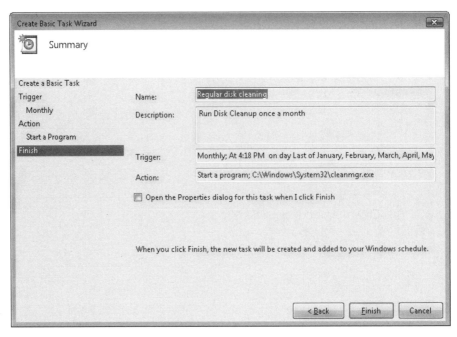

15. On the **Summary** page, click **Finish** to create the new task and add it to your Windows schedule.

16. Scroll the middle pane to display the Active Tasks area. Then scroll the list of tasks, which includes the Regular Disk Cleaning task you just created.

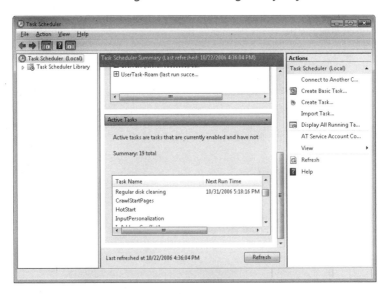

 CLOSE the Task Scheduler window and Control Panel.

Consolidating Files on Your Hard Disk

There can be times when there is nothing specifically wrong with your computer, but it is not operating at its peak efficiency. You might think that your computer is simply not as fast as it used to be, and although perceived speed can be a function of your own level of patience, it might be true that your system has slowed down since it was new. Unlike a sewing machine or a blender, a slow computer probably isn't due to the parts getting old and worn out; it might simply be that your hard disk has become cluttered and its contents *fragmented*.

Each time you save information to your hard disk, Windows Vista writes the information to the currently available space on the disk. When you delete information, the space that information used to occupy becomes free, and more information can take its place. When a file that you save to your hard disk doesn't entirely fit in one empty space, it is divided into "fragments" across multiple spaces. Accessing fragmented information takes more time than accessing the same information when it is stored contiguously.

You can use *Disk Defragmenter* to analyze all the data stored on your hard disk and then consolidate fragmented files into contiguous chunks. The benefits are faster file access and larger areas of available space in which to store new files. Each drive on your computer can be *defragmented* separately. By default, Windows Vista runs Disk Defragmenter every week. You can change this schedule, or you can run the program manually at any time.

> **Tip** Depending on the size of your hard disk, Disk Defragmenter can take up to an hour to run.

In this exercise, you will change the schedule for running Disk Defragmenter on your computer, and then you will see how to run it manually. There are no practice files for this exercise.

BE SURE TO display Control Panel before beginning this exercise.

1. In **Control Panel**, click **System and Maintenance**, scroll the window if necessary, and then under **Administrative Tools**, click the **Defragment your hard drive** task. In the **User Account Control** dialog box, if you're logged on as an administrator, click **Continue**. Otherwise, enter an administrator password, and then click **OK**.

   The Disk Defragmenter window opens.

By default, Windows Vista runs Disk Defragmenter once each week.

> **Tip** If your computer has more than one hard disk drive, each will be listed in the Disk Defragmenter window with its own schedule.

2. Click **Modify schedule**.

3. In the **Disk Defragmenter: Modify Schedule** dialog box, click the **How often** arrow, and in the list, click **Monthly**. Then click **OK**.

   The Disk Defragmenter window shows the updated details of the scheduled defragmentation.

4. If you want, click **Defragment now**.

   Disk Defragmenter begins the defragmentation process.

5. When the defragmentation process is complete, click **OK** to close the **Disk Defragmenter** window.

CLOSE the System And Maintenance window.

Key Points

- You can decrease the time it takes your computer to start up by removing any unnecessary programs and services from the startup process.

- Turning off some visual effects and optimizing your power settings are two other ways to increase performance.

- You might be able to improve the performance of your computer system by turning off Windows features that you do not use.

- Deleting unnecessary files and defragmenting your hard disk are easy ways to increase hard disk access speeds.

- Keeping your computer physically clean inside and out is another way to ensure that it operates at peak efficiency.

Keyboard Shortcuts

Press this	To do this
Delete	Delete the selected item and move it to the Recycle Bin
Shift+Delete	Delete the selected item without moving it to the Recycle Bin first
Ctrl+Esc	Open the Start menu
Windows logo key	Open or close the Start menu

Chapter at a Glance

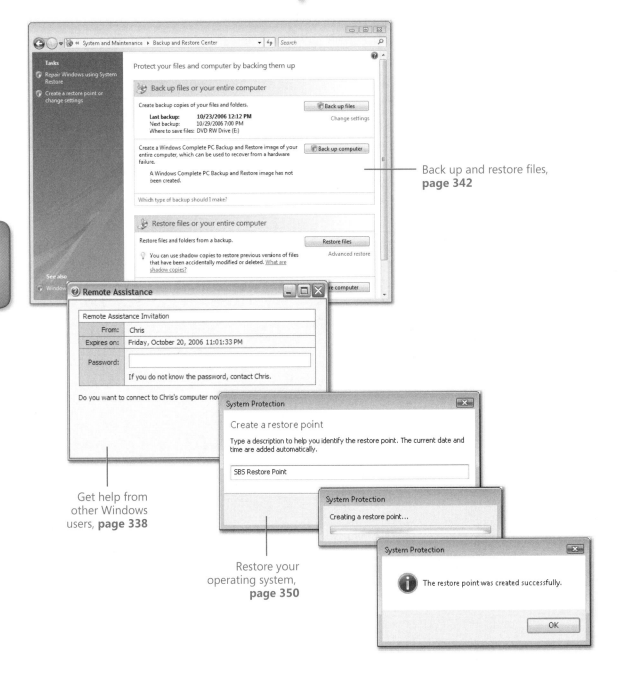

Back up and restore files,
page 342

Get help from
other Windows
users, **page 338**

Restore your
operating system,
page 350

12 Identifying and Solving Problems

In this chapter, you will learn to:

- ✔ Find solutions to common problems.
- ✔ Find information through a newsgroup.
- ✔ Get help from other Windows users.
- ✔ Back up and restore files.
- ✔ Restore your operating system.
- ✔ Transfer software, settings, and files to another computer.

It's easier than ever to find and use the Windows Vista tools and features that can help you maintain your computer. However, the fact that maintenance is easy doesn't mean that you won't ever experience a problem while using your computer. One of the first things you learn about skiing is how to recover safely and gracefully from a fall; this is also a good thing to learn in computing. Knowing where to look for solutions to problems is the key to safe recovery. It is also wise to take a few precautions to help you avoid problems as much as you can.

If you do run into technical difficulty with your Windows Vista computer, your first recourse is to look in Windows Help And Support for information. For more complex problems, you might need to seek help from other computer users. And if your system has become really unstable, you might need to restore it to a point in the past where it worked reliably.

Computer problems are frustrating, but most stop short of being disasters unless they involve loss of data. Windows Vista goes to great lengths to make it easy for you to regularly back up and restore your valuable files. It also makes it easy to transfer your system setup, programs, and files to a new computer so that you can be up and running in the least possible time.

In this chapter, you will learn how to use the available free support options. For those times when nothing seems to solve an operating system problem, you will learn how to roll your system back to its state before the problem occurred. Then you will learn how to back up files stored on your computer, and how to transfer programs, settings, and files from one computer running Windows Vista to another.

See Also Do you need only a quick refresher on the topics in this chapter? See the Quick Reference entries on pages xxxix–lxxiii.

> **Important** Before you can use the practice files in this chapter, you need to install them from the book's companion CD to their default location. See "Using the Book's CD" on page xxix for more information.

Finding Solutions to Common Problems

It is fairly common for people to purchase furniture, toys, bikes, or other things that require assembly, and then neglect to read the instruction manual until they actually have a problem. Along the same lines, many people never consult a program's Help file, because they don't realize how much good information can be found there.

Windows Help And Support is the place to go when you're having trouble. This is more than just a common Help file. It includes general and task-oriented articles cross-referenced to related articles and resources, a comprehensive glossary, tutorials and demonstrations, and links to most of the tools that you need to keep your computer running smoothly. You can choose from a list of common topics on its main page, search by keyword or phrase, or look up specific topics in the table of contents. If the information you need isn't in Windows Help And Support, you can at least find pointers to other resources.

Windows Help And Support displays static content that is stored on your computer, and dynamic content that it accesses over the Internet. By including online content resources in your searches, you can be confident that you are getting current information.

If your question is of a more technical nature, you can follow a link from Windows Help And Support to the Microsoft Help And Support site, which hosts an in-depth library of Knowledge Base articles written in response to customer inquiries.

You open Windows Help And Support by clicking the Help And Support link on the Start menu. Many Windows Vista windows and dialog boxes contain links to context-sensitive Help files that provide information about the currently displayed feature or program, and assist you in deciding which options you should choose.

> **Tip** Pressing the F1 key opens Windows Help And Support to a related topic, or opens the Help file for the currently active Microsoft program. Pressing the F1 key from within a Microsoft Office Word file opens the Word Help file, pressing the F1 key from within a Microsoft Office Excel file opens the Excel Help file, and so on. Many software manufacturers have made their context-sensitive help available through the F1 key, which is why context-sensitive help is often referred to as F1 Help.

In this exercise, you will open Windows Help And Support and search for useful information. There are no practice files for this exercise.

> **BE SURE TO** log on to Windows before beginning this exercise.

1. On the **Start** menu, click **Help and Support**.

   The Windows Help And Support window opens. You can display categories of information by clicking the icons under Find An Answer and explore support options by clicking the links under Ask Someone. To locate topics containing a specific word or phrase, enter the word or phrase in the Search Help box, and then click the Search Help button or press Enter.

2. At the right end of the toolbar at the top of the window, click **Options**, and then in the list, click **Settings**.

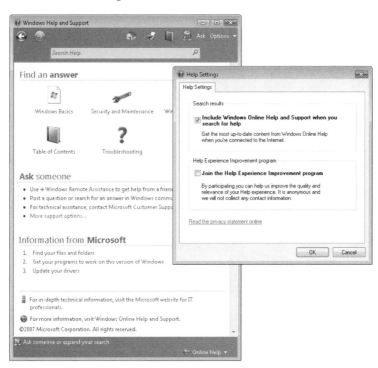

3. In the **Help Settings** dialog box, ensure that the **Include Windows Online Help and Support** check box is selected. Then click **OK**.

Browse Help

4. On the toolbar, click the **Browse Help** button.

   If you don't know precisely what information you are looking for, you can locate information by general topic from this page.

5. Click **Getting started**, click **If you are new to Windows—the basics**, and then click **Help and support**.

   Notice that the path you followed to get to this page is displayed above the topic list. You can click any link in the path to return to that page.

Maximize

6. On the **Help and support** page, click **Getting help (overview)**. Then in the **Windows Help and Support** window, click the **Maximize** button.

   The displayed topic contains in-depth information about ways of getting help with Windows Vista.

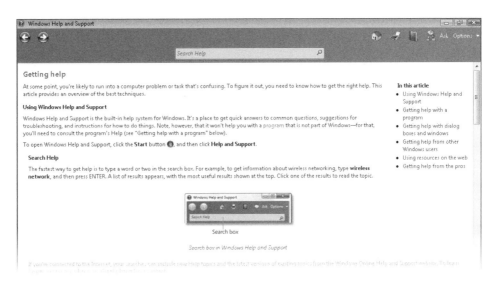

Search Help

7. Scan the topic. When you finish, type getting help in the **Search Help** box, and then click the **Search Help** button.

> **Tip** Search terms are not case-sensitive; typing *Getting Help* produces the same results.

A list of the first 30 topics that fit your search term appears. At the bottom of the list is a link to the next 30 topics.

Back

8. Click any topic link that interests you. Then in the upper-left corner of the **Windows Help and Support** window, click the **Back** button.

You can move back and forth between visited topics in the same way that you do in Windows Explorer and Windows Internet Explorer.

Home

9. On the toolbar, click the **Home** button to return to the starting page. Then explore on your own.

> **Tip** At the bottom of most Help topics, you have the opportunity to provide feedback about the usefulness of the information provided in the topic. Click the appropriate button, provide any additional information requested, and then click Finish to send your comments to the Microsoft support team, who continually refine the Help topics based on this feedback.

 CLOSE Windows Help And Support when you finish browsing the Help file.

Reporting Problems

When your computer experiences a hardware or software problem, Windows Vista creates a problem report containing information such as when the problem occurred and what software program or hardware device was involved, and sends the report to Microsoft. If you prefer, you can have the tool ask you before sending the problem reports. In some cases, the problem-reporting tool might request permission to send additional information that will help to identify the problem and develop a solution. You are always given the opportunity to view the additional information before you give permission to send it, and you can deny permission. Personal information from your computer is not transmitted, unless it is contained in a document you specifically authorize the tool to send.

If the Microsoft support database contains a solution to or other information about your reported problem, the problem-reporting tool returns with the information. You can choose whether to implement any reported solutions.

You can view transmitted and unsent problem reports and collected solutions in the Problem Reports And Solutions window. You can send the collected reports manually at any time.

To display the Problem Reports And Solutions window:

→ In **Control Panel**, click **System and Maintenance**, and then click **Problem Reports and Solutions**.

To turn off automatic reporting:

1. In the **Problem Reports and Solutions** window, click **Change settings**.

2. On the **Choose how to check for solutions to computer problems** page, select the **Ask me to check if a problem occurs** option, and then click **OK**.

To manually submit problem reports:

→ In the **Problem Reports and Solutions** window, click the **Check for new solutions** task.

Windows Vista sends reports about the currently logged issues to Microsoft, and reports any solutions that it finds.

You can implement any of the reported solutions; Windows Vista does not implement them for you.

Finding Information Through a Newsgroup

Windows Vista newsgroups are online forums where Windows Vista users and experts from around the world interact to discuss their experiences with the operating system and all manners of problems and solutions. These newsgroups are not officially monitored by Microsoft, and Microsoft is not responsible for any of the information available there. You can find discussion threads about many common and uncommon problems. You might find an answer to a question or an interesting discussion that you want to keep up with or join.

Newsgroups are free of charge, and you can join or quit them at any time. You can follow a link to the newsgroups through Microsoft Windows Mail or through a Web-based newsgroup reader. After joining the newsgroup, you can interact with a newsgroup in several different ways:

- You can visit a newsgroup to read messages.
- You can post a new message and wait for a response.
- You can post a reply to a message to the newsgroup; your message then becomes part of the discussion thread and is available to anyone who visits the newsgroup.
- You can send an e-mail message to the person who posted a specific message, or forward the message to someone else through e-mail.
- You can subscribe to a newsgroup and have all its messages sent to you via e-mail.
- You can subscribe to a specific discussion thread, in which case you will receive an e-mail message notifying you when a new message has been posted to the thread.

A word of warning about newsgroups: Some people see them as a forum for blowing off steam without actually communicating information that is useful or interesting to anyone else. You might find that it takes quite a while to wade through all the available messages before you find information that is pertinent to your situation. On the bright side, although Microsoft does not officially monitor the newsgroups, there do appear to be a fair number of "experts" who post useful information or respond to valid queries.

To locate Windows Vista newsgroups:

1. On the **Start** menu, click **Help and Support**.

   The Windows Help And Support window opens.

2. Under **Ask someone**, click **Windows communities**.

   The Windows Vista Newsgroups page opens in your default Web browser.

You can search for a newsgroup by topic, or click Getting Started With The Web-Based Newsreader for more information about using the newsgroup interface.

Getting Help from Microsoft Product Support

If you can't solve a problem by searching the Windows Help And Support topics, you can click the Microsoft Customer Support link under Ask Someone in the Windows Help And Support window to log specific problems with the Microsoft support staff, who then reply to your problem online. This method of handling product support is very efficient, both for you and for Microsoft.

Along with a description of your problem, you will be asked to send information about your computer that the product support technician might need to diagnose the problem and offer a useful solution. You can either allow your system information to be collected automatically by tools that come with Windows Vista, or you can stipulate which information can be sent to Microsoft. You are not required to send anything other than your product key, but because known issues often affect only certain computer models, sound cards, graphics cards, and so on, information about your computer can be useful.

Your problem report is assigned a tracking number so that you can follow up on your request for help. You can return to the Online Assisted Support site at any time to view the status of your support request, or you can ask to be notified by e-mail when an answer has been posted.

Getting Help from Other Windows Users

If you've tried to solve a problem on your own and have not been successful, you can turn to a friend or co-worker for help. Simple problems can frequently be diagnosed in a phone, e-mail, or instant messaging (IM) conversation; others are difficult for other people to identify or fix when they are not working on the affected computer. If it isn't convenient for someone to physically work with your computer to troubleshoot the problem, you can allow him or her to take control of your computer from another Windows computer by using the Windows Remote Assistance feature. By the same means, you can offer assistance to other Windows Vista users. (If you ask for assistance from Microsoft product support staff, a product support technician might also use Remote Assistance to troubleshoot technical problems with your computer.)

You initiate a *remote assistance* session by sending an invitation. To protect your computer from unauthorized access, the invitation is valid for a specific length of time—from 1 minute to 99 days—and can require a password, which you would send separately. You can send a remote assistance invitation through e-mail or IM to anyone with a computer running Windows Vista or Microsoft Windows XP.

> **Tip** If you are running Windows Live Messenger, you can request remote assistance directly through the instant messaging program.

In this exercise, you will request remote assistance. There are no practice files for this exercise.

BE SURE TO enlist the help of a friend or co-worker running Windows Vista or Windows XP.

1. On the **Start** menu, point to **All Programs**, click **Maintenance**, and then click **Windows Remote Assistance**.

   Windows Remote Assistance starts.

2. Click **Invite someone you trust to help you**.

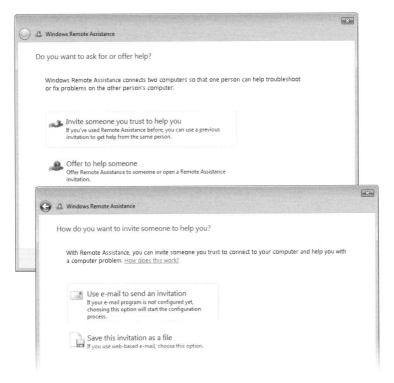

3. If you have configured Windows Mail, Microsoft Office Outlook, or another e-mail program on your Windows Vista computer, click **Use e-mail to send an invitation**, enter and confirm the password you want your remote assistant to use, and click **Next**; then skip to Step 6. Otherwise, click **Save this invitation as a file**.

Windows Remote Assistance creates an invitation file containing the information another computer needs to begin a remote assistance session.

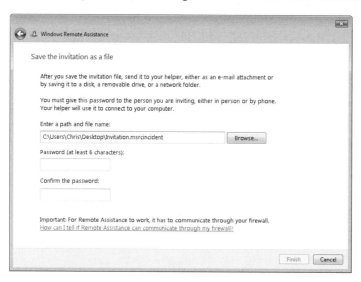

By default, the invitation file is saved to your desktop, but you can save it to another location if you prefer.

4. In the **Password** box, type a string of six or more characters you want your remote assistant to enter in order to gain access to your computer. Then click **Finish**.

The Windows Remote Assistance dashboard opens, and the remote assistance invitation file is created and saved to your desktop.

5. Start or switch to your e-mail program, and send the remote assistance invitation file to the person you want to assist you. Then contact him or her separately with the remote assistance password.

When your remote assistant receives the invitation, she or he accepts the invitation by entering the password, and then clicking Yes.

6. After the invitation is accepted, click **Yes** to allow your remote assistant to view your screen and chat with you.

   The Windows Remote Assistance window opens on your computer.

   A window also opens on the remote assistant's computer. At this point, the two of you can chat by typing messages, or if you both have microphones and speakers, by talking. You can also send files. Your remote assistant can see everything you do on your computer, so you can open files or demonstrate the steps that lead up to a problem and then ask for advice.

7. On the toolbar, click the **Chat** button, and in the box at the bottom of the window, tell your remote assistant to take control of your computer.

   He or she will need to click the Request Control button on the Remote Assistance toolbar. You will then receive a message asking if you would like to share control of your computer.

8. Click **Yes**.

   You both now have control of the mouse on your computer. However, you should not both try to move it at the same time.

9. When you decide that you no longer want to share control of your computer, on the toolbar, click the **Stop sharing** button.

You now have exclusive control of your mouse.

10. When you finish the Remote Assistance session, click the **Disconnect** button.

CLOSE the Windows Remote Assistance window.

Backing Up and Restoring Files

When *file* and *folder* were terms used to describe things made of paper, it was possible for your important documents to be permanently destroyed by fire, water, coffee, toddlers, accidental shredding, or a variety of other natural and unnatural disasters. With the advent of electronic files and folders, it is still possible for the files containing your information to be destroyed, but if you have recently backed up the information, you can recover from the loss with relatively little trouble.

Backing up is the process of creating a copy of your files somewhere other than on your computer so that you can restore them if an event such as a virus attack, hard disk failure, theft of a laptop, fire, or other loss should occur. Most people aren't convinced of the necessity of backing up the various types of information they create and work with until they suffer a disaster—and then they become evangelists. Your organization should have an automated system in place to regularly back up all the information stored on servers, but might or might not back up information stored on each and every individual computer—and few people have a system set up at home to protect family records, correspondence, digital photographs, and other personal information.

One key factor in useful data backups is frequency—information that has not been backed up is not protected. For continuous data protection, you can rely on an online data backup service such as Datacastle (*www.datacastlecorp.com*), which securely backs up incremental changes from your computer over the Internet at regular intervals. Implementing this type of solution ensures that you never lose more than a few minutes' work, and addresses another key factor in useful data backups—the storage location. Backing up your information to a CD, DVD, tape, or removable hard drive protects you from data loss only if the backup is also protected. For example, if you store your backup in your laptop bag and your laptop bag is stolen, you are not protected. Similarly, storing your backup in a location where it might be damaged or destroyed by environmental factors does not provide adequate protection.

Enabling and Disabling Remote Assistance

The Remote Assistance option is turned on by default. If you are uncomfortable with the idea that other people might be able to access your computer over the Internet, you can block Remote Assistance connections to your Windows Vista computer.

If you want, you can stipulate the number of minutes, hours, or days a remote assistance invitation that you send to another Windows user is valid, and you can limit remote assistance to only computers running Windows Vista.

To display the Remote Assistance settings:

→ In **Control Panel**, click **System and Maintenance**. Then under **System**, click the **Allow remote access** task. In the **User Account Control** dialog box, if you're logged on as an administrator, click **Continue**. Otherwise, enter an administrator password, and click **OK**.

The System Properties dialog box opens, displaying the Remote tab.

To completely disable Remote Assistance:

→ In the **Remote Assistance** area, clear the **Allow Remote Assistance connections to this computer** check box, and then click **OK**.

To limit Remote Assistance access:

1. In the **Remote Assistance** area, click **Advanced**.

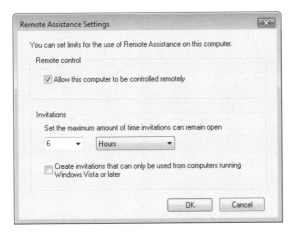

2. In the **Remote Assistance Settings** dialog box, set the access level, invitation duration, and access type as you want, and then click **OK**.

If you prefer to back up information to physical media such as CDs or DVDs, or to another computer on your network, you can do so by using Windows Backup. You can back up information manually, or have Windows Vista do it automatically according to a schedule you establish.

> **Tip** Automatic backups are not available with Windows Vista Home Basic Edition.

The backup schedule you choose should reflect the rate at which you create and change files. If you work on your computer only on weekends, a daily backup will probably not be necessary. On the other hand, if you work from your home office, store all your work on your computer, and could lose significant time or income if your computer crashes, a daily backup is a good idea. You can schedule automatic backups on a regular basis, and supplement them with manual backups when important. Keep in mind that your computer must be turned on at the scheduled time for Windows to be able to complete the backup.

You should routinely back up only the files you create, not program files or system files. Program files do not change very often and can usually be reinstalled from the original installation CDs. You can make a backup of your system files, but this is usually necessary only in rare circumstances.

If your computer is connected to other computers over a network or if you have more than one hard drive, you can choose one of those locations for the backup. If your computer is not connected to other computers and has only one hard drive, the computer must have a CD or DVD burner to create a backup. You cannot back up to a flash drive, to the disk containing the files you are backing up, or to the disk that Windows is installed on. If you are backing up to a CD or DVD, you must be present to insert a new disk when the backup is scheduled to occur. If you are not, Windows will put the backup on hold and will prompt you to insert the CD or DVD to continue the process.

> **Tip** Even if you have more than one internal hard drive, you might want to back up to a location away from your computer in case of disaster.

When you back up your files, Windows creates a folder in the designated backup location called *Backup Set [date] [time]*. The first time you create a backup, Windows performs a full backup of all files of the designated type. Thereafter, it updates the backup set with the files that you have created or changed since the last backup. You might want to create a new full backup periodically to start afresh.

If you need to restore a file from a backup set, you display the Backup And Restore Center, indicate the required files or folders and the restoration location, and Windows does the rest.

> **Tip** If you have made changes to a file and need to revert to a previous version, you might not need to restore it from a backup. If you have used System Protection to create a restore point, Windows automatically saves "shadow" copies of your files as part of the restore point. These copies are listed on the Previous Versions tab of each file's Properties dialog box. You can right-click the file and then click Restore Previous Version to display this tab of the dialog box, where you can select the version you want. The previous version then overwrites the current version.

In this exercise, you will back up a document to a removable storage device. You will also set a schedule for future backups. Then you will delete a file and restore it from the backup.

> **Troubleshooting** You must be logged in as an administrator to back up or restore files.

 BE SURE TO log on to Windows as an administrator and have a blank writable CD or DVD or the location of a network computer available before beginning this exercise.

USE the *04_BookBeat* document. This practice file is located in the *Chapter12* subfolder under *SBS_WindowsVista*.

1. Display **Control Panel**, and then under **System and Maintenance**, click **Back up your computer**.

The Backup And Restore Center opens.

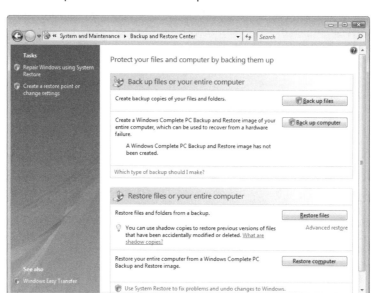

> **Troubleshooting** If automatic backup is already set up on your computer, your Backup And Restore Center will look different. To the right of Create Backup Copies Of Your Files And Folders, click Back Up Files, and when the process is complete, click **OK**. Then skip to Step 9.

2. Under **Back up files or your entire computer**, click **Back up files**. Then in the **User Account Control** dialog box, click **Continue**.

The Back Up Files wizard searches your system for an appropriate backup device—either an alternative hard disk drive, a CD writer, or a DVD writer.

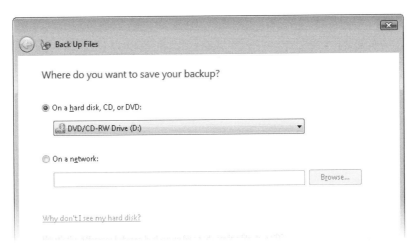

3. Select the hard disk or other drive where you want to save the backup, and then click **Next**.

    The Back Up Files wizard indicates the types of files you might want to back up. Pointing to a category displays a description in the Category Details box.

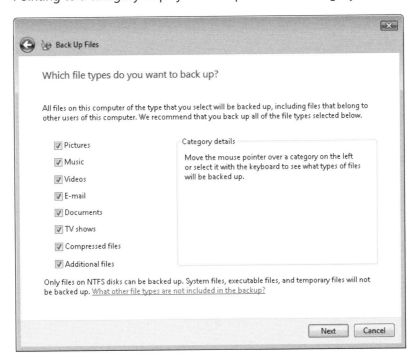

4. For the purposes of this exercise, clear all the check boxes except **Documents**, and then click **Next**.

You are prompted to establish a schedule for backing up the selected types of files.

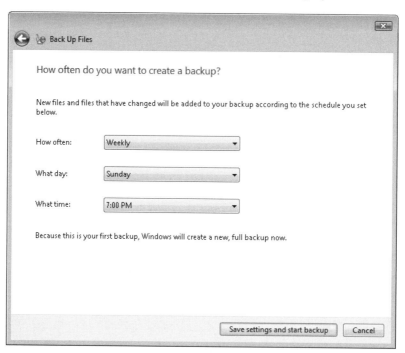

5. Adjust the **How often**, **What day**, and **What time** settings to the way you want them by clicking each one in turn and selecting from the list.

6. If you are backing up to a CD or DVD, insert a blank disk into your CD or DVD drive; otherwise skip this step.

7. Click **Save settings and start backup**.

The backup starts, and a progress box displays the status of the backup process.

> **Troubleshooting** If you are asked to insert a blank disk or to format the disk, click OK.

8. When the process is complete, close the **Backup Status and Configuration** dialog box.

The Backup And Restore Center provides information about the most recent backup and the next scheduled backup.

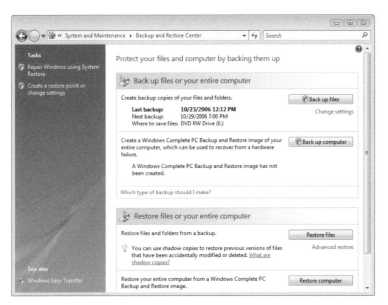

9. Open your **Documents** folder in Windows Explorer, navigate to the *MSP\SBS_WindowsVista\Chapter12* folder, and then delete the *04_BookBeat* document. Leave the window open.

   Now you will restore the file from your backup.

10. On the Windows taskbar, click the **Backup and Restore Center** taskbar button.

11. Under **Restore files or your entire computer**, click **Restore files**.

    The Restore Files wizard asks what you want to restore.

12. With the **Files from the latest backup** option selected, click **Next**.

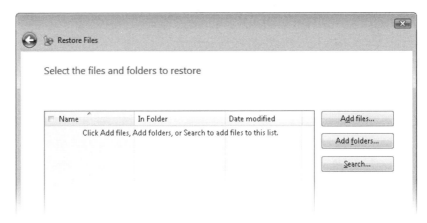

13. On the wizard's next page, click **Add files**. Then with the contents of your Documents folder displayed in the **Add files to restore** dialog box, navigate to the *MSP\SBS_WindowsVista\Chapter12* folder, double-click the *04_BookBeat* document, and then click **Next**.

14. On the next page, leave **In the original location** selected, and then click **Start restore**.

15. When Windows reports that the file has been successfully restored, click **Finish**.

16. Close the **Backup and Restore Center**.

In the Windows Explorer window, you can see that the file has been restored from the backup.

 CLOSE the Windows Explorer window.

Restoring Your Operating System

In the beginning, you start with a clean computer with a brand new operating system. As time goes by, you install new programs, delete programs, change your system settings, and upgrade to new versions of programs. Gradually, things change, and sometimes things fail, and you might find yourself wishing you could go back to the way things were. Now you can! You can use System Restore to roll back your system to the condition it was in at a prior point in time. You can roll back to any of these types of checkpoints and restoration points:

● Windows Vista creates an install restore point each time you install a program or device driver, and each time Windows Update installs an update.

● Windows Vista creates a system checkpoint when you back up or restore your computer.

● You can create a manual restore point at any time.

You can turn System Restore on or off for each hard disk in your computer, as long as the disk is at least 1 GB. (System Restore will not run on smaller disks.) Each hard disk must have 15 percent of its total space free for its restore points, which are saved on the individual disks. When the allocated restore point storage space is full, older restore points are deleted.

Restoring your computer restores Windows Vista and the programs that are installed on your computer to the state they were in at the time of the selected restore point. Your personal files (including your saved documents, e-mail messages, address book, Windows Internet Explorer Favorites, and History list) are not affected. All the changes made by System Restore are completely reversible, so if you don't like the results, you can restore the previous settings and try again.

System Restore also creates shadow copies of files and folders that have been changed since the previous restore point. If you make a change to a file or folder that you wish you hadn't, you can open the shadow copy and save it as a new file. Similarly, you can open versions of files that have been saved during a backup. To view available shadow copies and backup versions, right-click the file or folder, click Properties, and then in the Properties dialog box, click the Previous Versions tab.

> **Tip** Each of the System Restore checkpoints and restoration points is the equivalent of a large-scale file backup. If a virus-infected file is stored as part of a restoration point, it could inadvertently be restored along with the rest of your system settings if you choose to restore your system to that particular restoration point.
>
> While the System Restore feature is enabled, the backup files are protected from detection or cure by virus scanning programs. Prior to running a system-wide virus checker, disable the System Restore feature to ensure that all files are checked and cured or deleted as appropriate.

In this exercise, you will create a manual restore point and see how to restore your computer to a previous state. There are no practice files for this exercise.

> **BE SURE TO** display Control Panel before beginning this exercise.

1. In **Control Panel**, click **System and Maintenance**, and then click **System**.

2. In the **Tasks** list on the left side of the **System** window, click **System protection**. In the **User Account Control** dialog box, if you're logged on as an administrator, click **Continue**. Otherwise, enter an administrator password, and click **OK**.

> **Tip** You can also access System Restore by clicking Undo Changes To Your Computer With System Restore in Windows Help And Support, or by clicking System Restore in the See Also area of the Performance And Maintenance window.

The System Properties dialog box opens, displaying the System Protection tab.

3. Click **Create**, and then in the **System Protection** box, type SBS Restore Point to identify the purpose of the restore point.

4. In the **System Protection** box, click **Create**.

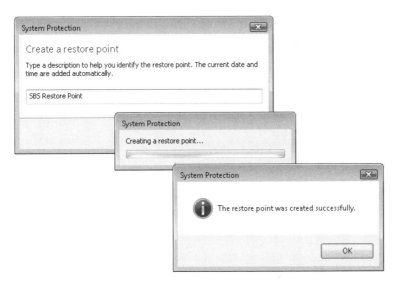

5. After Windows Vista creates the restore point, click **OK** in the **System Protection** box.

6. In the **System Properties** dialog box, click **System Restore**.

The System Restore wizard starts.

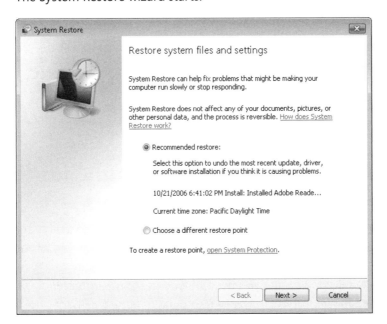

The restore point of the most recent software or driver installation is selected as the recommended restore point.

7. Select the **Choose a different restore point** option, and then click **Next**.

The System Restore wizard displays the available restore points and checkpoints.

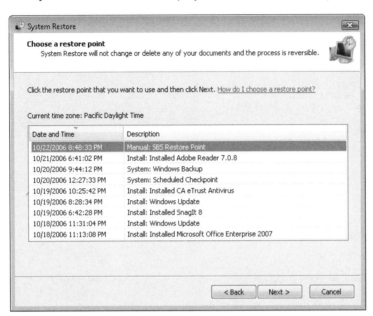

You can restore your computer to any of these points.

8. On the **Choose a restore point** page, click **Cancel** to exit the wizard without restoring your computer to a previous point.

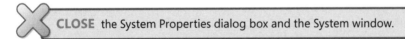

CLOSE the System Properties dialog box and the System window.

Transferring Software, Settings, and Files to Another Computer

Have you put off purchasing a new computer or switching to a different one because you dread the task of installing all the programs you use, customizing all your settings, and moving all your data files? You might not even be sure exactly what you should transfer in order to have everything you need. *Windows Easy Transfer* helps you choose what to transfer and leads you step by step through the process. It does not delete information from the old computer, so you don't need to worry that accidentally transferring the wrong file means it is lost forever.

You can transfer the following types of files and settings from a computer running Windows XP or Windows Vista to a computer running Windows Vista:

● Folders and files

● E-mail settings, contacts, and messages

● Program settings

● User accounts and settings

● Internet settings and favorites

You can transfer files, but not settings, from a computer running Windows 2000 to a computer running Windows Vista.

You can use several methods to get the information from one computer to the other, including over a network; via DVD, CD, or USB flash drive; or by using an *Easy Transfer Cable* (a USB cable that connects two computers together).

> **Troubleshooting** While the transfer is taking place, you will not be able to use either computer. Because the transfer can take several hours, you cannot start the process from a mobile computer that is running on battery power; you must first plug it in.

To begin the transfer process:

1. Log on to your computer as an administrator.

2. On the **Start** menu, point to **All Programs**, click **Accessories**, click **System Tools**, and then click **Windows Easy Transfer**. Then in the **User Account Control** dialog box, click **Continue**.

3. Follow the instructions in the **Windows Easy Transfer** wizard to specify the transfer media or method, the information you want to transfer, and the password for recovering that information.

4. If you are transferring files and settings via removable media, start Windows Easy Transfer on the second computer, and click **Continue transfer in progress**.

5. Provide the information requested by the wizard. When prompted to do so, insert the transfer disk into the second computer, select the destination drive, enter the password, and then click **Next**.

   The files transfer to the new computer.

Key Points

- If you need help with Windows Vista, you can find locally stored and online information through Windows Help And Support.

- You can get help from other people through a newsgroup, from an online product support provider, or by inviting a person to provide Remote Assistance.

- It is a good idea to periodically back up your important files. If you have a serious computer problem, you can restore files or even your entire operating system to an earlier state.

- Setting up a new computer is no longer a daunting task with Windows Easy Transfer, which helps you transfer all your programs, settings, and files from a computer running Windows XP or Windows Vista to another computer running Windows Vista.

Keyboard Shortcuts

In Windows Help And Support, press this	To do this
Alt+C	Display the Table of Contents
Alt+N	Display the Connection Settings menu
F10	Display the Options menu
Alt+Left Arrow	Move back to the previously viewed topic
Alt+Right Arrow	Move forward to the next (previously viewed) topic
Alt+A	Display the customer support page
Alt+Home	Display the Windows Help And Support home page
Home	Move to the beginning of a topic
End	Move to the end of a topic
Ctrl+F	Search the current topic
Ctrl+P	Print the current topic
F3	Move to the Search box

Glossary

activating A security measure that requires you to validate your copy of Windows Vista online or by telephone within 30 days of first use.

ActiveX control A set of technologies that enables software components to interact with one another in a networked environment, regardless of the language in which the components were created.

Address bar In Windows Explorer, a text box containing the navigation path to the current folder, beginning with the Windows symbol representing the overall Windows storage structure. The arrow after each folder name links to a list of its subfolders. In Windows Internet Explorer, a text box containing the Web address of the currently displayed Web page.

administrative privileges The highest level of permissions that can be granted to a user account. A computer administrator can perform tasks affecting the computer and all the user accounts on it. Administrative privileges are required to perform any tasks relating to or affecting computer security.

aspect ratio In computer displays and graphics, the ratio of the width of an image or image area to its height.

Audio Description A Windows Vista accessibility program that narrates videos as they play, if this feature is available within the video file.

autorun file A file that automatically starts an installation program when you insert the installation disc or browse to the folder containing it.

background tabs In Internet Explorer tabbed browsing, a page tab that opens in the background, so that the tab you are currently working with stays in the foreground.

backing up The process of creating a copy of your files somewhere other than on your computer so that you can restore them if an event such as a virus attack, hard disk failure, theft of a laptop, fire, or other loss should occur.

bitmap (BMP) A data structure in memory that represents information in the form of a collection of individual bits. A bitmap image represents images as dots, or pixels, on the screen and is saved in the bitmap (.bmp) format.

blog Short for Weblog. A personal Web site created for the purpose of sharing information and opinions with other Internet users. Blogs range from personal diaries and ways for communities to keep in touch to sources of information on a specific topic.

BMP See *bitmap (BMP)*.

browser See *Web browser*.

browsing Navigating through a folder hierarchy, for example in a dialog box or in Windows Explorer, to select a folder or file.

burning Copying a file, such as an image or audio file, to a CD or DVD.

byte A unit of information that is the equivalent of one character.

cable A type of broadband Internet connection that uses cable television lines. Access speeds vary greatly, with a maximum speed of 10 megabits per second (Mbps).

caching The process of storing information in a computer's memory, or storing a Web page on a computer's hard disk, for rapid retrieval at a later time.

CD key A unique combination of letters and numbers that identifies a product license.

clicking The action of pressing and releasing the primary mouse button.

command An instruction to the computer's operating system.

compressing To reduce the size of a set of data, such as a file or a communications message, so that it can be stored in less space or transmitted with less bandwidth.

computer system A complete, working computer, including the hardware, the operating system, and any other software or peripheral devices that are necessary to make the computer function.

content pane Displays files and folders stored in the currently selected folder or storage device.

context menu A context-sensitive menu of commands that appears when you right-click an item.

credentials The user name and password you use to connect to a domain, Web site, folder, or other secure location.

defragmentation The process of consolidating data stored on a hard disk drive into contiguous chunks, for the purpose of increasing file access speed.

desktop An on-screen work area that uses icons and menus to simulate the top of a desk.

desktop shortcuts See *shortcuts*.

device driver A software component that permits a computer system to communicate with a device.

DHCP server A computer running the Microsoft DHCP service, which allows IP addresses to change as needed.

dialog box A window that contains buttons and various kinds of options through which the user can carry out a particular command or task.

dial-up connection A connection from your computer to another computer using two modems and an ordinary telephone line. The remote computer usually belongs to the Internet service provider (ISP) with whom you have set up your user account.

Digital Subscriber Line (DSL) A type of high-speed Internet connection using standard telephone wires; also referred to as a broadband connection..

Disk Cleanup A program that frees up space on your hard disk by removing downloaded program files, temporary files, and offline files; compressing old files; and emptying the Recycle Bin.

Disk Defragmenter A program that analyzes all the data stored on your hard disk and then consolidates fragmented files into contiguous chunks. The benefits are faster file access and larger areas of available space in which to store new files.

DLL See *dynamic-link library (DLL)*.

DNS See *domain name system*.

docking To move a toolbar to the edge of an application window so that it attaches to and becomes a part of the application window.

domain A logical (rather than physical) group of resources—computers, servers, and other hardware devices—on a network, that are centrally administered through Microsoft Windows Server.

domain name system (DNS) The hierarchical system by which hosts on the Internet have both domain name addresses and IP addresses. The domain name address is used by human users and is automatically translated into the numerical IP address, which is used by the packet-routing software.

double-clicking The process of pressing and releasing the primary mouse button twice in quick succession to give the computer a command.

dragging The process of moving an item to another place on the screen by selecting the item and then pressing and holding down the mouse button while moving the mouse.

driver See *device driver*.

DSL See *digital subscriber line (DSL)*.

dynamic-link library (DLL) An operating system feature that allows executable routines to be stored separately as files with DLL extensions and to be loaded only when needed by a program.

Easy Transfer Cable A USB cable that connects two computers together.

executable file A program file that can be run. Files that have *.exe* extensions are executable.

expansion slot A socket in a computer, designed to hold expansion boards and connect them to the system bus (data pathway) as a means of adding or enhancing the computer's features and capabilities.

external peripherals Devices installed by connecting them to ports without having to open up your computer. Examples are your computer's monitor, keyboard, mouse, and speakers.

Filter Keys A keyboard feature that causes Windows to ignore brief or repeated keystrokes, or slows the repeat rate.

fragmentation The scattering of parts of the same file over different areas of the disk. Fragmentation occurs as files on a disk are deleted and new files are added. It slows disk access and degrades the overall performance of disk operations, although usually not severely.

gadget A device displayed in Windows Sidebar that provides constantly updated information, such as the time.

GB See *gigabyte (GB)*.

GIF See *graphics interchange format (GIF)*.

gigabyte (GB) 1,024 megabytes, though often interpreted as approximately one billion bytes.

Graphic Interchange Format (GIF) A graphics file format developed by CompuServe and used for transmitting raster images on the Internet. An image in this format may contain up to 256 colors, including a transparent color. The size of the file depends on the number of colors actually used.

graphical user interface (GUI) User interface incorporating visual elements such as a desktop, icons, and menus.

group An account that contains other accounts, called *members*. Permissions and rights granted to a group are also granted to its members.

hacker A person who attempts to gain access to computers or software programs through illegal means, often with the malicious intent of damaging computer data through the introduction of a virus.

hardware The physical components of a computer system, including any peripheral equipment such as printers, modems, and mouse devices.

High Contrast A program that changes the display of your screen from the usual muted Windows colors to a starker color scheme to make individual items on the screen stand out more from others.

home page In Internet Explorer, the page or pages that open automatically when you start your browser. For Web sites, the first page displayed when you connect to a site.

hub In a network, a device joining communication lines at a central location, providing a common connection to all devices on the network.

hyperlink A link from a text or graphic element to another location in the document, to another document, or to a Web page.

icon A small image displayed on the screen to represent an object that can be manipulated by the user. Icons serve as visual mnemonics and are used to control certain computer actions without the user having to remember commands or enter them through the keyboard.

IEEE 1394 A port used for the high-speed transfer of audio and video data.

Information Bar A bar that appears at the top of the Internet Explorer content pane, notifying you when potentially risky actions, such as downloading an ActiveX control, require your permission to continue.

input language A Regional And Language Options setting that specifies the combination of the language being entered and the keyboard layout, IME, speech-to-text converter, or other device being used to enter it.

instant messaging (IM) A real-time electronic communication system that allows you to "chat" with contacts by typing in a window on your computer screen.

internal peripherals Devices that have to be installed inside your computer. The internal component might be in the form of a card that provides a new connection at the back of the computer, or it might be a new hard disk drive, DVD drive, or tape backup drive that is accessed from the front of the computer.

Internet protocol (IP) address See *IP address*.

Internet service provider (ISP) A business that supplies Internet connectivity services to individuals, businesses, and other organizations.

IP address A 32-bit address used to identify a node on an IP network. Each node on the IP network must be assigned a unique IP address, which is made up of the network ID and a unique host ID. This address is typically represented with the decimal value of each 8 bits separated by a period (for example, 192.168.7.27).

ISDN A digital phone line used to provide a high-bandwidth Internet connection. An ISDN line must be installed by the telephone company at both the calling site and the called site.

ISP See *Internet service provider (ISP)*.

Joint Photographic Expert Group (JPEG) An image compression mechanism designed for compressing either full-color or grayscale still images. It works well on photographs, naturalistic artwork, and similar material. Images saved in this format have .jpg or .jpeg file extensions.

JPEG See *Joint Photographic Expert Group (JPEG)*.

KB See *kilobyte (KB)*.

keyboard shortcut A combination of keys that when pressed will quickly perform an action within an application that would normally require several user actions, such as menu selections.

kilobyte (KB) 1,024 bytes of data storage; in reference to data transfer rates, 1,000 bytes.

LAN See *local area network (LAN)*.

license terms The terms defining the legal relationship between you and the manufacturer of a software program, the terms under which you may use the software, and the extent of the manufacturer's liability, that you must agree to before installing or running a software program.

local area network (LAN) The process of connecting to a computer on your network that has been set up to provide Internet access; connections to upstream providers are handled for you by that computer.

local printer A printer that is connected directly to your computer.

local/locally A term referring to the computer you are currently using.

locking Making your Windows desktop inaccessible to other people; most effective when your user account is protected by a password.

logging off The process of disconnecting a computer from a network domain without affecting other users' sessions.

logging on The process of starting a computer session.

Magnifier See *Microsoft Magnifier*.

mapping a drive The process of assigning a drive letter to a specific computer or shared folder on your network. This is commonly done to create a constant connection to a network share but can also be used to maintain a connection to an Internet location.

MB See *megabyte (MB)*.

megabyte (MB) 1,024 kilobytes of data storage; in reference to data transfer rates, 1,000 kilobytes.

menu bar The toolbar from which users can access the menus of commands.

Microsoft Magnifier A Windows Vista accessibility program that opens a magnification panel in which the screen under the mouse pointer is displayed, magnified up to nine times. You can adjust the size and location of the magnification panel.

Microsoft Narrator A Windows Vista accessibility tool that converts on-screen text to spoken audio in order to read menu commands, dialog box options, and other screen features out loud. It also reads keystrokes as they're typed and identifies the location as you move around.

Microsoft Paint A drawing program with which users can create simple or elaborate drawings. These drawings can be either black and white or color, and can be saved as bitmap files. It can also be used to work with *.jpg* and *.gif* files. Paint pictures can be pasted into another document, or used as a desktop background.

Microsoft Windows Firewall A built-in firewall in Windows Vista that protects you from dangerous software and unwanted communications.

Microsoft Windows Update A utility that scans your computer, confers with the Microsoft Update online database, and recommends or installs any updates that are available for your operating system, your software programs, or your hardware.

middleware A type of software that connects two or more otherwise separate applications, which could be software programs or system applications.

modem A device that allows computer information to be transmitted and received over a telephone line. The transmitting modem translates digital computer data into analog signals that can be carried over a phone line. The receiving modem translates the analog signals back to digital form.

Mouse Keys A Windows Vista accessibility tool that allows you to move the cursor around the screen by pressing the Arrow keys on the numeric keypad.

Narrator See *Microsoft Narrator.*

Navigation pane Displays your personal folders and when you expand the Folders list, displays a hierarchical view of the entire storage structure of your computer.

network A group of computers that communicate with each other through a wired or wireless connection.

network printer A printer that is not connected directly to your computer. Instead, you access the printer through a network or workgroup as a free-standing networked printer, through someone else's computer, through a print server, or through a printer hub.

network share A folder on a different computer on your network.

newsgroup A collection of messages posted by individuals to a news server (a computer that can host thousands of newsgroups).

Notepad A basic text editor used to create simple documents or Web pages.

notification area The area on the taskbar to the right of the taskbar buttons that displays information about the status of programs, including those running in the background (programs you don't need to interact with), as well as links to certain system commands.

OEM See *original equipment manufacturer (OEM).*

On-Screen Keyboard A Windows Vista tool that displays a visual representation of a keyboard from which you can select individual keys by using your mouse, pen, or other device.

operating system The underlying program that tells your computer what to do and how to do it. The operating system coordinates interactions among the computer system components, acts as the interface between you and your computer, enables your computer to communicate with other computers and peripheral devices, and interacts with programs installed on your computer.

original equipment manufacturer (OEM) The maker of a piece of equipment.

Paint See *Microsoft Paint.*

parallel port An input/output connector that sends and receives data 8 bits at a time, in parallel, between a computer and a peripheral device.

password A security measure used to restrict access to user accounts, computer systems, and resources. A password is a unique string of characters that must be provided before access is authorized.

password reset disk A disk (or other piece of removable media, such as a USB flash drive) created by the user from within Windows Vista. When a password has been forgotten or lost, the disk allows the user to create a new password.

path The route followed by the operating system through the directories in finding, sorting, and retrieving files on a disk.

peripheral device A device, such as a disk drive, printer, modem, or joystick, that is connected to a computer and is controlled by the computer's microprocessor.

personal folder A folder that you open by clicking your user name at the top of the Start menu. You can save documents, spreadsheets, graphics, and other files in your personal folder. As you work on your computer and personalize Windows, it saves information and settings specific to your individual user profile in this folder.

pinned programs area A special area at the top of the left side of the Start menu to which users can drag program icons and shortcuts.

pixel The individual dots that make up the picture displayed on your computer. Each pixel displays one color. See also *screen resolution.*

play list A compilation of tracks from various CDs and other sources.

Plug and Play A phrase meaning that the operating system can locate any necessary drivers itself.

PNG See *Portable Network Graphics (PNG).*

pointing Moving the mouse pointer over an object.

POP3 See *Post Office Protocol 3 (Pop3).*

pop-up The small Web browser window that opens on top of (or sometimes below) the Web browser window when you display a Web site or click an advertising link.

port An interface through which data is transferred between a computer and other devices, a network, or a direct connection to another computer.

Portable Network Graphics (PNG) A file format for bitmapped graphic images, designed to be a replacement for the GIF format, without the legal restrictions associated with GIF.

Post Office Protocol 3 (POP3) A popular protocol used for receiving e-mail messages. This protocol is often used by ISPs. In contrast to IMAP servers, which provide access to multiple server-side folders, POP3 servers allow access to a single inbox.

primary display In a multi-monitor setup, the monitor that includes the Windows logon screen and the taskbar.

printer driver A software program designed to enable other programs to work with a particular printer without concerning themselves with the specifics of the printer's hardware and internal language.

product key A unique combination of letters and numbers that identifies a program's product license.

program icon See *icon.*

program shortcut See *shortcut.*

Quick Launch toolbar A customizable toolbar optionally displayed on the Windows taskbar, from which users can or start programs or utilities with a single click.

recently opened programs list A list on the Start menu of the last several programs started by the user.

Recycle Bin The place where Windows temporarily stores files you delete. When the Recycle Bin is empty, the icon depicts an empty trash can; when you delete items (but don't empty the Recycle Bin), the icon depicts pieces of paper in the trash can.

remote access server A host on a LAN that is equipped with modems so that users can connect to the network over telephone lines.

remote assistance A convenient way for a friend or trusted person to connect to a local computer from a remote computer and help troubleshoot a problem. To protect your computer from unauthorized access, the invitation is valid for a specific length of time—from 1 minute to 99 days—and can require a password, which is sent separately.

Remote Desktop A means of accessing a Windows session that is running on one computer from another computer.

restore point A snapshot of your computer system settings taken by Windows Vista at regular intervals as well as prior to any major change such as installing a program or updating system files. If you experience problems with your system, you can restore it to any saved restore point without undoing changes to your personal files.

right-clicking The action of pressing and releasing the secondary mouse button.

root The highest or uppermost level in a hierarchically organized set of information. The root is the point from which subsets branch in a logical sequence that moves from a broad or general focus to narrower perspectives.

root directory The place where folders and files are stored directly on a drive. The root directory often contains system files that should not be modified or moved in any way.

router A device connecting computers on a network or connecting multiple networks, that receives data and forwards it.

screen resolution The fineness of detail attained by a monitor in producing an image, measured in pixels, expressed as the number of pixels wide by the number of pixels high. See also *pixels*.

screen saver Static or moving images that are displayed on your computer after some period of inactivity.

ScreenTip The small text box that appears when pointing to an icon (positioning the mouse pointer over it), and contains identifying information.

secondary display In a multi-monitor setup, the monitor on to which you can expand programs so that you can expand your work area.

shared drive A drive that has been made available for other people on a network to access.

shared folder A folder that has been made available for other people on a network to access.

shortcut An icon on the desktop that a user can double-click to immediately access a program, a text or data file, or a Web page.

shortcut menu See *context menu*.

shutting down A process that closes all your open applications and files, ends your computing session, closes network connections, stops system processes, stops the hard disk, and turns off the computer.

Simple Mail Transfer Protocol (SMTP) A member of a suite of protocols that governs the exchange of electronic mail between message transfer agents.

Sleep mode A Windows Vista feature that saves any open files and the state of any running programs to memory and to your hard disk, and then puts your computer into a power-saving state.

SMTP See *Simple Mail Transfer Protocol (SMTP)*.

software See *software programs*.

software piracy The illegal reproduction and distribution of software applications.

sound card A type of expansion board on PC-compatible computers that allows the playback and recording of sound.

Sound Sentry A Windows Vista feature that flashes the screen element you specify (your choices are the active caption bar, active window, or desktop) every time the system's built-in speaker plays a sound.

Speech Recognition Allows you to control Windows, control open programs, and dictate text by speaking into a microphone.

Start menu A list of options that is your central link to all the programs installed on your computer, as well as to all the tasks you can carry out with Windows Vista.

Sticky Keys A Windows Vista accessibility feature that makes it easier to use the keyboard with one hand by causing the Ctrl, Shift, and Alt keys to "stick" down until you press the next key.

surfing the Web To browse information on the Internet.

switch box An enclosure that contains a selector switch. It looks similar to a hub but allows only one active connection at a time.

system cache An area in computer memory where Windows Vista stores information it might need to access quickly.

system date The current date according to the operating system.

system folders The folders created when Windows Vista was installed. The folders are Program Files, Users, and Windows. See the index to locate specific information about each of these folders.

system time The current time according to the operating system. The system time controls a number of behind-the-scenes settings and is also used by Windows and your programs to maintain an accurate record of happenings on your computer.

tabbed browsing A feature in Internet Explorer with which you can browse different Web sites on different tabs, easily and quickly switching between them.

tabs Multiple windows located within the Internet Explorer program window that can each display a different Web site.

task pane A fixed pane that appears on one side of a program window, containing options related to the completion of a specific task.

Task Scheduler Program with which you can schedule regular hard disk maintenance tasks.

taskbar Displays buttons you can click to run programs, utilities, and commands, as well as buttons representing the windows of open programs and files.

taskbar buttons Buttons on the taskbar representing each open window, file, or program.

theme A set of visual elements that applies a unified look for the computer desktop. Each theme can include a desktop background color or picture; a color scheme that affects title bars and labels; specific fonts used on title bars, labels, and buttons; sounds associated with specific actions; and other elements.

tilt-wheel mouse A mouse that incorporates a wheel that scrolls not only vertically, but also horizontally.

time server A computer that periodically synchronizes the time on all computers within a network. This ensures that the time used by network services and local functions remains accurate.

title bar The horizontal bar at the top of a window that contains the name of the window. On many windows, the title bar also contains the program icon, the Maximize, Minimize, and Close buttons, and the optional question mark button for context-sensitive Help. To display a menu with commands such as Restore and Move, right-click the title bar.

Toggle Keys A Windows Vista accessibility feature that sounds an audio signal when you press the Caps Lock, Num Lock, or Scroll Lock key. A high-pitched sound plays when the keys are activated, and a low-pitched sound plays when the keys are deactivated.

toolbar Presents menus and buttons specific to the content of the current window. When more buttons are available than can be shown, a chevron (>>) appears at the right end of the toolbar; clicking the chevron displays a list of other commands.

turning off The process of shutting down Windows so users can safely turn off the computer power. Many computers turn the power off automatically.

UI See *user interface (UI)*.

UNC See *Universal Naming Convention (UNC)*.

Uniform Resource Locator (URL) An address for a resource on the Internet. URLs are used by Web browsers to locate Internet resources.

Universal Naming Convention (UNC) The system of naming files among computers on a network so that a file on a given computer will have the same path when accessed from any of the other computers on the network.

Universal Serial Bus (USB) A connection that provides both data transfer capabilities and power to a peripheral device.

upgrading The process of updating your computer's operating system files to a newer version, without disturbing information that is stored on your computer, such as documents, spreadsheets, and data files.

URL See *Uniform Resource Locator (URL)*.

USB See *Universal Serial Bus (USB)*.

USB flash drive A portable flash memory card that plugs into a computer's USB port and stores up to 2 GB of data.

user account On a secure or multi-user computer system, an established means for an individual to gain access to the system and its resources.

User Account Control A Windows Vista security feature that requires specific acknowledgment and an administrator password when accessing settings that could disrupt your computer or affect its users.

user account name See *user name*.

user account picture An individual graphic representing a specific computer user account. User account pictures are available only on computers that are members of a workgroup or are stand-alone, and are not available on computers that are members of a network domain.

user interface (UI) The portion of a software program with which a user interacts.

user name A unique name identifying a user's account to Windows. An account's user name must be unique among the other group names and user names within its own domain or workgroup.

user profile A computer-based record maintained about an authorized user of a multi-user computer system. It describes the way the computer environment looks and operates for that particular user.

users A collective term used to refer to people who use computers.

utility A small program that provides additional features to the computer user; for example, the Magnifier utility that enlarges a portion of the screen in a separate window.

virtual private network (VPN) The extension of a private network. VPN connections provide remote access and routed connections to private networks over the Internet.

virus A program that infects computer files or other programs by inserting copies of itself into the files, and might execute some harmful or inconvenient action. A program that inserts itself into an e-mail program and sends copies of itself to everyone in the address book is an example of a virus.

VPN See *virtual private network (VPN)*.

Web An abbreviated term for *World Wide Web*; a worldwide network consisting of millions of smaller networks that send and receive data among each other.

Web browser Software that lets a user view HTML documents.

Welcome screen The screen that appears when you start your computer, containing links to each of the active user accounts.

wildcard character A keyboard character that can be used to represent one or many characters when conducting a query. The question mark (?) represents a single character, and the asterisk (*) represents any number of characters.

window A portion of the screen where programs and processes can be run. Users can open several windows at the same time. Windows can be closed, resized, moved, minimized to a button on the taskbar, or maximized to take up the whole screen.

Windows Classic The menu style found in Windows 2000 and earlier. If you are unable to adjust to the changed look of the Windows Vista menu, you have the option of changing back to the Classic version.

Windows Defender A Windows Vista security feature that helps you detect software that might pose a potential threat to your privacy or your computer..

Windows Easy Transfer A program that leads you step by step through the process of transferring files to a new computer.

Windows Experience Index Measures hardware and assigns a base score that reflects the lowest of a set of subscores for your processor, memory, graphics card, and hard disk.

Windows Firewall A Windows Vista security feature that helps you prevent unauthorized transmissions to and from your computer.

Windows ReadyBoost A Windows Vista feature that makes it possible to increase the available system memory by using USB flash drives as memory-expansion devices.

Windows Security Center A Windows Vista security feature that monitors the types of protection on your system.

Windows Sidebar A desktop pane that keeps useful tools and current information readily accessible.

Windows Update See *Microsoft Windows Update*.

wizard A program that walks you through the steps necessary to accomplish a particular task.

workgroup A logical group of computers that is not centrally administered but communicates through a network.

Index

A

access to files and folders, limiting, 79
Accessibility dialog box, 180
accessibility features. See also Ease Of Access
    center
  defined, 21
  recommendations on, 24
accounts. See user accounts
activating Windows, 7, 10
  checking status of, 9
  defined, 357
  grace period for, 7
ActiveX controls, 357
activity reports, lxv, lxvi
ad hoc wireless networks, 240
ad windows, blocking. See Internet Explorer
    Pop-up Blocker
Add A Favorite dialog box, 183
Add button (Sidebar), lviii, 225
Add Folder To Gallery button, 257, 258
Add Input Language dialog box, 138
Add Or Change Home Page dialog box, 178
Add Printer wizard, 149
Add To Favorites button, 183
Address Bar
  defined, 39, 357
  displaying, 53
address book. See Windows Contacts
addresses, Web site. See URLs
administrative privileges
  defined, 357
  software installation and, 204
administrator account
  defined, 3
  permissions, 282
administrator tasks, 283
Advanced Sharing dialog box, lxii, 253
Aero. See Windows Aero
animations, turning off, 22
antivirus programs, 296
Appearance And Personalization window, 98
Appearance Settings dialog box, 105
applications. See software
appointments (Windows Calendar), 215

approved sites in Content Advisor, 195
arranging shortcuts and icons, 57
arranging windows, 46
aspect ratio for viewing movies on screen, 126, 357
assistance, remote
  chatting during, lxx, 341
  defined, 363
  disabling, 343
  disconnecting, lxx, 341–42
  initiating, 338
  limiting access to, lxxi, 343
  requesting control, 341
  setting up, lxx, 340
  settings, displaying, lxxi, 343
  starting, lxx, 339
  Windows Live Messenger and, 339
Audio Description, 21, 357
audio devices
  portable, syncing with Windows Media Player, 266
  speakers, 157, 159
audio files, sharing, 275
audio input jack, 161
AutoComplete for Tablet PCs, turning on/off, 145
automatically starting software, 207
AutoPlay dialog box, 262, 263
autorun files, 203, 357. See also software
  installation

B

Back button, 86, 88, 173
  (Windows Explorer), 63, 68, 72
  (Windows Help And Support), lxix, 335
Back Up Files wizard, 346
background colors on Web pages, 180
background, desktop
  changing, xlvi, 108–109
  default, 7
  pictures as, 110
  pictures as, turning off, 22
  solid color as, 111
background tabs, 173, 357. See also tabbed
  browsing

D

Q

R

S

Z

What do you think of this book?

We want to hear from you!

Do you have a few minutes to participate in a brief online survey?

Microsoft is interested in hearing your feedback so we can continually improve our books and learning resources for you.

To participate in our survey, please visit:

www.microsoft.com/learning/booksurvey/

...and enter this book's ISBN-10 number (appears above barcode on back cover*). As a thank-you to survey participants in the United States and Canada, each month we'll randomly select five respondents to win one of five $100 gift certificates from a leading online merchant. At the conclusion of the survey, you can enter the drawing by providing your e-mail address, which will be used for prize notification only.

Thanks in advance for your input. Your opinion counts!

* Where to find the ISBN-10 on back cover

ISBN-13: 000-0-0000-00000
ISBN-10: 0-0000-00000

Example only. Each book has unique ISBN.

Microsoft
Press

No purchase necessary. Void where prohibited. Open only to residents of the 50 United States (includes District of Columbia) and Canada (void in Quebec). For official rules and entry dates see:

www.microsoft.com/learning/booksurvey/